817389

D1321417

B.C.H.E. - LIBRARY

00106942

The canal boatmen, 1760–1914

# HARRY HANSON

# *The canal boatmen*
## *1760–1914*

There is a vivid charm about all migratory people, and in vagabond life we find the breadth and color which elevate the commonplace into the romantic.

William H. Rideing
'The waterways of New York' in *Harper's New Monthly Magazine*, vol. 48, December 1873, p. 4.

There should be many contented spirits on board, for such a life is both to travel and to stay at home . . . and for the bargee, in his floating home, 'travelling abed', it is merely as if he were listening to another man's story or turning the leaves of a picture book in which he had no concern.

R. L. Stevenson
*An Inland Voyage* (1919 ed.), pp. 10–11.

Manchester University Press

© 1975 HARRY HANSON

*All rights reserved*

Published by
MANCHESTER UNIVERSITY PRESS
Oxford Road
Manchester M13 9PL


ISBN 0 7190 0575 2

BATH COLLEGE
OF
HIGHER EDUCATION
NEWTON PARK
LIBRARY

CLASS
No. 301·550942 HAN

ACC.
No. 817389

DISCARD

Photoset, printed and bound
in Great Britain by
REDWOOD BURN LIMITED
Trowbridge & Esher

# CONTENTS

# TABLES

# ILLUSTRATIONS

The thanks of the author and publisher are due to the following who supplied photographs: R. J. Wilson for plates 1 and 2 taken from the Susan Hambridge/ Robert Wilson Photography Collection; the Director of the NSPCC, 4; Mr E. W. Foskett and Mr M. M. Braide of the Manchester Public Health Department, 6; Mr A. J. Lewery, 8, 9, 12. Plates 3, 5, 11 and 15 are reproduced by courtesy of the Manchester Cultural Committee. Our greatest thanks are due to Mr Edward Paget-Tomlinson, who devoted a great deal of time to finding and supplying photographs and in particular plates 7 (reproduced by courtesy of Mr W. Mayo), 10 (Mr J. Stevenson), 13 (Waterways Museum) and 14 (Mrs H. Theobolds).

# ABBREVIATIONS

Birm R.L.—Birmingham Central Reference Library.
Br. Mus.—British Museum.
C. *or* Cd.—Command.
C.R.O.—Cheshire County Record Office.
D.R.O.—Derbyshire County Record Office.
H.C.—House of Commons.
H.L.—House of Lords.
H.L.R.O.—House of Lords Record Office.
*J.H.C.—Journal of the House of Commons.*
L.G.B.—Local Government Board.
L.R.O.—Lancashire County Record Office.
Le. R.O.—Leicestershire County Record Office.
Mins. of Evid.—Minutes of Evidence.
MS.—Manuscript.
N.R.O.—Nottinghamshire County Record Office.
P.R.O.—Public Record Office.
R.C.—Royal Commission.
S.C.—Select Committee.
S.R.O.—Staffordshire County Record Office.
St. Br.—British Waterways Museum, Stoke Bruerne.
W.R.O.—Warwickshire County Record Office.

The documents at the British Transport Historical Records Office (B.T.H.R.) are codes rather than abbreviations. B.T.H.R. has not generally been added to these codes in the footnotes as they are thought to be sufficiently distinctive without. These documents are now the responsibility of the Public Record Office.

BCN—Documents relating to the Birmingham Canal Navigations.
BLC—Birmingham and Liverpool Junction Canal.
GEN—General documents.
GJC—Grand Junction Canal.
OXC—Oxford Canal.
PIC—Pickfords.
STW—Staffordshire and Worcestershire Canal.
SURC—Shropshire Union Railways and Canal Company.
WOBC—Worcester and Birmingham Canal.

# ACKNOWLEDGEMENTS

This study, adapted from a thesis presented for the degree of M.A. at the University of Manchester, was made possible by an award from the Social Science Research Council.

I am indebted to the staffs of many libraries, record offices and museums throughout the country for their invaluable assistance. The librarians of the Central Reference Library in Manchester deserve special thanks. The staff of the House of Lords Record Office were especially helpful. I found the Public Health Inspectors of this country to be an interesting, knowledgeable and helpful body of men. Mr Nash in Birmingham was very informative about the boat people. My thanks are due not only to the inspectors of the various towns mentioned in the text but also to those who gave me information as to the fate of their Canal Boat Registers, and to those whose offices were visited, although the material obtained there was not, in the end, used. Mr Braide, in Manchester, who falls into this category, was especially helpful in the early stages of this study.

Other individuals who assisted me were Mr E. Atherden who drew the diagrams and map, Mr D. Campbell, Miss M. Grey, Mr C. Hadfield, Mr J. Hemelryk, Mr C. Hugues, Mr Hutchings of the British Waterways Museum at Stoke Bruerne, Miss F. M. Martin, Mr E. Rosbottom, Mr J. C. Sledge of Pickfords Limited, Mr G. L. Turnbull of Leeds University, Mr A. Walkden and Mr R. Warde. I must also thank others whose offers of assistance I was unfortunately unable to avail myself of.

I am especially grateful to Mrs Margaret Barnes who in typing the manuscript produced order from chaos with such speed and efficiency.

My greatest debt is owed to Professor A. E. Musson of Manchester University whom I was indeed fortunate to have as my supervisor during the preparation of the original thesis, when his help, guidance and encouragement were so important to its successful completion. He might then have claimed, with justification, that his labours were at an end. Instead it was his unfailing enthusiasm and cheerful willingness to offer further advice and practical help which have made the publication of this book possible. In particular his reading of the revised manuscript with such painstaking thoroughness resulted in many invaluable suggestions and the elimination of numerous errors. Much of any merit which this book may have is due to him. The errors which remain are, of course, my own.

# INTRODUCTION

MODERN WORKS WRITTEN UPON the subject of canals usually discuss not only these purely artificial waterways but also the English river system and those 'navigations', such as the Weaver and the Aire and Calder, which hover between canal and river status. It is often difficult to separate canal boatmen from river boatmen, since there was much connection between the two systems. Hence this is a study of watermen in general, but about one especially distinctive group in particular, i.e. the boatmen who navigated in 'narrow' boats (c. 6ft 10in–7ft wide) over an extended area of the midlands. Even where 'wide' boatmen, or bargemen (i.e. men working boats of about 14ft in width), can be said to be truly *canal* boatmen, as on the Leeds and Liverpool and Rochdale canals, they have not received so much attention as the 'narrow' boatmen.

This study begins by looking critically at some of the theories put forward in recent years as to the likely origins of canal boatmen, and suggests an alternative possibility. It then goes on to discuss the economic and social standing of these men, including their importance or otherwise as boat owners, their character, and the modes of working that they came to be involved with, although this is not a technical book. The remainder of the work describes the changes which took place in these particulars from the early years of canal development down to 1914.

Details of the expansion of the size and scope of the canal system in the half century or so before the 1840s, and of the impact of the railways in the half century or so after, are given to throw light upon the changing role and condition of the boatman, and his family, in the nineteenth century. It was during the first period that the special way of life which was peculiar to the canals began to emerge, and the reasons for this development are discussed. Characteristics of this distinctive waterway sub-culture appear in later chapters, and the final chapter is a study of the life style of these interesting people, as it blossomed from the earliest years of the nineteenth century, and as it was recorded in contemporary literature and records.

Attention is drawn to the evils which were said to flourish with canal-boat life, such as drunkenness, dishonesty, violence, immorality, ill-treatment of children and others. An attempt is made to establish how far there was truth in such suggestions. An effort is also made to try to establish the actual number involved in work on canal boats in the second half of the nineteenth century.

It should be made clear that, owing to the wandering nature of boating life, the statistics which were increasingly throwing light upon the lives of the rest of the population did not usually include details of the boating population, or they are too fragmented to permit meaningful study. Much of the knowledge of boatmen which comes to light in the nineteenth century is often based on the opinions of subjective observers. This study attempts to interpret the validity, or otherwise, of such opinions.

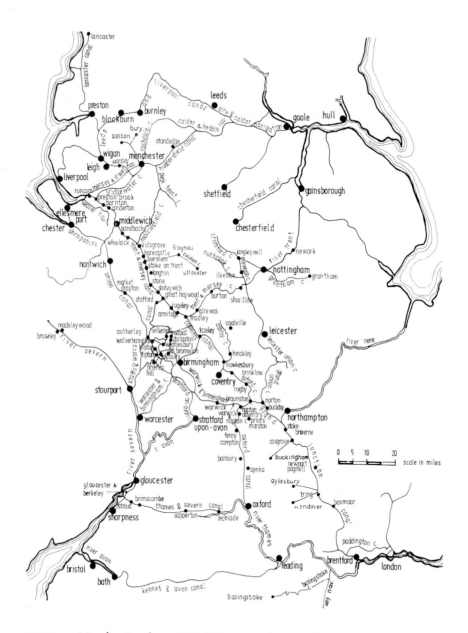

FIGURE 1    Map showing the main English canals and some of the places mentioned in the text

# I

## *Origins*

WRITERS UPON CANAL BOATMEN have, in the past, been eager to trace the origins of these people to some specific source, thereby adding a note of colour, an air of mystery and a spice of romance. We read that the first canal boatmen were Romanies, whose wanderings came to embrace the inland waterways as well as the open road. Or sailors from coastal vessels swashbuckled their way along the canals, the moonlight glittering on the gold rings in their ears, bringing with them their love of polished brass and colourful decoration. Alternatively they were river boatmen, long established, who retreated from currents and tides and shifting shoals to these waveless inland navigations. Another theory sees the earliest narrow-boat men emerging from among the ranks of the Duke of Bridgewater's miners, who, it is claimed, when they had completed so many weeks' work at the face, and being judged of good character, were allowed to act as boatmen who showed visitors round the underground workings at Worsley. They might graduate then on to one of the trading boats on the duke's canal. Again, the navvies, having gouged out these meandering channels, between bouts of drinking themselves unconscious, knocking each other insensible and ravishing the local maidens, came to people the boats which traded upon them.

### GYPSIES

Of the various theories, that of the gypsy origin has been the most popular, perhaps as much owing to the appeal of gypsy lore as to any real historical evidence. Joseph Phipkin, the owner of the *Flower of Gloster*, confirmed Temple Thurston's suspicions in 1911 when he confided, 'you'll find all these people are dark—dark hair, dark eyes, that browny sort of skin, winter and summer. It ain't the sun.' Temple Thurston seems finally to have mused himself to the conclusion that the boatmen were gypsies of Spanish origins.[1] A few years later Aubertin was more cautious. 'I am convinced', he wrote, 'that half of them . . . are of gypsy blood.' However, the other half were not true bargees but mere 'hangers-on'.[2] L. T. C.

Rolt, in his 1939–40 cruise along the waterways, recorded in *Narrow Boat*, similarly began to wonder if the first canal boatman had not been some Romany who had exchanged his caravan for the cabin of a narrow boat.[3] By 1950 the imaginative Rolt had evolved an ingenious, if tentative, theory to justify his assertion that many were of gypsy origin. The first master boatman was, he claimed, a gypsy encamped upon Trafford Moss, who, along with his fellows, had been assisting the Duke of Bridgewater in the completion of his aquatic masterpiece. When it was finished he and his tribe, 'fresh from the Balkans', exchanged their brightly painted caravans for the brightly painted cabins of the narrow boats. Hands which had wielded spades came to grasp the tiller, as he 'followed the network of still waterways as they spread eastwards and southwards across the midlands, bringing his customs and traditions with him', and 'it is surely more than a coincidence that there are Stanleys, Taylors, Lees and Boswells on the canals', Rolt declared.[4]

This view of the earliest origins of the boatmen has not been without its critics. Charles Hadfield concluded:

> One sees no reason to accept such a suggestion, or to assume that they were recruited in ways other than those normally used to draw men to the new industrial areas of the late eighteenth and early nineteenth centuries.[5]

The survival of the Registers of Boats and Barges for Lancashire, Cheshire, Staffordshire, Warwickshire, Gloucestershire, Derbyshire and Leicestershire, resulting from an Act of 1795, adds weight to criticisms of this imaginative theory.[6] The names of 898 masters of boats are registered,[7] of which 103 may be described as gypsy names, according to a list of such names prepared by Leland, the first president of the Gypsy Lore Society.[8] These figures suggest that not more than 11–12 per cent[9] were, in fact, gypsies, or ever had been, since the incidence of gypsy names can be used in this way only in a negative sense. According to Clébert, many of the gypsies, on first 'settling' in this country, in accordance with custom adopted a local name, generally the commonest, and thus they became Smiths, Grays, Hernes, Boswells, Jones and so on. Obviously there were many thousands of people with such names who were not of gypsy extraction. Again, many gypsies took the name of their occupation. Thus the tinsmiths, coppersmiths and blacksmiths became Smiths, but of course there were many smiths who were not gypsies.[10] In short, if Leland's list is comprehensive, we can assume that most gypsies were named thus, but not all people (or boatmen) with such names were gypsies. In consequence, we can say with some certainty that far fewer than 11–12 per cent of these captains of boats, at the end of the eighteenth century, were in fact gypsies. Significantly, while it is true that there are several Taylors (thirteen) among the boatmen listed, Stanleys (two), Lees (three) and Boswells (none) are very thin on the ground.

Rolt's theory also assumes that the narrow boat became the home of the gypsy and his family, yet in those counties where the registers make clear where the boatman lived, i.e. Lancashire, Cheshire, Staffordshire and Gloucestershire, out of a total of 571 masters only 6 per cent lived wholly on board their boats. Of these thirty-two captains with no shore homes, only four had gypsy names, representing a mere $\frac{3}{4}$ per cent of the total masters in these four counties.

It is possible that in the years after 1798 the wanderings of a waterway life attracted gypsies in increasing numbers sufficient to justify some of the assumptions of twentieth-century writers, but again the surviving registers, resulting from the 1877 Canal Boats Act, provide little substantiation for this.[11] The percentages of gypsy names to the total of masters registered in various places between 1879 and 1884 are listed in table 1.[12]

TABLE I   *Boatmen with gypsy names, 1879–84*

| Place | Boatmen | with gypsy names | |
|-------|---------|--------|----|
| | | Number | % |
| Burnley | 35 | 1 | 3·0 |
| Chester | 266 | 38 | 14·0 |
| Coventry | 100 | 7 | 7·0 |
| Daventry | 38 | 7 | 18·5 |
| Hinckley | 29 | 4 | 14·0 |
| Ilkeston | 23 | 4 | 17·5 |
| Nottingham | 31 | 3 | 9·5 |
| Paddington | 120 | 11 | 9·0 |
| Oxford | 28 | 1 | 3·5 |
| Tring | 24 | 2 | 8·0 |
| Wigan | 127 | 13 | 10·0 |

The proximity of Wales to the Chester registration district, and the fact that half of the gypsy names listed there are either Jones, Williams, Roberts or Davies, must render the 14 per cent there highly suspect. Elsewhere, the paucity of gypsy names hardly makes the resulting percentages meaningful and, since the strictures which applied to our exercise with the 1795 names apply equally here, it would appear that very few gypsies ever became boatmen. Equally, before 1911, 'gypsy origin' was not a phrase which flowed from the pen of writers upon canal life, or tumbled from the lips of the innumerable witnesses before the various committees in the last quarter of the nineteenth century—not even from the most eager lips and the most ardent pen of them all, those of the reforming George Smith who was, at the same time as he struggled on behalf of the boat people, working to improve the lot of the gypsies as well. And the Reverend Frederick Wade, in 1841, could go so far as to say:

> I should know a Boatman wherever I see him, his Features, Dress and everything marks him as a distinct Being in Society. There can be almost no mistaking his Appearance,[13]

yet he seemed to see no reason to remark upon any gypsy origins or gypsiness about the canal-boat population.

Finally, if the connection with the Romany had been so close, one might perhaps have expected at least a sprinkling of those exotic gypsy forenames which Leland remarked upon. The Boswells had been known to adorn themselves with such distinctive names as Opi, Plato and Happy. Others answered to Spico, Wacker and Gilderoy, to name but a few. One gypsy is reputed to have debated upon Vesuvius as a suitable name for his child.[14] Among the boat masters of the 1790s, only Onley Heath of Stone[15] and Randle Scragg of Middlewich[16] were able to sport a name of distinction, where they passed and repassed each other on the Trent and Mersey canal. A Benbow Jones navigated the Thames and Severn Canal Company's barge *Littleton* between Brimscombe and Stourport.[17] As for the remaining 895 masters it was William and Thomas, James and John and the like who exchanged courtesies or curses as they toiled in the movement of England's goods. Apart from Hamlet Mills (1800–44), of Barnton in Cheshire,[18] boatmen in the nineteenth century seem to have been no less conservative than their ancestors had been, a truth verified by the lists of names thrown up by the registers resulting from the Canal Boats Act of 1877.

It would, then, perhaps not be too adventurous to assert that, of the early (and later) boatmen, rather than a majority being of gypsy origin, it was an extremely small percentage who might have come from this source. Rolt, on reflection, came to the conclusion that

> the early carrying company's boats appear to have been manned by all male crews who could afford to house their families ashore, and it was not until railway competition brought hard times to the canals that the boatman was compelled to take his wife and family on to the boats with him.

It was only then that we see 'the starting point of elaborate decoration and that it does not pre-date the coming of railway competition'.[19] It had been these colourful 'roses and castles', with which narrow boats were copiously adorned, which had first tempted him to embark upon his gypsy hypothesis.

By comparison, Hadfield's assumptions appear more sensible if less exciting.

> Many doubtless came from river and coasting craft to the canals, many had probably been navvies who took to the waterways they had built, many came from the canalside towns and villages, places where the building and loading and passing of boats was a familiar thing.[20]

## RIVER BOATMEN

There can be little doubt that many of the early broad canals attracted existing coastal and river craft upon them, especially in the north, where many such canals were extensions of, or links with, navigable rivers or estuaries. The Sankey canal in 1757 opened up a section of the south Lancashire coalfield to the flats of the Mersey and Weaver. No doubt, also, many of the men who came to work the vessels on the Bridgewater canal were drawn from the ranks of existing flatmen, since Mersey flats, in journeying between Liverpool and Manchester, passed along the canal. However, it must be pointed out that it was not until 1776 that flats entering the canal from the river were able to navigate more than a few miles beyond Runcorn, owing to the intransigence of Sir Richard Brooke at Norton Priory. Before then considerable numbers of the diminutive 'starvationers' were bringing coal from Worsley to Manchester, and, also, much of the trade upon the canal soon came to be carried on in 'lighters', open vessels holding 40–50 tons and probably descended from the 'tuns' of 1772 described by Miss Malley.[21] The Duke of Bridgewater owned forty-four lighters by 1795.[22] Neither of these types of vessel was suited to enter the Mersey, and it is quite possible that 'inland' men, with no nautical experience, made up the first crews here. The boatmen on the duke's canal may have come from inland or existing river sources, and probably came from both.

In Yorkshire, as the waterways extended, established Humber keels were able to penetrate further into the hinterland, and even to cross the Pennines through the Rochdale canal from 1804.

In the south, Severn trowmen could navigate inland to Brimscombe, by the Stroudwater navigation and the Thames and Severn canal, by 1785, and Thames boatmen, in their 'Western' barges, could cross the watershed between the two rivers through the Thames and Severn canal, from around 1790, although the trade passing between the canal and the Thames seems never to have been very brisk, and lock dimensions restricted entry from the Severn above Brimscombe.[23] Also, it was the reluctance of the carriers on the rivers Severn and Thames to enter into trade on the canal which had compelled the Thames and Severn Canal Company to develop its own carrying business, but some river men did bring their barges on to the canal. Richard Gearing, probably the son of the Burcot lock keeper on the Thames, was in 1795 trading his two barges between Lechlade and London and Lechlade and Brimscombe.[24] It is significant also that when the company ceased to carry, the bulk of the trade was taken over by long-established river carriers.[25] Even if the river boats passing on the canal were few, it seems more than likely that the company's bargemen would be recruited from among the ranks of the river men.

### THE NARROW-BOAT AREAS

It is on the narrow-boat routes of the midlands, from Preston Brook to Oxford, unexposed to river and maritime influences, that the origins of the canal boatmen has aroused the greatest interest. The survival of material relating to the third canal to be opened (but the first narrow canal), the Birmingham,[26] does make possible some suggestions upon the likely origins of these inland boatmen, especially since the company carried in its own boats for some years. Here, too, there is some evidence to suggest that river boatmen may have peopled these canals in the first instance, for on 10 November, 1796 it was resolved that 'Mr Beck be immediately sent to Broseley and Madeley Wood [on the Severn] to endeavour to procure two proper persons to steer and three to stow the Company's Boats',[27] but there is no evidence to suggest that the financial inducements offered tempted anyone to come. On the contrary it would appear that no one did come, for on 15 November it was resolved that 'Mr Garbett be requested to write to Mr Gilbert at the Duke of Bridgewater's to lend the Company a boy or two to steer the Boats',[28] and Mr Garbett's request seems to have been complied with by 5 January 1770.[29]

The employment of the duke's steerers might be thought to confirm, in part, the theory that the earliest canal boatmen emerged from the gloom of the Worsley mines, but this is not really a tenable proposition since young boys were hardly transformed miners. At the same time there were many boats coming on to the Birmingham canal other than those of the canal company itself, and on to other partially completed canals, and it would seem unlikely that the Duke of Bridgewater provided more than a few of the steerers, if only because there would have been none left to steer the duke's boats. We might also note, in the same connection, that Rolt's idea, that boatmen first employed on the Bridgewater canal spread on to other canals, can be denied by three facts. It is now firmly established that for many years the duke's boats rarely left his canal and that most of the goods carried on that canal were carried in his boats only, except for the goods of a few large carriers, which excludes the possibility of the boats of small carriers, or owner-boatmen, being free to roam at will in significant numbers from the Bridgewater canal.[30] Nor, for that matter, was there a physical connection with other canals for several crucial years. Of course, a few of the duke's employees may have migrated, but it seems more likely that boatmen were recruited in the midlands area where the spread of canals was mainly occurring in the early 1770s. The Staffordshire and Worcestershire canal had been fully completed by 21 September 1772, making a junction with the Birmingham canal at Aldersley, and the Trent and Mersey canal at Great Haywood.[31] This last canal had been built from the Trent northward.[32] It seems not to have been until around September 1775 that any connection was made with the duke's canal, and then only for four miles, from Preston Brook to Acton,[33] and it was not until 1777 that boats could use the whole length of the waterway. It is to the Birmingham region that we must turn for any meaningful discussion of the origins of the narrow-boat men.

From the numerous accidents and sinkings in the opening months of the Birmingham canal it would seem most likely that men of little nautical experience picked up the new techniques as they went along. Hadfield's suggestion, that many were local people living near the canals, would bring on to these waterways just such an untrained labour force in the first instance, and the Cheshire and Staffordshire registers of 1795 do reveal that the boatmen working along the Grand Trunk and Staffordshire and Worcestershire canals, for example, had homes fairly evenly spread among the towns and villages on the banks of the two canals. Since Redford's conclusion (that migration generally only involved short-distance movements of population during the industrial revolution) is still widely accepted, the inference must be that they had not come from very far away.[34]

## NAVVIES

Unfortunately this might not be true if large numbers of boatmen emerged from the class of navvies who had built the canals, for it is often believed that such men travelled around the country, working on public undertakings, far from their native home. And, on the face of it, there is evidence to suggest that at least some of the navvies who worked on the Birmingham canal did in fact become boatmen, since the names of men receiving payments for such work do often appear as boatmen, in the 1795 registers and elsewhere. On the other hand, while much has been made of the navvy as a 'wanderer on the face of the earth, owning no tie and fearing no law',[35] there is some doubt as to when such men began to travel in significant numbers. Hadfield concluded that, for the building of the earlier canals,

> there was not yet sufficient public works contracting in existence for a class of professional contractors' men to have been created. Therefore it seems probable that the older canals were cut by men who worked in the neighbourhood of their homes, having been recruited by small local contractors known to them.[36]

There is evidence to confirm that many local men were, indeed, involved in the construction of the earliest canals, as there is also for those canals being built as late as the 1790s (although special conditions resulting from the French wars may have been responsible for this). On the other hand, as early as 1772 the Duke of Bridgewater brought forty labourers from Yorkshire.[37] John Proctor, who was labouring on the Trent and Mersey canal at Barnton in 1776, having previously worked on a canal at Chester, had originally been a farm labourer at Elland in Yorkshire.[38] There is, also, the possibility that some canal labourers had been drawn from the corps of migratory harvest labourers, whose seasonal migration patterns were long-established. By the second half of the eighteenth century such groups were made up mainly of Scottish, Welsh and particularly Irish harvesters.[39]

Given the existing state of research on this question, even though it would seem reasonable to assume that the bulk of canal construction was carried on by local men, we cannot rule out the presence of large numbers of strangers there even from the earliest days. Either group could have taken to the boats. If the people who took up this new mobile way of life did have any common origins in significant numbers, we are still no wiser as to what they might be. They could have been agricultural labourers escaping from the miseries of seasonal unemployment, perhaps having been introduced to the canal milieu as labourers there, thereby picking up the rudiments of boating as they were built. They might just as well have included cordwainers from Stone down on their luck, unemployed potters from Stoke, or adventurous ironworkers from Birmingham. Some of the navvies from far off could have stayed behind when their colleagues moved on. It may not have been coincidence, for example, that there was a boatman named John Proctor navigating the boat of William Davies, between Tipton and Fazeley, in 1795.[40] However, the registers of 1795 reveal that the names of few boatmen are easily recognisable as being Irish or Scottish, thus ruling out any significant recruitment from that source, at least.

## CARTERS

A closer examination of those men presumed to be navvies who had received payments during the building of the Birmingham canal and later reappeared as boatmen reveals that they were probably not navvies at all as such, but men of some small local substance who worked in the construction of the canal as carters, and, as the water flooded into the completed sections, they transferred from carting to boating, and then came to take up this new occupation permanently. Their boat was a floating cart. For example, in the record of payments made during the building of the second section of the Birmingham canal, from Bilston to Autherley, completed in 1772, men such as William Mountain were paid for the 'carriage of sundrys' and for 'boating materials'.[41] Job Lloyd received payments for the 'carriage' of materials and for 'boating' bricks, clay and sand.[42] Joseph Rowley was also involved in both, as were Jeremiah Whitehouse and James Jukes.[43] Others were paid substantial sums for carriage, although not all are immediately traceable as boatmen, which is not to say that they did not take up such employment.[44] Again, there were others paid for 'boating' who are not recorded as having 'carried' for the company, and while it would be unwise to assert that these were men who had already disposed of their carts and become full-time boatmen, none the less, the fact that they are all listed by name[45] does perhaps indicate that they were local men of some small standing, for there were others boating who were not named. 'James Place for 36 men boating clay etc.', for example, received £13 8s 1½d [£13 41p].[46] Given this possibility for the Birmingham canal, there seems to be no reason why there should not have been a similar emergence of boatmen from carters upon other canals. It also becomes possible to explain all manner of puzzling phenomena regarding the early years of canal transport.

Such men might own their horse and cart, but they could not usually afford the high cost of a new boat. One early estimate of the cost of the boat which would navigate on the proposed Trent and Mersey canal was £20.[47] The following year they were going to be

> seventy feet in length, six feet wide, to draw near thirty inches of water and to carry twenty tons burthen. They are to be constructed as to sail with either end foremost, by removing the rudder; and to cost about thirty pounds each.[48]

Expensive though this must have seemed to such men, it was, in fact, an optimistic forecast, for this increasingly popular (and increasingly inefficient) narrow boat seems to have cost much more than this, both at that time and subsequently. In 1770 eight boats built by the Birmingham Canal Company had cost £63 each.[49] In 1788, four boats, 70ft by 7ft, were to be built by the Oxford Canal Company at a cost of £70 each.[50] In 1794 boats of the same dimensions on the Chesterfield canal cost £90–£100 each.[51] Vessels upon the broader canals were costing around £150 in 1791–2.[52]

Consequently, there grew up the rather inflexible tradition of the boatman providing the necessary labour and haulage power while the carrying company supplied the boat. This was a convenient way of doing things, also, for the

Birmingham company at least, since that company was, in the first instance, short of horses. An advertisement tempted

> Such persons as are inclined to supply the Company with Horses towing the Boats from and to Wednesbury by Trip or Journey (viz to bring a loaded Boat from Wednesbury to Birmingham and take an empty one back).[53]

It was commonplace for boatmen to be caught towing the boat without a helm or steerer, just as they would lead a horse pulling a cart. The 'starvationer' boats, 47ft long and 4ft 6in wide, were, for example, in the early days, sent loaded with eight tons or so of coal from the Worsley mines 'where four, five or six of them are linked together and drawn by one horse or two mules, by the side of the canal, to Manchester or other places'. The propensity of the boats to bounce from side to side of the canal, cannoning into bridges, lock walls and gates, probably caused a decline in this practice and an increasing reliance to be placed on 'broad boats that hold about fifty tons', of which there were already a considerable number in 1766 carrying coal singly to Manchester and elsewhere.[54] On the Ketley canal in Shropshire, the only other waterway where boats were operated without a steerer, smooth rails had to be fixed to keep the boats from damaging the canal structure.[55]

Most canal companies, benefiting perhaps from the experience of the Bridgewater or their own canal, soon made it one of the by-laws that boats should have a helm, a mast (for the towing line) and a steerer. The additional expense incurred in employing a steerer tempted boatmen to continue to evade the regulations. It was resolved on 24 May 1776 that,

> Mr Meredith do write to Mr Kendrick and inform him that Normans the Steerer suffers his Boat to be taken along the Canal without proper assistance and by that means, the Banks and the works of the Canal are much damaged.[56]

Such occurrences were common upon this and other canals, and it was many years before the need for two people to manage a boat became completely accepted by the boatmen. Opportunities for evasion, or hard times, were always liable to produce a crop of such infringements. The rising price of horse feed in the years before 1799 was probably one factor leading to dispensing with the services of steerers in that year to reduce costs.[57]

### SMALL FARMERS

The possibilities do not rest with these men being mere carters, for there is a strong likelihood of at least some of them being small farmers as well. Increasingly it has become recognised by historians that for many decades before the industrial revolution the short-distance transport requirements of the country were met by farmers on a part-time basis, on a scale which was every bit as important as the professional carriers' contribution.[58] As early as 1600 the close connection between agriculture and land carriage was criticised.[59] Later, in Cheshire, the

> farmers and freeholders of Bucklow Hundred opposed the Weaver Bill because they

employed themselves and their servants in carrying coals in summer, with which they supplied the wiches in winter, while the farmers of Frodsham declared that land carriage alone enabled them to pay their rents.[60]

Professor Willan's later researches led him to conclude that such carriers, in Cheshire, were generally small tenant farmers.[61] Others provide evidence to show that the practice was common elsewhere in the eighteenth century.[62]

The interest of farmers in carriage varied. There were those who did a casual day here and there, or used their carts and waggons at times when there was little to do on the land, or backloaded them casually from the market towns. For others, carrying made up an important and regular part of their income, and for some, farming was largely geared to the carriage business. Here the dividing line between the part-time and the professional carrier becomes somewhat blurred.

R. A. Lewis has demonstrated that such farmers, with varying sizes of farm and interest in carrying, carted materials for forges and coal mines near the line of the future Staffordshire and Worcestershire canal in the years before that canal was opened. The practice was to continue in areas untouched by waterways. Farmers' waggons and carts continued to be loaded with coal as a back carriage after bringing hay and straw into Birmingham even as late as 1839.[63] In 1826 John Clare, a coal proprietor at Sankey, when asked what kind of people transported coal from Prescot to Liverpool, replied,

> The Farmers and many that are not exactly Farmers . . . they take back manure to their lands or any other goods which are to go into the interior of the Neighbourhood . . . they are Poor Fellows who have one horse carts, and if they cannot get Five Shillings a day with that one Horse, they are obliged to get Four Shillings or what they can.[64]

Although difficult to prove conclusively, it seems probable that the hard core of the early boatmen, in the midlands at least, may well have come from the ranks of just such small farmers, who were probably mainly tenant farmers. At least, this theory overcomes one of the main drawbacks of most of the other theories, that they lack any real awareness of the continuity which accompanies seemingly dramatic changes in this country during and since the industrial revolution. Speaking of the nineteenth century, F. C. Mather has recently remarked:

> Old institutions, manners, and techniques lingered when the conditions which created them declined, and were often adapted to accord with progress rather than displaced by it.

Nowhere is this more true than in the field of transport history. If Dr Kitson Clark could observe that 'Survivals are in fact to be found round every Victorian corner', no doubt we can find just as many lurking around eighteenth-century corners.[65]

Of course, some of the boatmen probably came from other sources. No doubt some carters employed by the larger farmers, whose interest in transport was strong, transferred on to the canals with their employers. Again, some of the carters and waggoners of existing professional carriers probably converted themselves into boatmen, as their employers bought boats, like Pickford, who began operations on the canals in 1786.[66] Carters of colliery owners, local manufacturers and merchants no doubt occasionally did the same, although there were probably not many such men who had their own transport before the canal era. In addition there were probably other avenues on to the water, for example through navvying. But the evidence pointing to these men emerging principally from the ranks of small farmers is strong in other directions. The tradition of the boatman providing his own horse must signify that they were men of some small standing. A navvy would seem to be the least likely person to own a horse; a carter, through his knowledge of and connections with horses, might come to possess one with greater facility, but there remains the problem of where he could obtain the necessary capital to buy it. A small farmer, however, seems to be an obvious horse owner.

There is other evidence to tie the boatmen in closely with the agricultural scene both at the outset and for many years afterwards. 'Our trade is generally slack in Harvest Time' wrote John Houghton, secretary of the Birmingham Canal Company, to his opposite number on the Oxford, on 11 July 1797.[67] On 11 March 1799 he suggested that the best time to make a stoppage would be at the 'Hay Harvest when the Carriers have but little to do and when but few coals are conveyed upon Canals'.[68] Might this not suggest that during the summer months the boatmen devoted all their attention to their farms? As trade increased and as coal became relatively less important as a cargo, as voyages became longer and as the boatmen were recruited from less agricultural sources, no doubt this practice died out, whereas in the U.S.A., where winter brought a long enforced stoppage upon the canals, it was still common practice for boatmen to be farmers. 'The boatman calculates to make six round trips in a season, and at the end he retires to his farmhouse, if he has one, and passes the winter in the bosom of his family', it was noted in 1881.[69]

Nor would it be so unusual for farmers to combine two occupations. A point which emerges from Dr Iredale's detailed study of Barnton is that in eighteenth-century villages, and even small towns, there was not yet sufficient demand for traders and craftsmen to be employed exclusively at their business, and many—such as tailors, shoemakers, blacksmiths and, of course, carriers—combined their trade with farming. Sometimes they combined other trades, as in the case of John Pointon, who was an alehouse keeper and carpenter.[70] It was only in the two or three decades which spanned the turning of the century that, as a consequence of increased demand, people came to concentrate entirely on one business. After about 1820 dual occupations had largely died out.

Evidence of specific examples of farmers becoming boatmen remains elusive. Henry Round, an owner-boatman navigating between Tipton and Birmingham, had agricultural connections, because Mr Lee spotted 'a number of Hogs belonging to Henry Round being washed in the canal at Oldbury'.[71] Joseph Whitehouse who had been paid by the company for 'boating rock etc.', also received a payment for 'rent and trespass'.[72] Richard Whitehouse was paid under the Repairs Account for 'Plow$^g$ Sowing Oats etc.'.[73] The case of Richard Hipkiss perhaps highlights the dilemma of these small farmers, as some, no doubt, aspired to own their own boat. He tenanted the land of John Turton of Bristol,[74] and one must assume that it was his landlord who provided some of the resources with which Richard bought a boat, for 'Messrs Hipkiss and Turton's boat was declared of a form unfit for locks and already done much damage'.[75] It is clear that Hipkiss was not overendowed with capital, for shortly afterwards he applied to the canal committee to hire four of the company's boats, and was refused.[76] Having built up considerable debts, he was forced to cease trading and by April 1773 had become the company's wharfinger.[77] Shortly afterwards he died, compelling his wife Hannah to become a boatwoman to pay off his debt to the company.

### BOAT HANDS

To reduce expense and in consequence of the simpleness of the new operation, it was common for boys to be employed in steering the boat, with the man on the towpath leading the horse, as was the expected duty and responsibility of a carter. Gradually the converted carter came to realise that he was doing all the hard work as the boy idled at the tiller, and no doubt a reversal of duties took place, with the master holding on to the helm and the boy being ejected on to the towpath. Driving the horse became boys' work, for, as anticipated in 1766, many of the narrow boats were crewed by a man and a boy.[78] In the 1795 registers at least 1,318 crewmen are listed, though not by name, in the seven counties. Of these at least 253 are recognisable as boys, i.e. around 20 per cent. In these 1,318 are included the crews of five 'thoroughmen' found on the Trent barges, the more adult flatmen of the Weaver, the Thames and Severn canal bargemen, and the Severn trowmen, thus disguising how numerous were the boys on the narrow canals. In Warwickshire, where no river or broad boats were registered, 88 per cent of the crews was made up of boys. None the less, we can see from the Staffordshire registers that the larger carriers, and especially those whose boats travelled longer distances, had come, by 1795, to crew their boats exclusively with men. Such carriers as Hugh Henshall & Co. of Stone (the carrying company of the Trent and Mersey Canal Company), the Burton Boat Company, Joseph Smith and Son of Horninglow Wharf, John Gilbert of Clough Hall and John Sparrow of Cockshead, employed two men, the master and a hand, on their boats.[79]

### CONCLUSION

In certain areas the earliest boatmen probably had an affinity with the nearby river or sea. For the rest, and particularly in the midland counties, the evidence points more strongly towards many of these men being small local farmers, who had traditionally been involved in local transport and who transferred on to the canal. The odds are that most of them were tenant farmers. This is not to deny that others, such as carters and waggoners employed by others, and even navvies (local or otherwise) in some instances did likewise. This last seems to be the least likely possibility. No doubt odd examples can also be found of men who arrived by other routes on to the waterways, but no common group seems as credible, given the available evidence, as does this possibility of their being small farmers. After the very earliest days, it would be unwise to be categoric about possible recruitment, beyond assuming that many entered the occupation as boys, from all kinds of backgrounds, but some obviously being the children of existing boatmen.

### NOTES TO CHAPTER ONE

[1] E. Temple Thurston, *The Flower of Gloster* (1911; 1968 ed.), pp. 29–30.

[2] C. J. Aubertin, *A Caravan Afloat* (*c.* 1918), p. 95.

[3] L. T. C. Rolt, *Narrow Boat* (1944; 1965 ed.), p. 24.

[4] L. T. C. Rolt, *Inland Waterways of England* (1950; 1962 ed.), pp. 174–7.

[5] Charles Hadfield, *British Canals* (1950; 1966 ed.), p. 73. Similar criticisms have come from Eric de Maré, *The Canals of England* (1950; 1962 ed.), p. 71, and D. D. Gladwin and J. M. White, *English Canals*, part III, *Boats and Boatmen* (1969), p. 64.

[6] 35 Geo. III, Cap. 58, 5 May, 1795. The Act was to operate until 1798. The registers are to be found in the various County Record Offices.

[7] See Appendix I, section (i).

[8] Charles C. Leland, *The Gypsies* (1882), pp. 304–9. See also Appendix I, section (ii).

[9] See Appendix I, section (iii).

[10] Jean Paul Clébert, *The Gypsies* (1963), pp. 80–1 (translated by Charles Duff).

[11] 40 and 41 Vict., c. 60. The registers were made available by kind permission of the Chief Public Health Officers for the towns concerned with whom they are to be found, with the exception of Chester and Coventry, where they are deposited in the city archives, and at Oxford and Ilkeston, where they are deposited in the Local History sections of the libraries of those towns.

[12] See Appendix I, section (iv).

[13] 'Select committee on Sunday trading on canals, navigable rivers and railways', in *House of Lords Journal*, 4th and 5th Victoria, vol. 73, 1841, appendix 2, (hereinafter *S. C. on Sunday Trading*, 1841), question 952.

[14] Leland, *op. cit.*, pp. 309–10.

[15] Register of Boats and Barges, 1795 (henceforward referred to as Boat Register 1795), No. 328, at Staffordshire County Record Office (abbreviated to S.R.O.), QR UB1.

[16] Register of Boats and Barges (henceforward Boat Register 1795), 1795, No. 61, at Cheshire County Record Office (C.R.O.).

[17] Register of Boats and Trows . . . , 1795 (henceforward Boat Register 1795), No. 34, at Gloucestershire County Record Office (G.R.O.), Q/RR 1.

[18] D. A. Iredale, 'Canal settlement: a study of the origin and growth of the canal settlement at Barnton in Cheshire between 1775 and 1845', unpublished Ph.D. thesis, Leicester University, 1966, p. 99 (abbreviated to 'Canal settlement: Barnton, 1775–1845'). I am indebted to Dr Chaloner for bringing this thesis to my attention.

[19] L. T. C. Rolt, *Navigable Waterways* (1969), p. 153.

[20] Hadfield, *op. cit.*, p. 73.

[21] Edith Malley, 'The financial administration of the Bridgewater estates, 1780–1800', unpublished M.A. thesis, Manchester University, 1929, p. 35, quoting from Raffald's *Directory of Manchester*, 1772 and 1773.

[22] Register of Boats, Barges and Vessels . . . , 1795 (henceforward Boat Register 1795), Nos. 3–12 and 1–34, at Lancashire County Record Office (L.R.O.), QDV/16/1.

[23] Humphrey Household, *The Thames and Severn Canal: Birth and Death of a Canal* (1969), pp. 93–4.

[24] F. S. Thacker, *The Thames Highway*, vol. II, *Locks and Weirs* (1920; 1968 ed.), p. 44; Boat Register 1795, 43, 46, G.R.O.

[25] Household, *op. cit.*, p. 120; Boat Register 1795, 40–1, G.R.O.

[26] Opened from Birmingham to Wednesbury on 6 November 1769.

[27] BCN 1/1, Birmingham Canal Committee Minute Book, 1767–71, p. 124, British Transport Historical Records (henceforward referred to as B.T.H.R.). Since 1 April 1972 these records have become the responsibility of the Public Record Office (P.R.O.).

[28] *Ibid.*, p. 130, minute 10.

[29] *Ibid.*, p. 147.

[30] Malley, *op. cit.*, pp. 52, 55; F. C. Mather, *After the Canal Duke: A Study of the Industrial Estates administered by the Trustees of the Third Duke of Bridgewater in the Age of Railway Building, 1825–72* (1970), p. 145.

[31] *Aris's Birmingham Gazette*, 5 October 1772. I am indebted to Mr C. P. Weaver's 'Extracts from *Aris's Birmingham Gazette*, 1760–1809, relating to canals', B.T.H.R., GEN 4/857/1–4, which have saved much time-consuming toil. All references to the *Gazette* in this study derive from this source. This particular reference is in GEN 4/857/1.

[32] *Ibid.*, 23 April 1770, 18 and 25 November 1771, 12 April 1773, 17 April 1775.

[33] *Ibid.*, 9 October 1775.

[34] A. Redford, *Labour Migration in England, 1800–50* (1926; 1964 ed., edited and revised by W. H. Chaloner), p. vii.

[35] J. Francis, *History of the English Railway, 1820–45*, vol. II (1851), p. 75.

[36] Hadfield, *The Canal Age* (1968), p. 57.

[37] Malley, *op. cit.*, p. 21. Skilled men (masons, etc.) were also attracted from distant places, in large numbers, from the earliest days, but it is unlikely that they would give up their trade to become boatmen.

[38] Poor Law Papers, C.R.O., P.C. 16/5/44.

[39] Redford, *op. cit.*, pp. 86, 133.

[40] See above. Register of Boats and Barges 1795 (henceforward Boat Register 1795), No. 292, at Warwickshire Record Office (W.R.O.), QS. 95/1–9.

[41] BCN 4/29, Journal, 1770–1, September–October 1770, and elsewhere therein.

[42] BCN 4/30, Journal, 1771–2, particularly May–September 1771.

[43] *Ibid.*, May–December especially.

[44] BCN 4/131, Cash Book, 1771.

[45] BCN 4/29 and 4/30.

[46] *Ibid.*, November 1770, p. 104.

[47] *Aris's Birmingham Gazette*, 6 May 1765; GEN 4/857/1.

[48] Anon, *History of Inland Navigation* (1766), p. 58.

[49] BCN 4/29, p. 64.

[50] OXC 1/4, p. 41.

[51] Abraham Rees, *Cyclopaedia*, vol. VI (1819), article 'Canals' (*c.* 1806). There are no page numbers. If numbered from the beginning of the article the page number of the reference would be 84.

[52] Household, *op. cit.*, pp. 93, 217; Vine, *London's Lost Route to Basingstoke* (1968), p. 72.

[53] *Aris's Birmingham Gazette*, 12 March 1770; GEN 4/857/1.

[54] Anon, *History of Inland Navigation* (1766), p. 51.

[55] Rees, *op. cit.*, p. 63 (my numbering).

[56] BCN 1/4, p. 34.

[57] Hay and oat prices rose by 16 per cent and 23 per cent respectively from 1793 to 1799, and from 1799 to 1800 increased by one third; W. Albert, 'The justices rates for land carriage, 1748–1827, reconsidered', *Transport History*, vol. I (1968), p. 119; BCN 1/7A, 14 and 19 April 1799.

[58] And in some cases long-distance transport as well. See Albert, *op. cit.*

[59] T. S. Willan, *River Navigation in England 1600–1750* (1936; 1964 ed.), p. 39.

[60] *Ibid.*, p. 47.

[61] Willan, *The Navigation of the River Weaver in the Eighteenth Century* (1951), pp. 5–6.

[62] Albert, *op. cit.*; Alfred Fell, *The Early Iron Industry of Furness and District*, Ulverston, (1908); R. A. Lewis, 'Transport for eighteenth century ironworks', *Economica*, N.S., vol. 18, August 1951, pp. 278–84; Vine, *London's Lost Route to the Sea* (1965), p. 17, quoting *J. H. C.* 5 February 1759.

[63] House of Lords Record Office (H.L.R.O.), MS., Mins. of Evid., H.C., 1839, vol. 3, Birmingham Canal Bill, 21 April 1839, pp. 201–2 (henceforward Birmingham Canal Bill, 1839).

[64] H.L.R.O., MS., Mins. of Evid., H.L., 1826, Liverpool and Manchester Railway Bill, 21 April 1826, pp. 163, 171.

[65] F. C. Mather, *After the Canal Duke* (1970), p. vii.

[66] Information supplied by Mr G. L. Turnbull of Leeds University. I am indebted to Mr Turnbull for his invaluable assistance in matters relating to Pickfords.

[67] BCN 4/371B, Houghton to Dunsford.

[68] *Ibid.*, Houghton to Woodcock.

[69] Rideing, 'The waterways of New York', *Harpers New Monthly Magazine*, vol. 48, December 1873, p. 16.

[70] Iredale, 'Canal settlement: Barnton, 1775–1845', especially pp. 46–7.

[71] Boat Register 1795, 311, W.R.O; BCN 1/7A, 11 April 1794.

[72] BCN 4/29, December 1770, p. 113.

[73] BCN 4/33, 17 May 1777, p. 54.

[74] BCN 1/3, p. 12; BCN 1/2, 25 July 1771.

[75] BCN 1/1, 13 April 1770, p. 173.

[76] *Ibid.*, 25 May 1770, p. 182.

[77] BCN 4/32, 3 April 1773, p. 31.

[78] Anon, *History of Inland Navigation* (1766), p. 58.

[79] Boat Register, 1795, S.R.O.

II

# Ownership of boats
## in the first phase
## of canal development
### 1760–c.1800

'ORIGINALLY most craft were owned by the boatmen themselves who took great pride in the condition and appearance of their possessions', de Maré asserted confidently in 1950.[1] Rolt was equally certain: 'In the past the bulk of the canal traffic was handled by these independents [owner-boatmen], the carrying company being a comparatively recent development'.[2] By 1950 he had become more catholic in his assumptions:

> traffic during the heyday of the canals was handled either by independent carriers, the majority of whom were small owner-boatmen, or by merchants or manufacturers who made use of water transport for their own trade.[3]

Gradually, according to these two writers, these early, happy, independent, sturdy (etc.) waterway peasants came to be downtrodden, dependent and defeated until, 'Today [1950] there are few owner boatmen, or Number Ones, left on the cut'.[4]

### THE LARGE CANAL CARRIERS

In fact in 1795, which must be bordering upon Rolt's 'heyday of the canals', most boats were owned not by the boatmen but by substantial capitalists. Over one quarter of all the boats (28 per cent) in the five counties where it is possible to work out the ownership[5] were owned by twelve carrying firms, none of which owned fewer than thirteen boats.[6] The fact that 20 per cent (242) of all the boats were owned by canal companies themselves[7] is another significant figure, and confirms the opinions of more recent canal historians that the canal companies did, in fact, in the early days take an active part in canal carrying, although they usually, and rapidly, found it to be unprofitable and abandoned it. Thus 31 per cent (399) of all the boats were owned by ten canal companies, and nine large independent carriers.

Even more significant is the fact that 60 per cent of the boats were owned by men, companies and partnerships owning more than five boats. Among these owners of numerous boats it is possible to ascertain that most were men of substantial capital, and had probably been so before they moved on to the waterways. Many of them were, as Rolt suggested, coal-mine owners and iron founders, manufacturers and merchants, in particular salt merchants. One such was Charles Moore who owned eight boats in 1795, ten by 1797, and a substantial salt works at Shirleywich—sending 60–80 tons of salt each week to Oxford alone—in 1799.[8] The famed John Gilbert (of Worsley), agent to the Duke of Bridgewater, owned a share in the Marston rock pits near Lawton in Cheshire, and owned seven boats in partnership with Cornelius Bourne, a Liverpool merchant, and Edward Mason, also of Liverpool, to take the salt along the Trent and Mersey canal to Runcorn.[9] Joseph Lane, who owned a colliery at Ettingshall in 1776, was probably the same person who, in 1795, owned nine boats travelling from that place to Birmingham, Stourport and Great Haywood.[10] Viscount Dudley, who had substantial coal measures under his Staffordshire estates, owned seven boats in 1795.[11] On the Nutbrook Canal, at around the same time,

> While there were obviously some private traders who saw profit in conveying the coal from West Hallam and Shipley, the collieries seem to have operated their own large fleets, "Mr Sutton's boats" far exceeding any others while the canal was only open to West Hallam and for some time afterwards.[12]

The Bickley family, owners of coal mines and furnaces (including the Bilstone (*sic*) furnace), since at least the opening years of the canal, owned six boats in 1795 in the name of William Bickley.[13] George Parker & Co. also had furnaces and coal mines at Tipton and Oldbury, and eight boats in 1795.[14] Robert Williamson of Longport, who owned six boats, was a substantial man, for at his marriage his uncle, Hugh Henshall, had settled on him 'estates, farms, mines, hereditaments and premises at Golden Hill and Ranscliffe in the Parish of Woolstanton', and on Henshall's death, on 13 November 1814, further wealth came to him from that source.[15] Matthew Pickford 'of Poynton', representing the long-established and prosperous land carriage firm, had registered ten boats in 1795, in operation between Manchester and Coventry.[16]

### THE SMALLER OPERATORS

None the less, there remained a substantial number of small men, in the sense that 39 per cent of the boats (501) were owned or part-owned by men owning less than six boats. Was this group perhaps made up principally of owner-boatmen or of boatmen who, by dint of hard work, had acquired perhaps three, four or five boats? It would seem not. Many were again capitalists, who used their boats in the furtherance of substantial businesses. John Lowe of Middlewich, owning three boats in 1795, was a salt-pit proprietor, who had sent salt in them as far as Manchester since at least 1780, and also to Shardlow.[17] 'George Chesworth of Middlewich was another salt pit owner who carried for himself', owning three boats to take his salt to Derwent Mouth, Harecastle and Anderton in 1795, and four by 1798.[18] A man of some generosity, when he died on 18 November 1816, his will read:

> I give and bequeath out of the monies [*sic*] to arise as aforesaid to each Salt-Waller and Boatman and to such other men who shall have been in my employ twelve months at the time of my decease the sum of five pounds each.[19]

Edward Best & Co. of Bilston, with five boats, were colliery owners,[20] as was John Dumaresq of the Gospel Oak Colliery, with two.[21] John Wilkinson, presumably the famed Midas at whose touch all turned into iron, had three boats working between Autherley and Birmingham.[22] John Iddins was a substantial timber merchant (and landowner), long-established in Birmingham, who had come to possess five boats by 1796.[23] Some owners may have bought boats as an investment, rather than to further their own business interests. 'William Waldron Esq.' was in partnership for two boats travelling between Colebourn Park and Stourport.[24] William Whitehead of Sandbach, 'Gentleman', owned two,[25] as did the Marquis (*sic*) of Stafford.[26] They may of course have been used simply to service their estates. A more intensive search would also, no doubt, indicate that many of the owners listed as '& Co.' in the registers carried on substantial businesses, using the boats to transport their own goods or to bring coal to their works. Ralph Hales & Co., of Colbridge, was one of several companies owning three boats.[27]

A category of ownership which might in some cases be said to be of humble origins, though not necessarily coming from the ranks of the boatmen, was that where men had close connections with the canal world; men with a knowledge of canal trade and opportunity, perhaps, to acquire boats cheaply, to arrange special concessions and even to work 'fiddles'. This does not include the substantial proprietors and committee men who carried their goods on the canals in their own boats, but the more lowly wharfinger, agent, clerk and even lock keeper, i.e. paid employees of the canal company. Hence, it was recorded in the Oxford Canal Committee Book, in 1791:

> It appearing to the Committee that most if not all the wharfingers upon the line of the canal have been, or now are traders . . . Ordered that in future the Wharfinger shall not carry on or be interested in any trade . . . as . . . [it] may occasion jealousies and inconveniences amongst other traders using the canal by an interference of interests prejudicial to the Company and reduce the amount of Tonnage which might otherwise be obtained.[28]

This veto was extended to surveyors and collectors on 13 December 1791 after the good effects had become apparent.[29] Other companies were less rigid. For many years it seems to have been accepted that agents of the Birmingham Canal Company could have boats. On 28 June 1799,

> Mr Bache attended this meeting and stated that Mr Alsager the Company's agent at Fazeley being also the Agent at Fazeley of [other carriers] . . . and having Boats upon

the Canal employed in business of his own—had it in his power to draw a preference to himself and those for whom he was employed.[30]

Among the many malpractices of employees reported upon the Thames and Severn canal between 1801 and 1803 there was 'in particular the Brimscombe agent's preoccupation with a private trading venture of his own'.[31]

At a higher level, Thomas Bretell of Moor Lane, the clerk of the Stourbridge and Dudley Canal Companies, owned four boats trading between Moor Lane and Stourport in 1795, and was possibly in partnership with a Mr Pidcock for a further five.[32] At a still higher level, there was of course John Gilbert, with his salt boats. His son, the other partner in the firm of Worthington and Gilbert, probably found it no disadvantage to be the son of the duke's agent. In a category of his own was John Rooth, who seems to have emerged from a carrying business on the Huddersfield canal that was closely connected with the company to become superintendent of the whole canal in 1801, while still carrying on the boating business.[33]

### JOINT-STOCK COMPANIES AND PARTNERSHIPS

Capital for canal carrying was sometimes raised on a joint-stock basis. With the exception of joint-stock companies incorporated by Crown charter or by Act of Parliament (as were canal companies), the joint-stock company in the eighteenth and early nineteenth centuries was, strictly speaking, illegal from the Bubble Act of 1720 down to its repeal in 1825.

Corporate status gave business enterprise a definite commercial advantage.[34] Unfortunately, these advantages were not available to most commercial enterprises, since the process of obtaining incorporation by Act or charter was difficult and expensive, and, except in certain accepted forms of business, successful applications were few. Therefore, at a time of increasing industrial activity, business organisation was, in theory, cut off from the advantages which flowed from those 'Rivers which always continue the same though their waters are always changing', as one eighteenth-century legal adviser described the corporation.[35] Entrepreneurs, faced with the growing inadequacy of the one-man business or the partnership, were eager for the advantages of incorporation, and it was the achievement of shrewd eighteenth-century lawyers to create forms of unincorporated business companies which, while more unwieldy, gave many of the advantages of the incorporated company, by circumventing the law. It was in the Birmingham area, where the expanding mineral industries were demanding better means of raising capital and improved business organisation, that this 'stepchild of the law' flowered to the fullest extent.[36]

Quite apart from colliery and iron companies, which owned boats to transport their goods, there were canal carriage businesses which presumably represented the unincorporated company at about its fullest development, since several were clearly capitalised by the sale of freely transferable shares to a large number of people. An advertisement of 1800 was signed by twenty-three ex-shareholders of the Warwick Boat Company.[37] The Hockley Boat and Coal Company, owning five boats in 1796, 'in its infance has seldom divided less than twenty per cent of profit', it was claimed in 1797, when three shares of the company were to be sold by auction.[38] The famous carrying firm of Crowley and Hicklin would appear to have developed out of the Wolverhampton Boat Company, founded around 1803 by some inhabitants of that town.[39]

Another method of raising capital, which particularly suited the man of limited means who wished to become his own master, was the partnership, and there is evidence to show that a few humble boatmen acquired their boat in this way. For example, two Hanley men, Samuel Steele and John Prime, owned a boat in partnership in 1795, steered by Samuel Steele himself.[40] John Heath, of Milton, owned two boats in partnership with Benjamin Parr and George Cope, and himself steered one of the boats between Norton Colliery and Oxford.[41] The partnership, especially the multiple partnership, was particularly common with the more expensive Weaver flats. For a flat to have five owners was not unusual. But, just as here such part-owners are recognisable as being substantial capitalists, so, too, on the canals proper there is little evidence to show that more than an insignificant few part-owners of boats in 1795 were members of the boating class, or had risen from such beginnings.

In fact many partnerships exhibited features of the unincorporated business company. Dubois informs us that

> in the eighteenth century the distinction between a partnership and a joint-stock company was primarily a matter of size. The partnership, in which a small number of persons invested not too extensive a sum, shaded imperceptibly into the unincorporated joint stock company, when the individuals concerned and the capital were increased.[42]

Hence, the public were informed 'of the forming of a partnership under the name of the Gainsbro' Boat Co.' on 1 July 1793.[43] Later there was Pickford & Co. and Worthington & Co.

Although the label '& Co' may well have been a loose expression, used to abbreviate the title of even the most diminutive of joint affairs (two humble boatmen owning one boat in partnership, for example), nonetheless, wherever it was possible to discover more of a firm listed as '& Co.' it was found to be a substantial undertaking. The inference must be that such a title did have some significance as representing an organisation which had adopted some of the features of the unincorporated business company, and therefore indicated a business of some standing.[44] Our assumption is that '& Co.' would not describe a union of two simple boatmen, although the absence of such words need not deny the existence of a wealthier partnership.

### OWNERS OF ONE BOAT

Such an assumption helps us to assess the types of men who owned, or part-owned, one boat. There were 129 boats owned by one-boat owners and part-owners and, if it could be shown that boatmen had a substantial stake in the ownership of these 10 per cent of boats, it would still be a significant amount, and even go some little way towards justifying the assertions of de Maré and Rolt. But, again, this seems not to be, since the owners of one boat appear to have been much the same kinds of people as those who owned several, i.e. substantial businessmen.

Here, as elsewhere in the registers, owners of one boat were labelled '& Co.'[45] In addition, John Beebee of Willenhall was a mine owner and owned one boat.[46] Isaac Aston, of Tipton, used his one boat to transport the bricks he made at Bloomfield.[47] Again, country gentlemen appear. Richard Aston Esq., of Bescott Hall, James Barber Esq., of Barton-under-Needwood, and Thomas Lyon Esq. all owned or part-owned one boat.[48] Richard Rabone was a substantial farmer, of Smethwick, who had used the canal since the earliest days.[49] Others are known to have owned works such as Benjamin Gibbons & Co, of the Level Ironworks,[50] and John Izon & Co.[51] The Byerley of Etruria, who owned a boat in partnership with Josiah Wedgewood, was almost certainly Wedgewood's nephew.[52] John Baddeley of Shelton, part-owning a boat with Richard Simms, was also probably the potter described by Miss Meteyard.[53]

All the owners mentioned above employed boatmen to steer their boats, but there were owner-boatmen, 'number ones',[54] who steered their own boats, in 1795. There was George Alcock, of Tetton in Cheshire, who traded between the Pottery (presumably Stoke-on-Trent) and Runcorn, and between Shardlow and Manchester.[55] John Barlow, of Lawton in Cheshire, steered his own boat between Manchester and Birmingham,[56] as did Thomas Curtis between Tipton and Banbury.[57] There were others, but the most conclusive statistic to emerge from the registers of 1795 is that *less than 4 per cent of all the boats (some of them river boats) in the five counties were steered by their owners or part-owners*, representing about 6 per cent of all the masters in those same counties, which is hardly 'most craft' nor does it warrant the assumption, 'the majority of whom were owner boatmen'.

It might perhaps be suggested that already, by 1795, the 'number ones' were less numerous than at the inception of the earliest canals, to which perhaps de Maré's 'originally' may refer, but such evidence as exists for the early years of the Birmingham canal appears to contradict any such suggestion. The pattern of ownership seems to have been much the same as that established around 1795. In the early 1770s, of those paying tonnage to the canal company,[58] there were many coal-mine owners like Merrs Baker & Co., and Parkes & Co.[59] Messrs Ruston and Grew, Thomas Russell and Henry Venour were substantial shareholders.[60] The largest tonnages were carried by the canal company itself, and the Birmingham Boat Company. Others were listed as '& Co.': Aitkin & Co., Askey & Co., and so on, many of them probably being colliery firms.

It is clear, however, that some did emerge from the ranks of the boatmen to own their own boats, and that men of humble origins, whether boatmen or no, did graduate some little way and developed a small carrying business, but it is unlikely that many rose to fame and fortune in the carrying world as has sometimes been suggested. Although the price of new boats was prohibitive, no doubt second-hand boats came within the reach of small men, and there is evidence to show that after the first enthusiasm had worn away quite a few such boats began to come on to the market.[61] Failing that, there was always the expedient of hiring a boat or boats. William Barnett was hiring three and four boats a week from the Birmingham Canal Company in 1777 at 7s [35p] a week each, and by 1795 he owned ten trading between Birmingham, Tipton and Wednesbury.[62] Boats were specifically built 'to be let . . . (by the year)'.[63] It is doubtful if many men hiring boats were of humble origins; Lord Dudley also hired three boats in 1778 for bringing coals to Birmingham.[64] Richard Miller was probably exceptional. He had gone to Gloucestershire in 1793 as an apprentice in the office of the Thames and Severn Canal Company at Brimscombe Port. On completing his indentures he had left the company and hired one of their trows and two of their Thames barges to carry coal to Lechlade. He later bought these boats and by about 1812 he owned seven barges.[65] Others, sometimes boatmen, seem to have got the chance to begin trading on their own account when canal companies decided to abandon their unprofitable carrying businesses, as most of them did, leasing their boats or selling them at low prices.

### DIFFICULTIES FACING THE SMALL OPERATOR

One boatman who appears to have scraped together enough to buy a boat was Henry Wright, but the difficulties he faced show but one of the many problems with which the 'number one' had to contend. H. Rolls, of Priors Marston, informed the Oxford Canal Company, by a letter of 15 July 1794, that

Before the Oxford Canal was finished, I understand the Company erected a wharf near to Fenny Compton Bridge, at which a great deal of business was done, till the Tunnelling in Fenny Compton field was perfected after which it was nearly if not quite useless till within the last two or three years during which period Mr Jas. Griffin and Co. have used it and claims an exclusive right of so doing. One Henry Wright of Fenny Compton who had just a sufficiency to work a boat, some time since entered into the Coal Trade and says that by it he was likely to get a comfortable livelihood, but on account of the exclusive right of unloading at the Fenny Compton wharf, claimed by Mr James Griffin his trade will be wholly put a stop to, as there is no other place in or near to Fenny Compton where he can unload. Wright tells me that he has always been willing and has offered to pay Mr Griffin 3d [1p] per ton to permit him to unload at this wharf, but that his offer was always rejected, and therefore that he had for some time past unloaded upon the Turnpike Road leading from Southam to Banbury, the Herbage of which road I am informed, is rented by Mr Griffin, who in May last year gave Wright notice not to trespass their [*sic*], by either laying or stacking Coals thereon or otherwise—notwithstanding which Wright continued to unload there till within this fortnight, when an Action was commenced against him by Mr Griffin for unloading upon the said Turnpike Road—Wright has at this time some coals coming up which he dares not unload; . . . and if he [does] not he loses his Bread and the Coal Trade in the neighbourhood of Fenny Compton will be mono-polized to the injury of the County and the revinue of the Company. The cause of Mr Griffin thwarting Wright in the manner he does—is, I am told because Wright, who navigates his own Boat will, if his customers will meet him at the time he appoints, let them have coals at 1*d* [½p] cwt less than Mr Griffin generally sells at and this he says answers his purpose as he is then at liberty to go for more, and it answers the purpose of the Company as lowering the price induces people to come for Coals at a great distance from the Navigation than they otherwise would.[66]

Whatever the outcome, Henry Wright was still trading with his own boat in Sep-tember of the following year between Tipton and Fenny Compton, as was James Griffin with his two boats steered by James Heydon and Thomas Hickson, the latter also steering William Neale's boat along the same route.[67] Perhaps the pass-ing and repassing of the four boats was not always amicable.

Elsewhere small traders and owner-boatmen experienced similar difficulty in unloading their boats. It was not a problem confined to small men, but inevitably it was they who came off the worst. Loading and unloading facilities were often provided free by the canal company. The Paradise Street Wharf 'hath ever been free to the use of the Traders and public', John Houghton claimed.[68] Such free wharves were often seething with boats, jostling to find a berth to unload.[69] That small men were at a disadvantage is clear. Thus, on 2 June 1780 Mr Bourne, a wealthy coal master, successfully demanded a station at the Birmingham wharf at the expense of Izon, a small trader, and such a policy was continued.[70]

The larger companies were able to circumvent these difficulties by building their own wharves and warehouses, or by renting them on liberal terms from the company. Many canal companies, to get trade moving on their canals in the early days, and further to encourage it later, gave assistance by building warehouses and renting them to carriers; by providing cheap boat-building facilities;[71] by leasing boats or by selling them cheaply; and even with loans.[72] But, of course, canal com-panies were obviously keener to grant loans to, and provide facilities for, men who already possessed substantial amounts of capital, or were known to be men of some social standing and proved ability. Hence, probably, the refusal to allow Richard Hipkiss to hire boats.[73] The Thames and Severn Canal Company, on its withdrawal from carrying, insisted that only 'proper persons' should participate.[74]

The question of credit also favoured the larger boating firms, since they seemed a more reliable risk, if only because they had large visible assets which might make up any deficit in the event of a failure. For the same kind of reason the larger com-panies attracted the more valuable type of goods. As Baxendale put it later:

> If persons have Property of consequence, they would wish to put it into the Hands of
> Men of Property, so that if there is any Loss they can get, if not the whole at least 10*s*
> [50*p*] in the Pound, but if they are put into the Hands of a Man not worth a Bawbee,
> they can get nothing.[75]

Another consequence was that the 'number one' had to pay the tolls in cash at the locks, and the small owner had to trust his boatmen with the money, if he were unable to obtain the usual three months' credit. The large capitalist was able to save substantially by paying quarterly.

That the refusal of credit was a considerable inconvenience is demonstrated by the experience of Thomas Sherratt. In 1797 he wrote:

> Mr Dunsford writes me I must pay Mr Brown at Hawkesbury Stop [lock] every Boat this order. I hope you will in your goodness alter and let me have my account from Oxford as usual as I shall persevere until I can make my remittances for the tonnage to the satisfaction of the Committee . . . Please to pardon me but I shall be very hard press[d] to find money to work my boats for this next month.[76]

The difficulties of Messrs Orpington and Seal, Oxford coal merchants, before they obtained quarterly credit provide a further example. Apparently they could not trust all their boatmen, since a 5s [25p] loan to one of them 'would be sufficient for him until he could be trusted'. Consequently, they had to resort to sending money by letter to the points where their boatmen had to pay tonnage tolls. Inevitably, letters were late, and this steerer was held up for several days in Birmingham as a result.[77] Edward Atkins of Banbury was also having 'great difficulty in sending the money by the men'.[78]

Another problem presented itself with the competitive nature of canal carrying. There was strong competition between different boating companies on the same line, and with different boating firms running over different canal routes. In addition, there was competition from different modes of transport in the form of coastal shipping, land transport and—of course, much later—the railways. On the same line of waterway there were always those trying to steal a march on their rivals. William Ellis and Joseph Bowerman offered to sell best Staffordshire or Tipton coal, at Witney on the Oxford canal, for £1 7s [£1 35p] per ton, 'provided you will allow us a drawback of three shillings [15p] per Tun of coals sold at Ensham wharf by us. And not make the same allowance to any other person or persons.'[79] Charles Moore had for some years been sending his salt from Shirley-wich to Oxford at rock bottom prices in an attempt to wrest the trade from the Droitwich salt masters, but in sending their salt through the Thames and Severn canal they were persistently able to undercut him.[80] No doubt carriage rates were pared to a minimum in the contest.

The midland carriers, anxious to capture the long-distance traffic from the north and midlands to the south of England, had forever to keep a weather eye open upon the route which loomed menacingly at their backs, via the Trent, through Gainsborough and Hull, and by coastal shipping to London, and thence (occasionally) up the Thames. Trade attracted from that route was liable to revert to its previous channel.

> I am afraid that the Cannon and Fire which is for Government and Twenty Tuns a week must be gave up and also much larger Quantitys of heavy Goods which have usually gone by way of Hull,

Thomas Sherratt complained in 1793.[81] Even after the opening of the Grand Junction canal, trade still moved from the north by river and coast, and, although the canal route came to have the advantage, this competition seems to have continued into the steamboat era before it was (perhaps temporarily) overcome.[82] The carriers upon the Basingstoke canal felt a chilling competitive draught from the coastal shipping of the south coast, abated for a time by the disruptions of the Napoleonic Wars, but renewed with vigour after Waterloo.[83]

Nor were the canals so all-conquering over the land carriers as is sometimes thought, especially over short distances. In 1791, of the 250,000 tons of coal brought annually into Birmingham, about 70,000 tons were brought by land, mainly from Wednesbury.[84] It would seem that farmers were not content to restrict their carrying activities to areas untouched by canals, but in some instances continued to carry along the line of a canal, at almost any price, rather than go to, or return from market empty-handed. On the Peak Forest and Ashton canals there was this type of competition.

> The parties who bring the lime are small Farmers in the neighbourhood of Chapel-on-Frith and they cart it at a very low price indeed as that enables them to come into the Manchester market.

However, Mr Meadows made clear that it was only 2,000 out of 29,000 tons which were brought by cart.[85]

More serious were the developments which resulted from the improvement and construction of roads, from the end of the eighteenth century, which brought greater competition from land carriage over longer distances. In Hampshire, for example, the carriers on the Basingstoke canal came under increasing pressure from road waggons.[86] The canals were particularly susceptible to land competition for three reasons. The first is clearly demonstrated by Bouverie's statement in 1841:

> [The Grand Junction Canal] is circuitous in the Neighbourhood of London, and therefore Towns probably only from Thirty to Forty miles from London by Road are as much as Sixty by Canal. The Road Waggons to such places, at Times have very much interfered with the Canal.[87]

The second is that, over short distances, where goods were not being moved from one station on the canal bank to another similarly situated, it was sometimes as cheap, and invariably faster, to send goods by cart and waggon from and to points reasonably distant from the canal, since, instead of goods having to be handled four times, with all the possible delays and expense involved, by land carriage this could be avoided.[88] Thirdly, although long-distance land carriage, was, and remained, more expensive, it was faster and more reliable.

Regularity and speed, for which a customer would often be prepared to forego the cheapest rate, presented another problem to the canal carrier. That the demand for this type of transit was considerable is evident by the rapid growth in the number of fly-boats in the first half of the nineteenth century. But to provide such a regular service could be a costly business, since this often meant that the boat was not carrying a pay load, and the existence of goods for back carriage invariably represented the difference between profit and ruin. Thomas Sherratt again had his troubles.

> If I cannot send goods enough to clear the barges from Oxford about every eight days then shall loose a part of my trade which pays you a higher tonnage and me a better freight.[89]

And there was an imbalance of trade on almost every waterway route.

Canal charges also became increasingly complex, the ordinary tolls being complicated by special rates. There would be a special rate for this, but not for that type of goods, on this route for nails, but on that for sugar, a cheaper rate on iron going down, but not coming up, or a part of a cargo at the reduced rate, but the rest at the full rate. In addition, there were the intricacies of the drawbacks (i.e. special reductions of tolls on long-distance goods), arranged with different canal companies, increasing the bewilderment. Since there was no canal clearing house, each canal company had to be dealt with separately. William Watts, the manager of Crowley & Co., was nearing the end of his patience in 1839:

> There are so many drawbacks that it is a puzzle to me and every other person in the Carrying Trade—there is more drawback on things of that sort than any man could know or remember.[90]

As Mr Turnbull points out, it must have needed an army of clerks to keep all these accounts in order, and Pickfords admitted that it was 'no light tax upon the drawbacks'.[91] The odds against humble semi-literate owner-boatmen being at ease in this jungle of rates were high. Obviously, too, the canal companies favoured making rate concessions to large carriers, thus bringing a perceptibly greater trade on to the canal. The small owner-boatman, passing once a week, or even less frequently, with a load of 20 tons, was hardly likely to be greatly favoured.

And there was always the hand of God, descending almost every year, sometimes aided by man's frailty, to bring ruin to the small man and grave disquiet to even the largest companies. It could happen that a canal might be closed for many weeks. Frost, for example, invariably closed the canal for a time each year in the eighteenth century, despite the often heroic efforts of the men of the canal company, and the boatmen, to keep it open.[92] Then the expensive expedient of continuing to send goods by land, by hiring waggons, had to be adopted or, failing that, a complete loss of revenue was sustained. Summer also was a time of dislocation caused by annual stoppages of various canals, often not synchronised, and even quite short dry spells could result in a shortage of water on most canals, if not a complete stoppage. Shortages of water led to delays, through boats being compelled to take turns at the locks, and to uneconomic loading, since boats could carry less, which in turn used up more water since more boats were needed. These water shortages sometimes resulted from the inadequacies of the canal companies.

> Their [sic] must be either inability in the engineer or he neglects is [sic] report to the

Committee or the Committee neglect giveing [*sic*] proper orders for the execution and Maintaining of it,

Thomas Sherratt wrote, in 1793, of the Oxford canal, for,

> I calculated my freight under the idea that I could carry 16 or 18 Tons in a Boat which to my very great injury I cannot gett over the Summit . . . with more than half that Burden and am obliged to hire the other half over which I pay from two to three pounds for each time.[93]

Most canals had similar problems at one time or another. Hugh Henshall, engineer of the Trent and Mersey canal, wrote in 1796 that, 'before the late rains Boats cou'd not pass with more than nine tons, which was a great delay and inconvenience to all canals that connected with the Grand Trunk'.[94]

The simple fact was that canal carrying, especially over long distances, was an extremely complex and competitive business, becoming increasingly so, and the bulk of the goods was carried by large carriers. This was equally true of short-distance transport, where the large users and sellers of the transported goods carried most of them. The few owner-boatmen were restricted to the sweepings left by these large companies (inhibited as they were by high overheads), in the carriage of low-value goods such as coal, stone, lime, ironstone and manure. Their principal occupation was probably the providing of a regular supply to small dealers and works, over a regular and reasonably short route, with occasional variations. Alternatively, they might be hired by the large companies during times of trade boom, to be discarded in times of slump, thus acting as a reserve pool of boats. It also sometimes happened that a canal company, anxious to get trade moving along its waters, would arrange a trade in which such men could participate. For example, the Warwick and Napton Canal Company made all the arrangements, after its opening in 1800, for coal to be moved from Staffordshire via its canal to stations along the Oxford canal. An agreement of 18 July 1800 between Peter Downing, a Birmingham coal dealer, and the company was swiftly followed by similar agreements[95] with other small men, such as Joseph Duffield, William Whitehouse[96] and William Beddington, all of Tipton, and William Westbury of Anyho, all of whom were probably owner-boatmen, as James Dunn of Tipton and his partner, Abraham Darby, certainly were.[97]

Thus the business life of the owner-boatman, and the small trader with his two or three boats, was a precarious one. It seems clear that many fell by the wayside. At least some of the earliest traders upon the Birmingham canal were small men, as shown in part (in the journals) by the few tons they carried each week.[98] Such names, over the years, came and went with considerable frequency. One boat, in 1795, was being operated by 'the Assignees of John and Samuel Hallen—bankrupts'.[99] In February 1794, the creditors of Joseph Warren were beating upon his door.[100] In 1799, Henry Betts, who had owned four boats in 1795, was in imminent danger of bankruptcy.[101] It was recorded that 'men navigating their own barges [on the Basingstoke canal] scarcely earn a subsistence',[102] and bankruptcies seem to have been frequent there,[103] as they were also on the Thames and

Severn canal, including that of Richard Miller before mentioned.[104] Seizures of boats and bankruptcies were a particularly common feature of the canal scene, as recorded in several canal company minute books, between 1816 and 1822, although failures were not, of course, a prerogative of boat owners during this period.

The difficulties of the small trader, especially one who had aspired towards the big league of carriers, are amply demonstrated by the experience of Thomas Sherratt. He appears to have risen from lowly beginnings, 'being with Messrs Henshall and Co when they established theirs from this town [Birmingham] to Liverpool and Hull',[105] probably as a clerk rather than as a boatman. He began to work boats in 1792, with two running between Birmingham and Oxford, 'for a considerable time with little or no loading'.[106] None the less, assisted by some special rate concessions from the Oxford and Coventry canal companies he had by 1795 'increased his boats to eight which are now in full work'.[107] By 1796 he had ten,[108] and by the end of 1797, he had 'gott eleven in the trade beside two hired ones which enable me to send a barge down every 7 or 8th day which gives that dispatch to the trade that I expect it to increase'.[109] But Sherratt's troubles, some of which we have already seen, were only just beginning. He was to have problems of finding adequate back-loading, of maintaining regularity, of competition, of high rates, of bad weather,[110] of wharfage space,[111] of shortage of capital, of loss of credit and of inefficient canal maintenance. Although he had acquired another boat by 1798,[112] by 1800 he was fearful of being arrested for debt.[113] He seems to have survived until 23 June 1806 when it was advertised that the firm of Thomas Sherratt, 'bankrupt', was being operated on behalf of the creditors.[114] He was compelled to advertise for the post of manager to a carrying firm in September and by October his boats had been bought by Judd and Sons with T. Sherratt acting as manager. In May 1807 a dividend of 3s [15p] in the pound was eventually paid to the creditors.[115]

Even larger firms were not without their problems. In 1800 the Warwick Boat Co. was apparently on the verge of failure,[116] and the mighty Pickford was in grave financial difficulty in 1816,[117] but of course the larger firms, usually well-endowed with capital from the outset, were in a much better position to ward off the many crises which were part and parcel of canal transportation. It would be wrong, of course, to give the impression that the canal carrier lived in perpetual gloom and that all teetered on the verge of bankruptcy, but it can be seen how the margin between success and failure could be very slim, faced as the carrier might be by so many difficulties beyond his control.

CONCLUSION

The capital for canal carriage seems to have come principally from the canal companies, in that they appear to have been the largest contributors, either through their own carrying businesses or through assistance, such as loans, to others. For the rest, it was raised from a variety of sources and by a variety of methods: from

industries involved in the use of canal transport; by the partnership; from inves-
tors, both through the medium of the joint-stock company or more directly from
people involved in canal management; and from existing carriers who transferred from land to water, e.g. Pickford.[118] Where there were profits they
were no doubt, also, ploughed back to finance further expansion. Last, and
almost certainly least, a little capital was generated from the savings of boatmen, but the evidence of widespread expansion from such a base is not very
abundant. Owner-boatmen were few and even fewer seem to have risen from
the ranks to become anything like substantial carriers.

### NOTES TO CHAPTER TWO

[1]  Eric de Maré, *The Canals of England* (1950; 1965 ed.), p. 15.

[2]  Rolt, *Narrow Boat* (1944; 1965 ed.), p. 32.

[3]  Rolt, *Inland Waterways of England* (1950; 1962 ed.), p. 145.

[4]  De Maré, *op. cit.*, p. 15.

[5]  Lancashire, Cheshire, Staffordshire, Warwickshire and Gloucestershire. The registers for
Derbyshire and Leicestershire do not give details of ownership.

[6]  Duke of Bridgewater, 81; Hugh Henshall & Co., 75; Thames & Severn Canal Co., 47;
Birmingham Coal Co., 25; Worthington & Gilbert, 23; Burton Boat Co. 19; John Gilbert ('of
Clough Hall Merchant'), 16; Thomas Honeyborn, 16; Charles Norton & Co., 16; Thomas Russell
& Co., 15; Joseph Smith & Son, 14; Hateley & Taylor, 13: total 360 boats. See also Appendix II, sec-
tions (i) and (ii).

[7]  Only a handful of these were maintenance boats.

[8]  Boat Register 1795, 203–10, 529, 531, S.R.O.; OXC 4/81/1, Moore to Dunsford, 2 April 1799;
OXC 4/80/6, Moore to Dunsford, 17th April 1798. See Appendix II, section (iii).

[9]  W. H. Chaloner 'Salt in Cheshire 1600–1870', Lancashire and Cheshire Antiquarian Society
*Transactions*, vol. LXXI, 1961, pp. 71–2; Boat Register 1795, 35–41, C.R.O. It is not certain that this
was the John Gilbert who was listed in Boat Register 1795, 333–48, S.R.O., as 'of Clough Hall, Merchant'.

[10]  BCN 1/4, 26 October 1776 p. 42; Boat Register 1795, 182–90, S.R.O.

[11]  *Ibid.* (Register), 427–33.

[12]  Peter Stevenson, *The Nutbrook Canal: Derbyshire* (1970), p. 80. John Sutton was the lessee of
Henry Hunloke's West Hallam collieries in the 1790s, *ibid,*, p. 21.

[13]  Boat Register 1795, 250–5, S.R.O.; BCN 1/1, 4 June 1770, p. 100, 12 April 1771, p. 255; BCN
1/3, 11 June 1773, p. 10, 23 June 1773, p. 11; BCN 1/7A, 1 April 1796; STW 1/4, 5 June 1806.

[14]  *Ibid.* (Register), 234–40, 456; BCN 4/371B, Houghton to Parker, July 1796, Houghton to
Parker, 16 May 1801.

[15]  *Ibid.* (Register) 447–51; Wills at Chester, Hugh Henshall of Longport, C.R.O., W.S., 14
October 1817.

[16]  Boat Register 1795, 74–83, C.R.O.

[17]  *Ibid.*, 49–51; Malley, 'Financial administration of the Bridgewater estates, 1780–1800' (1929), p.
59.

[18]  *Ibid.*, 60–2, 174; Malley, p. 59.

[19]  Wills at Chester, George Chesworth, C.R.O., W.S., 12 May 1817.

[20]  Boat Register 1795, 286–91, S.R.O.; BCN 1/7A, 10 June 1796, 7 September 1798; BCN
4/371B, Houghton to Best, 7 March 1801, Houghton to Best, 25 February 1804.

[21]  *Ibid.* (Register), 397–8; BCN 1/7A, 28 July 1797, 7 September 1798; BCN 4/371B, Houghton
to Dumaresq, 7 December 1798.

[22] *Ibid.* (Register), 367–9; BCN 4/371B, Houghton to Wilkinson, 21 October 1797.

[23] *Ibid.* (Register), 328, 351–4, W.R.O.; BCN 1/1, 15 April 1768, p. 31; BCN 1/4, 23 August 1782, p. 134; BCN 1/7A, 28 August 1795; BCN 4/371B, Houghton to Iddins, 9 March 1798.

[24] *Ibid.* (Register), 79–80, S.R.O.

[25] *Ibid.*, 149–50, C.R.O.

[26] *Ibid.*, 241–2, S.R.O.

[27] *Ibid.*, 351–3.

[28] OXC 1/4, 13 June 1791, p. 205.

[29] *Ibid.*, 13 December 1791, p. 259.

[30] BCN 1/7A, 28 June 1799.

[31] Household, *The Thames and Severn Canal* (1969), p. 114.

[32] Boat Register 1795, 310–13 and 305–9, S.R.O.; BCN 4/371B, Houghton to proprietors of Dudley Canal Navigation, early 1797; BCN 1/7A, 30 March 1798.

[33] Hadfield and Biddle, *The Canals of North West England* (1970), vol. II, pp. 326–7.

[34] See B. C. Hunt, *The Development of the Business Corporation in England 1800–67* (1936), p. 3.

[35] A. B. Dubois, *The English Business Company after the Bubble Act 1720–1800* (1938), p. 89.

[36] *Ibid.*, pp. 217, 231–6.

[37] *Aris's Birmingham Gazette*, 17 March 1800; GEN 4/857/3.

[38] *Ibid.*, 27 November 1797; Boat Register, 1795, 344–8, W.R.O.

[39] *S. C. on Sunday Trading*, 1841, 512–14.

[40] Boat Register, 1795, 458, S.R.O.

[41] *Ibid.*, 164–5.

[42] Dubois, *op. cit.*, p. 242, note 1.

[43] *Aris's Birmingham Gazette*, 29 July 1793; GEN 4/857/2.

[44] The various forms of unincorporated business companies are outlined in Dubois, *op. cit.*, chapter III, pp. 215–80.

[45] See for example Boat Register 1795, 350, 516, 399, S.R.O., and 271, W.R.O.

[46] Boat Register 1795, 366, S.R.O.; BCN 4/371B, Houghton to J. Beebee Esq., Willenhall, 10 April 1796; BCN 1/7A, 29 April 1796.

[47] *Ibid.* (Register), 495; BCN 1/7A, 24 February 1797.

[48] *Ibid.* (Register), 499–501, S.R.O., and 155, C.R.O.

[49] *Ibid.*, 272, W.R.O.; BCN 1/1, 25 March 1768, p. 23; BCN 4/371B, Houghton to Hanson, 20 March 1798, Houghton to Rabone, 15 June 1799; BCN 4/33, 17 March 1778, p. 195.

[50] Boat Register 1795, 457, S.R.O.

[51] *Ibid.*, 326, W.R.O.; BCN 1/7A, 27 May 1796.

[52] Boat Register 1795, 480, S.R.O.; Eliza Meteyard, *Life of Josiah Wedgewood*, vol. I (1865), pp. 326, 356.

[53] *Ibid.* (Register), 500; Meteyard, *op. cit.*, p. 357.

[54] It should be made clear that this expression does not appear in eighteenth and nineteenth century records.

[55] Boat Register 1795, 114, C.R.O.

[56] *Ibid.*, 161.

[57] *Ibid.*, 171, W.R.O.

[58] See the names listed under 'Tonnage Account' in the journals, as under BCN 4/29, 1770–1; BCN 4/30, 1771–2; BCN 4/31, 1772–3; BCN 4/32, 1773–4.

[59] BCN 1/1, 1 February 1771, p. 231; *ibid.*, 23 February 1770, p. 161.

[60] The share list is in BCN 1/1, 25 March 1768, p. 23.

[61] *Aris's Birmingham Gazette*, 29 August 1774; GEN 4/857/1.

[62] BCN 4/33, 5 April 1777, p. 23; Boat Register, 1795, 72–81, W.R.O.

[63] *Aris's Birmingham Gazette*, 23 February 1789; GEN 4/857/2.

[64] BCN 1/4, 1 May 1778, p. 72.

[65] Household, *op. cit.*, pp. 120–1.

[66] OXC 4/80/2, Rolls to Dunsford, 15 July 1794.

[67] Boat Register 1795, 202, 169–70, W.R.O.

[68] BCN 4/371B, Houghton to Woodcock, 7 December 1804.

[69] BCN 1/3, 29 July 1774, p. 66.

[70] BCN 1/4, 2 June 1780, p. 106; the treatment of Isaac Parkes provides a later example, Boat Register 1795, 319, W.R.O.; BCN 4/371B, Houghton to Parkes, 7 September 1804.

[71] BCN 1/1, 19 October 1770, p. 211 and BCN 4/29, 28 February 1771, for examples on the Birmingham canal.

[72] See Hadfield and Biddle, *op. cit.*, p. 326, for the favourable treatment accorded to John Rooth.

[73] See above p. 12.

[74] Household, *op. cit.*, p. 119.

[75] *S. C. on Sunday Trading*, 1841, q. 1261.

[76] OXC 4/80/5, Sherratt to Durrell, 18 December 1797 and OXC 4/80/6, Sherratt to Dunsford, 26 December 1797 (i.e. located in In-letters 1798).

[77] BCN 4/371B, Houghton to Orpwood and Seal, 5 September 1797.

[78] OXC 4/80/3, Atkins to Oxford Canal Company, 19 October 1795.

[79] OXC 4/80/2, Ellis and Bowerman to Parsons, 15 November 1794.

[80] OXC 4/81/1, Moore to Dunsford, 2 April 1799, Ward and Holland, and Brooks and Evetts to Oxford Canal Company, 9 April 1799.

[81] OXC 4/80/1, Sherratt to Dunsford, 2 November 1793; OXC 4/80/6, Sherratt to Dunsford, 6 February 1798.

[82] *S. C. on Sunday Trading*, 1841, qq. 11, 1045, 1094. See also q. 592 for competition from the Bristol-Liverpool coastwise trade.

[83] Vine, *London's Lost Route to Basingstoke* (1968), pp. 67, 99.

[84] H.L.R.O., MS., Mins. of Evid., H.L., 1791, Birmingham Canal Bill, 24 May 1791, p. 11.

[85] H.L.R.O., MS. Mins. of Evid., H.C., 1836, vol. 24, Manchester and Salford Canal Bill, 19 May 1836, pp. 88–90.

[86] Vine, *London's Lost Route to Basingstoke*, p. 103.

[87] *S. C. on Sunday Trading*, 1841, q. 1129.

[88] This was particularly true of the area in and around Manchester. The neglect of the Manchester Bolton and Bury canal by manufacturers provides but one example; H.L.R.O., MS., Mins. of Evid., H.C., 1844, vol. 27, Manchester Bury and Rossendale and the Leeds and Manchester (Bury Branch) Railway Bill, p. 241.

[89] OXC 4/80/6, Sherratt to Dunsford, 13 February 1798.

[90] Birmingham Canal Bill, 21 April 1839, p. 103.

[91] G. L. Turnbull, 'Pickfords and the canal carrying trade 1780–1850', *Transport History*, vol. VI (1973), p. 18, (kindly loaned by the author before publication).

[92] This problem can be exaggerated. By the nineteenth century the constant passage of boats and the improved methods of breaking ice kept most canals open, except in the severest winter. Several years might pass without a canal being closed through frost.

[93] OXC 4/80/1, Sherratt to Dunsford, 2 November 1793.

[94] OXC 4/80/4, Henshall to Oxford Canal Company, 20 October 1796.

[95] OXC 4/81/2, Memorandum of Agreement, 18 July 1800; *ibid.*, Hickling to Dunsford, 31 July, 25 July, 6 September 1800.

[96] William Whitehouse of Tipton had been one of Richard Bissell's boatmen, in 1795, navigating two boats between Autherley and Birmingham; Boat Register 1795, 418, S.R.O.

[97] Abraham Darby had been a boatman for Thomas Bailey of Sedgley in 1795, at which time James Dunn was already a 'number one'. By 1800 they owned two boats in partnership; Boat Register 1795, 384, S.R.O., and 206, W.R.O.

[98] See the names listed under 'Tonnage Account' in the various journals, BCN 4/29 (1770–1) to BCN 4/48 (1794–6).

[99] Boat Register 1795, 508, S.R.O.

[100] BCN 1/7A, 14 February 1794.

[101] Boat Register 1795, 129–31, 158, W.R.O.; BCN 4/371B, Houghton to Parr, 12 July 1799.

[102] Vine, *London's Lost Route to Basingstoke* (1968), p. 69.

[103] *Ibid.*, pp. 70, 101.

[104] Household, *op. cit.*, pp. 119–21.

[105] OXC 4/80/1, Sherratt to Dunsford, 2 November 1793.

[106] OXC 4/80/3, Sherratt to Chairman, Oxford Canal Company, 26 August 1795.

[107] *Ibid.*

[108] Boat Register 1795, 240–7 and 349–50, W.R.O.

[109] OXC 4/80/5, Sherratt to Durrell, 18 December 1797.

[110] *Aris's Birmingham Gazette*, 19 January 1795, 14 January 1799; GEN 4/857/3.

[111] OXC 4/81/2, Sherratt to Oxford Canal Company, 12 December 1798 (i.e. located in In-Letters for 1800).

[112] OXC 4/80/5, Sherratt to Durrell, 18 December 1797.

[113] OXC 4/81/2, Sherratt to Bignell, 8 February 1800.

[114] *Aris's Birmingham Gazette*, 23 June 1806; GEN 4/857/4.

[115] *Ibid.*, 22 September, 13 October 1806, 11 May 1807.

[116] *Ibid.*, 17 March 1800; GEN 4/857/3.

[117] GJC 1/1, 27 September 1816, p. 44, and 17 October 1816, p. 49.

[118] *Transport Saga 1646–1947: The History of Pickfords* (1947), p. 17 (kindly loaned by Pickfords Ltd.).

III

# Canal boatmen
# in the
# first phase

## THE CASUAL NATURE OF EMPLOYMENT

THE EMPLOYMENT OF BOATMEN from the earliest times was, seemingly, on a casual
basis, in that each master boatman contracted to do one or a number of voyages, at
a rate per voyage, usually providing the horse and any extra labour himself.
Although boatmen continued to be employed on a relatively casual footing down
to quite recent times, the constant employment of the same master boatmen by the
same employers did, in practice, come to mean that many boatmen were sufficiently regularly employed to be listed with a specific employer in the 1795
registers, although some boatmen steered the boats of several boat owners. For
instance, John Dent, of Calf Heath, was the master of four boats trading between
Heywood and Stourport, one of William Reynolds & Co., of Ketley, two of John
Lycett, of Weeping Cross, and one of John Legg, of Bilston.[1] This practice was
not restricted to short-haul traffic, for Thomas Fisher provides but one example of
a boatman who steered the boats of several employers over long distances, in this
case the 140 miles between Tipton and Oxford.[2] An indication that for many
boatmen casual labour was the rule is perhaps demonstrated by an advertisement
in the *Birmingham Gazette*, in 1798. It read:

> Men of approved character wanted who will engage to steer themselves anywhere
> may meet with constant employment by applying to Rock, Walkers and Rock's, . . .
> Birmingham.[3]

For many decades, if our theory of the farming origins of the boatmen is correct,
this casual arrangement probably suited both the employers and the boatmen,
especially in the seasonal transportation of such materials as coal, the main product
conveyed by canal. At off-season times, and perhaps on one or two days a week,
the boatman could concentrate on his small farm. At the same time, where a small
works owned only one boat to carry its produce or to bring supplies, it was often
not employed more than two or three days a week. As the boat lay idle it made
sense for several such firms to hire a boatman only when he was needed. For the

rest of the time he could be steering boats for similar firms, or attending to his farm. That this practice was widely accepted is demonstrated by the information to Mrs Hipkiss in 1779 that, as well as hauling the coals of the Birmingham Canal Company, she was 'at liberty to employ herself for other persons as well as for the Company'; and she also hired the company's boats to carry for herself.[4]

By 1795 more canals were opening, trade was quickening, distances were increasing and the larger carrying firms could not be content with this haphazard system, particularly if they travelled long distances. Hence Rocks' advertisement for men to travel anywhere. The boatmen employed by the big carriers, such as Hugh Henshall & Co, Worthington and Gilbert, Pickfords, etc., were exclusively employed by them.

Such firms apart, often one boatman had charge of a substantial number of boats. Joseph Lawrence was the master of four barges, owned by the Thames and Severn Canal Company, operating the 169 miles between Brimscombe and London.[5] He and others[6] were probably cost-bearers, who travelled, usually with two barges, arranging for the payment of toll charges and generally superintending their passage.[7] This, in fact, meant that each was the master of several barges, two actually on route, another perhaps being loaded at Brimscombe waiting for his return, while others waited hopefully for a cargo in London, the imbalance of trade on this canal making this a common occurrence.[8] This practice was common elsewhere. In the Warwickshire register of 1795 it was noted, 'Five boats belong to the Oxford Canal Co. and are registered as such as two boats are always loading six men only are employed in working the other three'.[9] Similar shift working had operated in the earliest days on the Birmingham canal, where two steerers navigated twelve boats from the Wednesbury collieries to Birmingham, whilst others loaded, unloaded and took them through the locks.[10] This system was particularly convenient for passing relatively short distances and it is apparent that many of the boats were operated in this way. The Duke of Bridgewater's thirty-four lighters working between Worsley, Manchester and Runcorn, and the thirty-seven smaller boats carrying coal between Worsley and Manchester, had no fixed master, some presumably being loaded, others moving, and others being unloaded.[11] As we have seen, it was a mode of operation carried on over long distances as well, if on a more limited scale. Abraham Haywood of Sedgley provides another example. He steered two boats belonging to Jeremiah Holloway of Ettingshall. As he navigated the one between Stourport and Oxford (170 miles), presumably the other was being loaded for him to operate between Burton and Stourport.[12]

Some boatmen are listed with such a large number of boats and owners that it seems unlikely, even if some of them were being loaded and others not used very often, that the boatmen named could have handled so many. John Tinsley was responsible for twelve boats, i.e. seven of Messrs Durrad and Sprig, four of Henry Betts, and one of Richard Rabone, the farmer.[13] Several of these men can be traced back to the earliest boatmen. William Walker, responsible for fifteen boats, was probably one of those who had been paid for boating in the early 1770s.[14] William

Mountain, who appeared regularly in letters and minutes, certainly was; he attended to eleven boats.[15] So, too, was Job Lloyd with twelve boats, one of them being his own.[16]

The possibility arises that some of the original boatmen, apart from hiring themselves, had also come to act as sub-contractors for a supply of steerers over the short-distance routes in and around Birmingham. A reference to damage caused by 'W^m. Mountain or one of his Men, Steerers to Messrs. Grew and Co',[17] may substantiate this. A system of sub-contracting was in common use in the building of canals, where one man contracted to carry out work and hired labour to execute it, and it is possible that, in this way, men such as William Mountain and Job Lloyd acted as agents to provide steerers. However, if this did happen, it never applied to long-distance boats.

Whether this possibility is true or not, the master of a boat invariably hired his own assistant, often a boy or young man, but by no means always. Such assistance varied from the casual day-men to those who were hired by the year, if the evidence thrown up at the beginning of the nineteenth century is typical of earlier years. In 1800, at the age of 11, George Cooke was first hired as a day-labourer to several boatmen for about three years. He must have proved sufficiently capable for he was then hired by one boatman, John Foster, of Shelford in Nottinghamshire, by the week, for about two and a half years, and eventually, in 1806, by the year.[18] Thomas Carnell began his boating career, in 1799 at the age of 18, being hired by the week on a boat going from Brinsley Pit to Grantham.[19] John Parker was also hired by the week on a Trent and Mersey canal boat from 1802.[20] Richard Widdowson, however, who took up boating in 1796 when he was 18, was paid by the voyage.[21] Yearly hirings were probably rare.

### CHARACTERISTIC MALPRACTICES

The early canal boatmen were not timid men. It was inevitable that lock keepers and toll collectors should become their natural enemies, just as they had been and were to the river boatmen, although there were probably fewer doddering old men or people with interests other than the navigation among their ranks. These canal guardians were exhorted to save water, to preserve the fabric of the canal, and to collect the just dues of the canal company on pain of dismissal. On the other hand, the boatmen, being paid by results, were eager to proceed on their way as quickly as possible and were often careless of wasted water and of canal property, and sometimes not beyond defrauding the canal company.

The boatmen were careless about the timing of the opening and closing of lock paddles. They often opened those which filled the lock before those which emptied it were closed, thus causing water to pass straight through. This was not merely carelessness, for the boatmen used the flush of water to shut the bottom gates.[22] This closed these ponderous barriers rapidly and effortlessly, saving precious seconds, but the resounding crash of wood on stone was unlikely to have improved the condition of either the gates or the lock walls. There was also a danger of the boat being nipped between the heavy gates. All of these possibilities, together with the waste of water, tended to displease the canal company. Thus the 'Walking Surveyor' on the Birmingham canal was observed to have made a note in his book, at the Wolverhampton locks, of 'An empty boat coming up the above Locks, the Steerer draw'd the upper paddles at two separate Locks before he shut the lower Gates of either Lock', and John Houghton was anxious to know why the boatman had not 'at least been reprimanded if not taken before a magistrate'.[23] Further incidents led to yet another circular being issued to the company's lock keepers.

> The Committee taking into consideration the damage which has been done in the Locks and waste of water occasioned by the carelessness and negligence of the Boatmen have directed me to inform you that you are expected to see to the Passage of every Boat through the Locks under your care and in case of any damage . . . or waste occasioned by the negligence of any of the Boatmen . . . that you do (on pain of dismission) . . . report the same . . . that the offenders may be dealt with according to Law.[24]

Such carelessness had not suddenly appeared in the 1790s, but had been a constant feature of canal life since the earliest days. In 1771,

> John Chambers one of the Company's Lock keepers complained that John Littleford had violently forced upon the Gates of one of the Locks, notwithstanding he was forbidden so to do and much injured the same.[25]

There were many other instances and the Birmingham company was still complaining bitterly much later.[26] In times of water shortage the problem of disobedient steerers became acute, and the altercations numerous. Brookes informed the Committee that

> there is a great loss of water sustained by the persons not observing Turns in passing the Locks,[27] and that though he has frequently urged . . . the necessity of their observing proper order in passing the Locks yet that they not only refuse to acquiesce but threaten to break open the Lock Gates.[28]

For if the lock keepers attempted to reprimand or delay the boatmen they were sometimes ill-used. Action was to be taken against 'Samuel Cofield for an assault against Thomas Crow one of the Company's Servants when attending his Proper Business'.[29] Richard Smith, lock keeper at Autherley, in 1776, seems to have had a difference of opinion with Mr Parke's steerer John Brown, who had 'thrown him over some rails and otherwise hurt and abused him'.[30] And so it went on. Clearly many hundreds of boats passed peaceably, but there are frequent references to suggest that boatmen as a class did not like to be impeded in their progress.

They were also accused increasingly of dishonest practices. At the outset, they seem to have been generally more honest and respectable than their predecessors and contemporaries on the rivers, who had never been noted for either quality. The Severn boatmen were said to have been as 'skilled in pillaging cargoes and poaching game as in exploiting the moods of their unbridled river'.[31] Professor

Willan gives examples of the 'lewed' character of the river men in the years before the canals were built, although he is anxious to conclude with the words of an anonymous pamphleteer. 'I know many water-men, and I know them to be like other men, some very honest men and some naves.'[32]

Although Miss Meteyard, in describing them as 'inland pirates', probably did an injustice to many river men, there can be no doubt that river-borne goods were subject to a great deal of thieving, and to a much greater extent than those sent by land.[33] Often one of the reasons put forward for the 'utility' of a proposed canal was the dishonesty of the existing watermen. Conveyance would be much swifter, canal supporters claimed, and because there would be fewer delays and interruptions, opportunities for pilfering would be much reduced.[34] There were also to be fewer men involved in canal transport, and it was therefore suggested that, 'as one man and a boy will be sufficient to attend the conveyance of goods along the canal . . . the number of dangerous visitors will be greatly decreased'.[35] Opponents of canals were not convinced, but judging from the absence of complaints about the dishonesty of canal boatmen in the early years, both as regards the cargo and the territory passed through, the fears of these pessimists were not justified.[36]

However, it would seem that by the closing years of the eighteenth century steerers had worked out various 'fiddles', one of which was the use of employers' boats, unknown to them, for private ventures of their own.[37] Boat loads of coal were also regularly lightened on their way from mine to market. Messrs Russell and Hunter, in querying a discrepancy of nearly three tons between the weight of coal that they had dispatched, in 1790, and the weight which had arrived at Oxford, were informed, 'The Steersman Lees acknowledge[s] that he had sold out by the way 2 Tons and in another conversation 3$^T$. was very anxious to know the w$^t$. of the cargo'.[38] Charles Handley, in 1800, expressed his opinion that, 'considering the character of these men in general they may possibly deliver less [coal] at Oxford than they may have on at Napton'.[39]

Part of the trouble stemmed from the remarkable liberality of the coal-mine owners with this commodity, for not only did they supply a little extra per ton, for loss in transit, but at times they were positively generous.

> The Committee are very desirous that all due encouragement should be given to the Traders and especially those at a distance who are more subject to losses on the road but since coals have been in so great plenty at the Mines and so much strife for Trade among the Coal Masters – The weights carried have been too unequal to pass without notice,

the Birmingham Canal Company's secretary complained.[40]

Although the canal companies were prepared to tolerate some discrepancy, in cargoes of coal at least, it was in order to prevent excessive cheating—by which they of course received less tolls—that a system of *gauging* boats was evolved to establish quickly the amount of cargo carried. Previously the laborious and time-consuming expedient of weighing each cargo had been used.[41]

Two methods of gauging, often complementary, were adopted. By the first, numerous metal strips, 'gauge indexes' were fixed to the corners of each boat, and from the four metal strips nearest to the waterline, the tonnage of the boat could be read off at a glance. The second method involved the measurement of the 'dry inches' between the waterline and the highest point on the hull, by means of a portable callibrated float. The tonnage of the boat could be worked out by reference to tables in a 'gauge book' equating tons with 'dry inches'. Each boat using the canal had a table under its name or number worked out at the canal company's graving dock before it began to use the canal.[42]

The first method had been adopted by the Birmingham company by 1773, but an exact account of the weight of cargo could not be guaranteed with this system.[43] It gave the toll collector only a rough idea of the accuracy of the bill of lading presented by the boatman. Hence, it would appear that, by the later years of the eighteenth century the sequence of events on many canals would be as follows. A boat would enter the lock or stop lock by the toll office, and the toll collector would examine the tonnage indexes on the boat. If these corresponded, roughly, with the declaration of tonnage issued by the colliery (or the owner of the boat) to the steerer, then it would be allowed to pass, on payment of the required toll (unless the owner had credit with the canal company). If the toll collector was not satisfied, the boat would be gauged 'by the rod' (method two), and any extra tonnage would have to be paid for or noted. In addition, an extra 2s 6d [$12\frac{1}{2}$p] would have to be paid to the man who did the gauging, and a possible fine of 10s [50p] for every ton overweight might be exacted.[44] This was not popular with the boatmen, since the process of gauging by the rod could take up some time, especially if it was carried out too zealously or to the detriment of other traffic. The Staffordshire and Worcestershire Canal Company's agent, at Autherley, became unpopular through

> Gauging the Boats going downwards in the 20th Lock . . . [which] greatly retards the Business of this Canal and often causeth many Boats to be in the Pound above said Lock waiting while others are gauged.[45]

Where a boat was found to be overloaded the extra weight was entered on the boatman's permit, to his displeasure, since the exact tonnage was now clearly indicated, and he no longer had an opportunity of selling the extra coal at public houses, to other boatmen, to lock keepers, or to relatives and friends on the way, without exposing himself to awkward questions. Thus Houghton explained to one puzzled owner, presented with a permit bearing two weights,

> The extra weight being entered in the Ticket gives the owner an opportunity of examining the fidelity of his boatmen without which entry it is possible that no such extra weight could reach the place of destination.[46]

However, the steerers continued to be one jump ahead. Houghton wrote to Lord Dudley's agent that he was aware that

> alterations in the weight [written on the permit] are very frequently made by the Boatmen,[47] and I have always apprehended the reason for them to have arisen from

the Bounty of the Coalmasters in the allowance they have made of extra weight—
the fear of detection when gauged by our agents and the expense and delay to which
they would thereby be subjected.

But, he had to admit, 'you have convinced me there may be another motive and I
think a worse and that our Agents may innocently and without design have been
accomplices in fraud'.[48] Either the boatmen were declaring only a part of the
excess, thereby lulling the suspicions of the busy toll collector, who duly noted
down the supposed extra weight or received payment for it, and the undeclared
portion was then sold or otherwise disposed of; or, since the ticket was collected
by the canal company, and presumably the carrier or customer did not see it unless
they specifically asked to do so at the canal company office, they paid for tolls on
coal which the boatman later sold.[49]

Where a ticket was carried throughout, or where the weights were carefully
checked on arrival, the boatman could still adopt the expedient of watering the
coal. The agreement with Peter Downing and others, in 1800, stipulated, 'the
boats to be as free from water and put in to such state as is most proper for ascertaining the weight fairly either by the index or gauging'.[50]

It seems clear that by the end of the eighteenth century the boatmen had convinced themselves at least that a free and not insubstantial supply of coal was one
of the perks of their trade. Commodities other than coal also began to receive the
attention of the boatmen. In 1790, the proprietors of the Trent and Mersey canal
informed the public of their intention to introduce lock-up boats, to protect wines
and liquors, in consequence of the increased pilfering.[51]

At the same time, it is only fair to point out that if boatmen were paid by the
ton, and they were carrying more than was declared on the ticket, they were not
themselves being paid for carrying such excess, and it is not surprising that many
of them looked upon this surplus as their own. With relatively unsaleable commodities, such as ironstone, pig iron, limestone, flagstones and manure, they were
understandably aggrieved to find that they were overloaded. One of Henshall &
Co's boatmen became excited about such a predicament in 1797. The agent at
Autherley noted:

> Henshall and Co's Boat no 2 is coming up the Locks with 20 Tons Pig Iron the steerer
> says he knows they have too much on by the Boat . . . the steerer intimated to him
> [Brookes the lock keeper] that he was carrying a considerable weight for which he
> should have nothing.[52]

Other steerers became less excited, but calmly pitched a part of the cargo overboard, especially if they ran aground. In 1796 the accumulation of twenty-six
years of such coal and iron deposits on the bed of the Birmingham canal meant
that boats loaded with only 16 tons of ironstone were having difficulty in getting
through.[53]

It is equally fair to draw attention to the fact that examples of dishonesty can be
found in similar abundance among boat owners, among men employed by the
canal companies, and no doubt among men having no connection with canals.

Indeed, sometimes it was the boat owner who encouraged the boatman to indulge in fraudulent practices on his behalf, but left him to take the consequences.[54] If anything, in the earlier years of the Birmingham canal, judging from the attempts at fraud detected, the boat owners were more dishonest than the boatmen. Important colliery owners had to be written to rather sharply over the matter of their using the canal without paying for it.[55] Stealing water from the canal for the use of a works was not uncommon. There were also malpractices in the gauging and indexing of boats. In 1775, Edwin Goodwin

> signified to the Committee that he has great reason to suspect that the Co. sustain a material loss in their Tonnage by the unjustness of the Indexes particularly in Mr Russell's and Mr Wall's Boats.[56]

Many canal company servants were loyal and dedicated men, who served the company all their lives and if they had a fault it was, perhaps, that they were over-zealous, but examples of dishonesty and inattention to duty are not difficult to find. Collusion with boatmen was prevented, as far as possible, by outlawing any form of transaction, other than the official ones, between boatmen and lock keepers. As early as 1770 the Birmingham Company had ordered that 'the lock keepers be not permitted upon any occasion to take coals for their own use off any of the Boats upon pain of being prosecuted',[57] and most other companies adopted and extended such prohibitions. The case of William Pate shows that not all obeyed, or were men of the best character. One boatman complained that he was 'more neglectful than any other Lockman—he is constantly begging Drink of every steerer w[h.] passes and he is a dealer in counterfeit halfpence',[58] allegations which were substantiated in part in the following year.[59] On the Thames and Severn canal 'it was well known that some [lock keepers] could be silenced by presents of meat and drink'.[60] Others were probably more subtle in their corruption. On the Staffordshire and Worcestershire canal, it was said

> that great and numerous frauds have been recently practised upon this Canal by false declarations of Steerers and irregularity of charges of tonnage in which great blame appears to attach to the Company's servants for their negligence,[61]

a negligence perhaps not the result of carelessness.

### WORKING CONDITIONS AND EARNINGS

In the very earliest days there were no cabins on the boats, merely a platform to stand on, it being ordered in 1769 that 'Mr Holloway do also see that a Stage is Built in each of the Company's Boats for the steersman to Stand upon'.[62] This was no great hardship in itself as the distances were short, with no necessity to sleep in the boat, and, apart from being compelled to stand for long hours in one place, the boatman was no worse off in this respect than the carter and waggoner, who were equally exposed to driving rain and numbing cold. He could always jump on to the towpath and drive the horse, to restore the circulation to a suffering body.

As more canals were opened distances lengthened and boatmen were away from home at night, but, even so, they were probably not away for days on end, as happened later. It was not until 1776 and 1777 that the Bridgewater and Trent and Mersey canals were completely finished. Only in 1789 was England first crossed in the south, by the Thames and Severn canal. The Oxford canal, creating the first north–south canal connection with London, via the Thames, was not fully operational until 1790 and, in fact, very little ever reached the capital by that route, it being quickly superceded by the Grand Junction canal, although this was not fully open until 1806.[63] Many canals had yet to be built in 1795. And, if it was becoming possible to send goods much further by the 1790s, there was still a great deal of transhipment, which kept journeys reasonably short.

None the less, distances of a hundred miles and more were being covered in 1795, such as from Manchester to Coventry and Tipton to Oxford, which obviously took several days at two to three miles an hour, and men were compelled to sleep away from home. Probably some slept as those still steering 'open boats' did in 1875.

> They have no shelter, and often sleep say one night on board, doing the best they can. Their fire is a huge open circular grate, such as we see at night on roads under repair, and it seems to me that the approved mode of taking a siesta is to lie flat on the back, with boots as near the fire as may be convenient.[64]

Others almost certainly slept at the canal-side inns which sprang up, usually built and owned by the canal company.[65] Here the boatmen stabled their horses, and it would seem unlikely that a man with any sense would see his horse warm and snug under cover, while he stoically suffered in rain, frost and chilling mists on the canal, especially as they were a race of men whose love of animals often did not embrace their horses.

It would seem that a few boats were built with cabins from the earliest days, in order to ensure the presence of a boatman at night to guard valuable cargoes. As early as 1775 steerer Robinson had a cabin on his boat. It had not, however, saved the cargoes from depredation for, on being caught stealing salt from another boat, a closer investigation of the affairs of Mr Robinson revealed that he was harbouring large amounts of stolen pottery in his cabin.[66]

As more goods of high value came to be carried, and as distances increased, cabins became more numerous, but it was probably not until the 1790s that they were in widespread use. It was 1790 before advertisements in the *Birmingham Gazette* talked of cabins. In that year, the Coventry Canal Company requested tenders for the building of boats, which were 'to have proper cabins on them', and subsequent advertisements for the sale of canal boats indicate that the cabin was becoming more common.[67] They were also becoming more substantial affairs. 'Mr Brough reported that . . . Some of the highest Oxfordshire Cabins had been obstructed in their passage under [a bridge]',[68] indicating that it was on the long-distance boats that the best accommodation facilities were to be found. Again, there were thirty-two captains shown to have no other home than their boats in the 1795 registers, pointing to a more frequent incidence and use of the canal-boat cabin. The appearance and expansion of the fly-boat service, in the 1790s, where boats travelled for many hours non-stop, necessitated more cabined boats, since it was essential for two of the crew to rest while the others hurried the boat forward.

It would appear that the early boatmen were reasonably well paid. In the journals and cash books of the Birmingham Canal Company for 1770–2 it is possible to trace weekly payments to some of the boatmen and thereby establish their income over a period. Job Lloyd provides a good example. Between 4 May 1771 and 7 September 1771 (excluding any payment on 4 May) he earned £33 9s [£33·45p] for boating various materials. For this sixteen-week period he thus earned an average of £2 1s 10d [£2·9p] per week. In addition he was paid £1 19s [£1·95p] for 'carriage' on 31 August, which would have raised his average to £2 4s 3d [£2·21p], but this we will ignore.[69] Out of this £2 1s 10d [£2·9p] he almost certainly had to provide his own horse and an assistant. Perhaps 10s [50p] might be a fair estimate of the weekly cost of his horse.[70] Since many of the early assistants were boys, and the cost of casual labour at that time was around 1s 6d [7½p] per day, the hand probably received 9s [45p] or less. Therefore, Job Lloyd's net earnings over this period were in the region of £1 3s [£1·15p] per week, from boating alone. Outside this period he appears less frequently, but this need not imply that he was unemployed in the intervals. Apart from Joseph Rowley,[71] James Jukes was another boatman who received relatively regular weekly payments of £1 14s 6d [£1·72½p].[72] In the period 5 October–23 November 1771, however, he earned a prodigious £25 16s 6d [£25·82½p] gross from boating bricks, which gave him an average of £3 13s 9d [£3·69p] gross weekly earnings from boating.[73]

It appears, then, that after all expenses were paid these men were earning in excess of 15s [75p] in most weeks, from boating, and at times considerably more than this. It should also be emphasised that most of those paid for boating were paid, in addition, for other services. Joseph Rowley for example was paid for carriage, for ice breaking and for labour; William Morgan for 'getting clay', unloading sand and loading a boat of turf. These men were well paid.

However, these payments were to men working upon the completion of the canal from Bilston to Autherley, and one might expect that rates would be higher here. The Journal of 1777–8 makes it clear that the sums paid for bringing coal, in the Birmingham Canal Company's boats, from Wednesbury and Tipton to Birmingham, were also substantial ones.[74] The total amount of £177 earned by the hard-working Hannah Hipkiss, Richard's widow, in the year covered by the journal, prove that boating could be a very prosperous occupation, since she averaged £3 6s 9½d [£3·34p] gross earnings weekly. Allowing for generous expenses she had a net income of £2 a week throughout the year from company boating alone, a figure well in excess of earnings in most other occupations at that time. It should be pointed out that much of her earnings probably went in paying off the debts of her husband,[75] where she found difficulty in paying off the interest, let alone the capital debt.[76] When the canal company ended its carrying business, in 1784,[77] Mrs Hipkiss, who lived next to the Navigation Inn, Paradise Street, on the wharf in Birmingham,[78] had to seek work elsewhere, but this indomitable woman turned up again in 1795, steering the boat of William Davies between Tipton and Oxford,[79] and she then went on to set up her sons in business.[80]

The figures quoted above may not be typical, since the earlier ones were of payments to men involved in building the canal, and Hannah Hipkiss may have had a special relationship with the company. They throw no light on long-distance wage rates or on regional variations. None the less, the wages paid to boatmen working on the building of the Thames and Severn canal in the 1780s, although lower than those on the Birmingham canal, confirm that boatmen were in the top league of wages paid to skilled men, even if they were not leading the field. Household noted that

> Day wages paid to men employed directly by the company were: carpenters 2/- 2/8 3/- [10p 13½p 15p]; masons 2/- 2/4 2/6 [10p 11½p 12½p]; miners 2/- 2/6 [10p 12½p]; *boatmen* 2/- [10p]; blacksmiths 1/6 1/9 [7½p 9p]; labourers and winders in pit sinking 1/6 [7½p]; labourers in open cutting 1/2 [6p].[81]

Aaron Yorke in 1791 gave *2s 8d* [13½p] a day as an estimate for the wages of canal boatmen, which continues to compare very favourably with other occupations.[82] Clearly canal boatmen, or, perhaps more accurately, master boatmen, could be very prosperous men.

### CONCLUSION

Although the very earliest canal boatmen were seen to be violent and destructive on occasion, this was invariably because they found their progress impeded. There was never any suggestion that they were intrinsically a violent set of men, or collectively drunken and disorderly, dishonest or immoral, as there had been of the river men, and as the canal boatmen themselves were to be denounced in a later age. Nathaniel Spencer had remarked on the 'civility of the boatmen' on the Duke of Bridgewater's canal in 1771.[83] The fact that many of the early boatmen were probably well-known local men, respectable and respected, not travelling far beyond their own neighbourhood, would provide a work force that differed little in virtues and vices from the local population. And boatmen had the advantage of being, generally, a more prosperous set of men.

That standards deteriorated is certain. The Oxford Canal Company was having trouble with the honesty of its steerers when it took over the carrying business in 1790.[84] The Birmingham Canal Company was becoming aware of some of the malpractices carried on in the transportation of coal in the 1790s, as were other companies and carriers with more valuable commodities. Owners were having greater difficulty in sending money by the steerers. Charles Handley had spoken in a derogatory way of 'the character of these men in general' in 1800.

The reasons for such a deterioration in standards of honesty are not difficult to guess at. As the numbers of boatmen increased, more were drawn from less respectable sources. As distances lengthened, more men travelled further from home, and by the end of the century we are beginning to see the emergence of a rootless class of men, increasingly cut off from the civilising effects of home, family and community. The casual nature of canal-boat employment may have contributed to the decline in standards. More valuable commodities were being carried in increasing volume. Boatmen over the years had learned techniques of pilferage. Above all, the introduction of the fly-boat in the 1790s, and its subsequent expansion in numbers and distance, was to create a special, and sometimes disreputable breed of men. But this process of decline was only just beginning in the 1790s. And critics of the boating class at this time appear to have confined themselves to deploring their dishonesty. It was only in later years that the floods of complaint included drunkenness, immorality, irreligion, illiteracy, cruelty and violence among the sins of canal boatmen.

### NOTES TO CHAPTER THREE

[1] Boat Register 1795, 201, 325–6, 494, S.R.O.

[2] *Ibid.*, 138, 291, W.R.O.

[3] *Aris's Birmingham Gazette*, 24 December 1798; GEN 4/857/3.

[4] BCN 1/4, 12 March 1779, p. 87; BCN 4/33, 2 August 1777, p. 87.

[5] Boat Register 1795, 17, 25, 61, 70, G.R.O.

[6] See also Nathaniel Lawrence, *ibid.*, 18, 24, 26, 66, 81; Thomas Beesley, 12, 14, 19, 62, 65, 67, 69; John Jackson, 11, 20, 27, 84; John Mills, 16, 21, 63, 79;

[7] Jonathan Sills, superintendent of the Thames and Severn Canal Company referred to 'our Cost-bearer Thomas Beesley', OXC 4/80/5, Sills to Oxford Canal Company, 11 December 1797.

[8] The westward flow was little more than 17 per cent of the whole trade. Barges were also kept waiting at London, since the Thames Commissioners charged the full toll whether barges were empty or full; Household, *Thames and Severn Canal* (1969), p. 98.

[9] Boat Register 1795, 1–5, W.R.O. In 1791 Mr Brown, for the Oxford Canal Company, had to enquire at the Wychen Colliery 'what *Empty* boats it w$^d$ be necessary to leave there in order to be loaded and ready for the Steerer to return with immediately on his Arrivel', Oxford Canal Company Letter Book, 1790–91, Davey to Brown, 7 January 1791, British Waterways Museum, Stoke Bruerne (abbreviated to St. Br.), WD 63/44.

[10] BCN 1/1, 17 November 1769, p. 132, minute 14.

[11] Boat Register 1795, 31 August 1795, L.R.O.

[12] *Ibid.*, 23, 523, S.R.O.

[13] *Ibid.*, 19–25, 129–31, 158, 272, W.R.O.

[14] *Ibid.*, 35, 64–7, 98–105, 159–62.

[15] *Ibid.*, 189–97, 323, 335.

[16] *Ibid.*, 97, 184–8, 239, 303–7, 337.

[17] BCN 1/3, 2 December 1774, p. 76.

[18] Poor Law Settlement Papers for Shelford, Nottinghamshire County Record Office (henceforward N.R.O.), PR. 85.

[19] *Ibid.*

[20] Poor Law Settlement Papers for Armitage, S.R.O., D 805/3/3.

[21] *Ibid.*, N.R.O., PR. 85.

[22] The opening of the lower paddles could also shut the upper gates through the increased water pressure above the gate.

[23] BCN 4/371B, Houghton to Brookes (Wolverhampton lock keeper), 25 June 1795.

[24] *Ibid.*, Houghton to lock keepers, 24 June 1797.

[25] BCN 1/1, 26 April 1771, p. 256.

[26] BCN 4/372, Houghton to Birmingham Coal Company, 21 June 1813; *ibid.*, Houghton to Robinson, 22 June 1813.

[27] i.e. two boats going in opposite directions would use only one lock full of water and consequently every boat had to wait for a partner.

[28] BCN 1/4, 24 May 1776.

[29] BCN 1/3, 4 November 1774, p. 73.

[30] BCN 1/4, 24 May 1776, p. 34.

[31] Household, *op. cit.*, pp. 27, 98.

[32] Willan, *River Navigation in England*, pp. 106–9.

[33] Meteyard, *Life of Josiah Wedgewood*, vol. I, p. 275.

[34] Anon, *History of Inland Navigation* (1766), p. 57.

[35] *Ibid.*, p. 74.

[36] *Ibid.*, p. 49.

[37] BCN 4/371B, Houghton to Barnes and Holland, 11 September 1794.

[38] Oxf. Canal Letter Book, Davey to Russell and Hunter, 31 December 1790, St. Br., WD 63/44.

[39] OXC 4/81/2, Handley to Dunsford, 10 August 1800.

[40] BCN 4/371B, Houghton to Hodgkinson, 25 April 1798.

[41] BCN 1/1, 23 March 1770, p. 166.

[42] Rees, *Cyclopaedia*, vol. VI (1819), article 'Canals'. (c. 1806), pp. 67–8 (my numbering).

[43] BCN 1/2, 13 November 1772.

[44] BCN 3/371B, Houghton to Hodgkinson, 25 April 1798; *ibid.*, Houghton to Watkins, 9 March 1799.

[45] BCN 1/4, 11 July 1777, p. 59.

[46] BCN 4/371B, Houghton to Watkins, 9 March 1799.

[47] Many boatmen must have been reasonably literate.

[48] BCN 4/371B, Houghton to Roberts, 7 March 1800.

[49] Houghton wrote, 'To prevent similar abuses of which you complain I can see no remedy but in the Coal Masters issuing duplicate Tickets and the Master, owner or purchaser of the Coals at the place of destination requiring such field duplicate' (*ibid.*).

[50] OXC 4/81/2, memorandum of Agreement, Downing and Handley, 18 July 1800.

[51] *Aris's Birmingham Gazette*, 1 November 1790; GEN 4/857/2.

[52] BCN 4/371B, Houghton to Robinson, 5 September 1797.

[53] *Ibid.*, Houghton to Jessom, 24 September 1796.

[54] See BCN 4/371B, Houghton to Cattell, 17 May 1798, for one example.

[55] BCN 1/1, 26 October 1770, p. 213; *ibid.*, 3 May 1771, p. 257; BCN 1/3, 24 March 1774, p. 47.

[56] BCN 1/4, 19 May 1775.

[57] BCN 1/1, 9 March 1770, p. 163.

[58] BCN 4/371B, 26 July 1794, back page.

[59] BCN 1/7A, 15 May 1795.

[60] Household, *op. cit.*, p. 79.

[61] STW 1/4, 4 July 1811.

[62] BCN 1/1, 10 November 1769, p. 124.

[63] 'The trade which used to come to Oxford is so diminished by going down the Grand Junction that the united parishes . . . have accepted a twelfth of the sum raised . . . instead of a tenth'; OXC 4/110, 1808, p. 32. This may have been the last straw for Thomas Sherratt, since the bulk of his trade was along the line of the Oxford canal.

[64] *Birmingham Daily Mail*, 12 March 1875, quoted in George Smith, *Our Canal Population* (1875; 1879 ed.), p. 75.

[65] The Staffordshire and Worcestershire Canal Company, for example, owned several; STW 1/4, 31 July 1817.

[66] *Aris's Birmingham Gazette*, 1 May 1775; GEN 4/857/1.

[67] *Ibid.*, 19 April 1790; GEN 4/857/3.

⁶⁸ BCN 1/7A, 13 March 1795.

⁶⁹ BCN 4/30, pp. 38–86.

⁷⁰ Joseph Rowley and William Morgan give some clues here. Joseph Rowley was paid, for his son and horse, what amounted to a weekly wage of £1 14s 6d [£1·72½p] between 11 April and 2 May inclusive, but William Morgan was paid, during the same period, £1 4s 6d [£1·27½p] a week, listed only as William Morgan and man; BCN 4/131, pp. 49–53.

⁷¹ See footnote 70.

⁷² BCN 4/30, pp. 86–122.

⁷³ *Ibid.*, pp. 100–11.

⁷⁴ BCN 4/33, 1 March 1777–7 March 1778.

⁷⁵ BCN 4/33, 1 March 1777, p. 7; BCN 1/7A 6 September 1799.

⁷⁶ BCN 4/371B, Houghton to Hipkiss, 18 October 1798; BCN 1/7A, 3 May 1799.

⁷⁷ BCN 1/4, 9 April 1784, p. 165.

⁷⁸ *Aris's Birmingham Gazette*, 11 October 1779; GEN 4/857/1.

⁷⁹ Boat Register 1795, 320, W.R.O.

⁸⁰ BCN 1/7A, 3 May 1799.

⁸¹ Household, *op. cit.*, Chapter IV note 7, p. 203.

⁸² H.L.R.O., MS., Mins of Evid., H.L., 1791, Birmingham Canal Bill, 24 May 1791, p. 3.

⁸³ Malley, 'The financial administration of the Bridgewater estates, 1780–1800' (1929), p. 90.

⁸⁴ Oxford Canal Letter Book, Davey to Russell, Hunter & Co., 31 December 1790, St. Br., WD 63/44; *ibid.*, Finch to Brown, 24 February 1791, Dunsford to Fowler and Rathbone, 14 May 1791. From this last it would seem that the steerer did not always go to the colliery that he was ordered to, thereby perhaps making a faster trip or receiving some secret bonus.

# IV

# The Canal Age
## and the canal boatmen
### 1795–1840

### GROWTH OF THE CANAL TRADE

IT WAS DURING THE 1790s that the canals began to be witness to the significant changes which were to have far-reaching effects upon the canal-boat labour force. Canal mileage increased considerably from this period. The figures compiled by Hadfield (which include rivers) clearly demonstrate this:[1]

| Year | Miles | Year | Miles |
|------|-------|------|-------|
| 1760 | $1398\frac{1}{4}$ | 1820 | $3691\frac{1}{4}$ |
| 1790 | $2223\frac{1}{4}$ | 1830 | $3875\frac{1}{2}$ |
| 1800 | $3074\frac{3}{4}$ | 1840 | 4003 |
| 1810 | $3456\frac{3}{8}$ | | |

As more canals were built and connected with others, so boats could travel greater distances and more boats were needed. The growing canal network was but an additional stimulus to an economy already expanding rapidly, and thus demanding a further multiplication of boats. In 1793 one hundred boats a day were said to pass over the Birmingham canal summit,[2] whereas in the autumn of 1821 Josiah Baxendale, in accompanying his son Joseph on his periodic inspection of Pickfords' stations, 'met and passed upwards of four hundred boats full or empty' in the six-and-a-half-hour journey over the same summit pound.[3]

Pressures of trade demanded that there should not only be more boats, but that carriers should provide a faster, more regular and more reliable service with these boats. The greatest pressure would seem to have been that exerted by the merchants and manufacturers who were involved in the rapidly growing export trade, where it was vital that the goods dispatched should arrive on board ship at the correct time.

The late arrival of goods to a vessel bound for some distant market could result in the payment of substantial warehouse charges at the port, perhaps for several months; the season might be over by the time the goods eventually reached their destination; or the order might be cancelled altogether.[4] For different seasonal reasons, winter brought trade with the north European countries to an end by November, but the demand for certain goods was at its greatest in the autumn months. There was a frantic rush to get consignments away before they were 'shut out by the See'.[5] Insurance rates on sea routes began to rise week by week in September.[6] The East India Company exacted a fine if goods arrived late at the port.[7]

Internally, merchants, manufacturers and retailers were demanding more rapid and reliable transit. Here too, late deliveries could lose orders,[8] or involve merchants in other losses.[9] Speed also was important because it became 'the principle of a large business to conduct it with as little capital as possible',[10] and hence it was of particular consequence for the transit of high-value goods, and especially for fashionable goods, which could lose a great deal of their value in two or three days.[11]

It was the inadequacy of canal transport for this last type of goods and for highly-perishable materials which was to force merchants thus involved to revert to the more expensive, but quicker and more reliable, land carriage, if indeed they had ever significantly abandoned this mode of transport. And it was the realisation that canals could not satisfactorily meet the needs of traders in these other directions, in particular in the 'want of certainty', which was to provide a part of the stimulus for the building of the railways. This, however, was a matter for the future. In addition to the commercial pressures that we have outlined that were building up at the close of the eighteenth century,[12] others were to result from the French Wars (1793–1815). Coastal shipping became vulnerable to enemy attack and, therefore, expensive. Land carriage rates rose dramatically because of the shortage of horses and horse feed, whereas canal carriage rates did not experience such a sharp upward movement. The canal boat was a much more economical user of the horse. Goods which had previously passed through other channels were forced on to the inland waterways.[13]

### THE FLY-BOAT SYSTEM AND INCREASING COMMERCIAL PRESSURES

The answer of the canal carriers to such demands was the fly-boat, which emerged in the 1790s, and grew rapidly in number. Pickfords' growth gives us a rough idea of the magnitude of expansion, since theirs was essentially a fly-trade. In 1795 Matthew Pickford registered ten such vessels, but by 1832 the firm owned nearly one hundred.[14] The fly-boat started at fixed times, usually carried 15 tons or less, and proceeded with all speed, night and day, to its destination (averaging about 3 m.p.h.), being drawn by relays of horses and worked by four men, two of them resting.

Canal companies came under increasing pressure to allow these boats to pass at all times unhindered. It was probably in the 1790s that it became more common for such vessels to travel in the night.[15] In 1799 the Birmingham Company decided that,

Messrs. Bache and Co Stage Boats between London and Manchester be permitted to pass the stop at Fazeley without interruption as do the boats belonging Messrs. Pickford and Company.[16]

The practice was becoming common, if not universal, by 1806, when Rees wrote, 'Light boats . . . are allowed on some canals to pass on during the night, their owner paying a specified sum for a license for such privilege'.[17] Many canal companies continued to resist any extension of this practice because of the 'waste of water and other inconveniences . . . [and] the Gross impositions which have been practiced [sic] by some Boat Men upon their employers',[18] but the 'increasing consequence of Water Conveyance and the importance of dispatch',[19] were to sweep away their resistance and allow all to have the special concessions previously held by a privileged few.[20] Paradoxically, however, it was the slump after the Napoleonic Wars which forced this development upon the reluctant canal companies, 'but such [was] the Strife and compleation [presumably competition] in Every Branch of Trade in the Country that Everything must give way to his [the fly-boat trader's] accommodation'.[21] Once established, the practice was there to stay, although John Houghton had hoped that it would not 'last longer than Stage Coach Contests usually do'.[22]

A complex system of fly-boat services therefore emerged and reached its most developed state in the third and fourth decades of the nineteenth century. Basically, the function of this system was to provide rapid lines of transit, for exported and imported goods, between the interior and the various ports. There were, of course, other fly-boat routes, which provided relatively cheap and rapid internal transportation for goods of medium value, into which fly-boats on the port routes dovetailed, since they dropped off and picked up consignments along the way, and particularly at such distribution centres as Braunston and Shardlow.[23] Exports were not necessarily sent through the port nearest to the place of manufacture, but through a port which might have the closest shipping connections with the recipient country—London for the Far East, Liverpool for the West Indies, Hull for Russia and so on. Much might depend on where a ship was available at any given time. And one Wolverhampton merchant preferred to send goods to Scotland by London, because of the delays and pilferage on the water route to Hull.[24] In short, fly-boats did not merely provide a speedy conveyance in the immediate hinterland of a port, but satisfied a demand for long-distance transportation, in connection with external as much as with internal trade.

It was inevitable that London, as the largest port and market, should draw in the greatest number of fly-boats from distant places to its wharves and warehouses. The most important route of all was that between Birmingham and London, where each week in 1832 twenty-five fly-boats started out in both directions. Those from Birmingham were usually loaded with about fifteen tons of finished metal and glass goods. As they neared Braunston their numbers were swollen by boats bringing metal goods from other midland towns, cotton goods from Manchester, Cheshire cheeses, earthenware and pottery goods from Staffordshire, woollens and cutlery from Yorkshire, and lace from Derbyshire and Nottinghamshire. In 1832 over one hundred such fly-boats each week had to force their way past eighty slow-boats (many laden with heavy midland iron goods), and 138 coal boats, as they moved slowly towards London on the Grand Junction canal south of Braunston. On their return these fly-boats would be loaded with about eight tons of colonial goods. The non-stop journey from Birmingham to London took three days and three nights.[25] There were other important fly-boat routes which it is not necessary to detail here.[26]

Slow-boat owners too were demanding that their boats should be allowed to pass for longer hours, and even all through the night. Heavy boats were being issued with red permits in 1822, permitting them to pass in the night on the Grand Junction canal, to the distress of the fly-boat operators,[27] and in 1836 it was decided that 'boats be allowed to pass at all hours without Red Permits'.[28] It had been many years before this that the locks at Farmers Bridge, on the Birmingham canal, had been thrown open to all, night and day and on Sunday, in an attempt to lessen the crush of boats which built up there.[29]

Sunday as a day of rest had been an early casualty of the growing weight of trade. In the early days Sunday trading was forbidden and the locks stayed firmly shut. 'No Boat of what sort so ever will be permitted to navigate upon the [Birmingham] Canal upon a Sunday', it was ordered in 1770,[30] but as trade and distances increased, by the end of the century the temptation to open the canals on Sunday became greater. At first it was for special cases. In 1798, a note to the Oxford Canal Company read, 'Mr Martins will esteem it as a particular favour if you will Let James Cox steer on Sunday as The grain is very mutch wanted'.[31] In the same year Thomas Sherratt was successfully demanding that the locks be opened on Sundays on the Birmingham canal.[32] Such intrusions on the Sabbath remained, in theory, special concessions.

> I have frequently been applied to by your Agents here and by your Boatmen in their names and sometimes as late as ten-o'-clock on Saturday nights . . . to permitt your boats to pass from hence to Fazeley on Sundays,

wrote John Houghton, and these boats were usually 'represented to have Goods on board which required extraordinary dispatch'. It is clear though that in practice the use of Sunday was becoming increasingly accepted.[33]

By 1832, Sunday work was almost universal,[34] and in 1841 recollection of things ever having been any different were vague. 'I believe they have always travelled on Sundays, I am not aware it ever was otherwise', Sir George Chetwynd thought, although Alexander Hordern had found, on inquiry, that, 'in former Days, Thirty Years ago, the trade along the Canal was of very limited Extent on Sundays'.[35]

EFFECTS OF GROWTH UPON THE CANAL-BOAT LABOUR FORCE

Such developments in the canal world, from the 1790s, obviously affected the labour force, not least because many more boatmen were needed. The manning of fly-boats, with their double crews, accounted for a significant growth in the boating population. Pickfords' boatmen had increased in number from forty in 1795[36] to around 400 in 1832[37] and to about 500 men and boys in the late 1830s.[38] Increasing numbers of slow-boats, some travelling further afield, also needed more men. In fact, the exact origins of the earliest boatmen, as discussed in the first chapter, is something of an academic, if an interesting, question, since in terms of numbers it was not really until towards the end of the eighteenth century that the boating population began to be of significant size.

The nature of the work was changing, too. Men were being expected to work for longer hours, to travel longer distances, and to be away from home for weeks on end rather than for a day or a few days. Working on the fly-boats became 'a most harrassing and wretched mode of Life; their Night and Day, travelling in the Way in which they do, must be exceedingly wretched'.[39] One missionary, in 1832, concluded that 'the men who work the fly-boats are little better than slaves; they toil and work, day and night, week and Sundays'. There was little rest on arrival at the terminus, for

> they arrive with their boats in London, and unload them; then re-load, obtain what drink they well can, lay in their stock of meat and peck loaves and off.[40]

The victualling of such a vessel, according to Hollingshead, consisted of

> shipping a sack of potatoes, a quantity of inferior tea, and about fifty pounds of meat at the beginning of the voyage; while large loaves of bread; weighing upwards of eight pounds, [can be] got at certain places on the line of canal.

The beef was all boiled off at once to ensure its keeping fresh.[41]

Sunday and night and day working, coupled with the rapid turn about at the termini, invariably meant that the men involved in this restless, sleepless occupation might not visit their home on land for weeks on end. George Thomas had only visited his parents' home once in the eleven years that he had been on the boats.[42] Captain Randle, whose land home was in Stoke, did not leave his fly-boat home to pay it a visit above three times a year.[43] Family life was inevitably very difficult.[44] Invariably the crews of fly-boats were young or unmarried or both, although the captains were often married.

Nor must fly-boat men be too timid. The captain had to account for any delays on the journey, the date and hour of departure being stamped on the passage bill, and, if not satisfactorily explained, he was liable to a fine.[45] The purchase of a licence for such boats was supposed to allow night passage and precedence over other craft, although this last concession was often not a legal right. Other boatmen were not always prepared to give precedence, and physical negotiation had to take place.[46] 'Mr Bouverie reported three instances in which there had arisen contests between the men navigating the Fly Boats and those in Slow Boats.'[47] Some slow-boat men demanded money for allowing the fly-boat to take their turn at the locks, and perhaps as much as £1 10s [£1·50p] might have to be paid to buy off the turns of a large number of boats. The making of such arrangements was often 'Everything but peaceable of course'.[48]

Similarly, work on the slow-boats could be almost as disagreeable. They could be away from home for much longer periods than a fly-boat. It took six or seven days to travel from Birmingham to London, although there was less travelling at night, there was not the brisk turn round at both ends, nor the same frantic haste all day and all night.[49] Even so, many slow-boat men were working very long hours each day with no let up on Sunday. In Birmingham some boatmen bringing coal were working twenty hours a day in 1839. 'My Steerers are very seldom a bed after one o'clock [in the morning]', one boat-owner admitted.[50]

What kind of men then came forward, and by what avenues, to crew England's growing fleet of canal boats? The details of a few such men have been preserved. Thomas Carnell, born in Granby in Nottinghamshire in 1781, had first started work for a shopkeeper when he was 15. He was discharged by him and was then employed by a farmer for less than a year, and then by another farmer, William Wilson of Shelford, for the year, and, although he ran away from there for several days, he returned to finish the term before going on the boats in 1799.[51] Richard Widdowson, born in 1778 at Burton, was first hired by a farmer for a year when he was 12, but was hired by several farmers in various places in the intervening years before he too became a boat hand at the age of 18.[52] George Cooke was 11 when he first went as a day-labourer on the boats in 1800, having served a year only of an apprenticeship with William Widdowson of Nottingham, frame-work knitter.[53] Thomas Perkins, born in 1778 at Lichfield, was the illegitimate son of William Chadbourn, of Armitage. At the age of 11 he went to live with John Chadbourn, a farmer of Hampton-in-Arden in Warwickshire, but for the next six years or so he seems to have spent his time working for him, or for another farmer of Hansacre, or running away from the one to the other. He eventually decided to work for William Barnes, of Kings Bromley, a wheelwright, until after five weeks with him a disagreement arose and he took to the boats in 1797.[54] John Parker had lived at Newport Pagnall, in Buckinghamshire, for most of his early life, although he had been born in Birmingham in 1787. When he was 12 or 13 bad times forced his father to remove himself voluntarily to Penkridge in Staffordshire, his parish of rightful settlement. John was found a place with Thomas Croydon, a farmer of Hatherton, after spending some time in the poor house, but when he was 15 or 16 he went on to the boats on the Trent and Mersey canal.[55] William Pickering had been a whitewasher in Birmingham before being employed by Pickfords when he was still in his teens, in the years immediately before 1822.[56] Hamlet Mills (1800–44), although the son of a boatman, worked as a salt labourer and rock getter before himself taking to the boats.[57] There were of course many other sons who followed their fathers on to the boats in this period, but clearly many came from other sources, and not particularly from the ranks of agricultural labourers.

There is no reason to assume that such examples, thrown up by the vagaries of time, were untypical of the kinds of people who became boaters in this second period of expansion. Were they men of good character, in whom

Birds of passage, beating northwards in the springtime . . . [had awoken] . . . a vague discontent with the routine of settled life and a longing to venture forth in quest of happier surroundings.[58]

On the contrary, our examples seem to confirm, rather than deny, the view later held of the kinds of people who were recruited into the boats. One witness in 1841 observed that,

> it is generally such Boys as those who have run away from their Parents, or committed some improper Act, and they come to the Banks of the Canal, and there they are sure of getting Employment; and frequently these Boys have robbed their Masters and then run away from them.[59]

A second witness informed the Committee that, 'whenever a Man loses his Character in the Neighbourhood, he says, "I will go and be a Boatman"'.[60]

In fact, canal boating was attracting to an increasing extent a lower class of man and boy. The bad conditions of service, the relatively low pay (for hands), coupled with the bad name that the canal world came to have, ensured that it was so. Certain canal centres were host to this kind of casual labour, waiting for endless hours in canal-side beer houses for some captain to hire them. J. C., fourteen years a fly-boat hand, confessed in 1839:

> I spent my time . . . lurking in fields where game lay, sometimes in beer-shops, public houses, and bawdy houses. When not in honest employ I was maintained by poaching and stealing.[61]

Such unsavoury characters no doubt accosted boat masters, as they passed through locks or important junctions, asking for work. Braunston, 'a most important and busy place' in 1821, because of its position at the junction between the Oxford and Grand Junction canals, and its nearness to others,[62] proved to be a centre to which boatmen gravitated to live as being near possible employment. It was also a convenient place for them to leave their families, being the place where they were most likely to see them. Braunston was a particular attraction to the shiftless, casual boat hands who arrived there, waited and departed. Hence, it was petitioned, in 1829:

> That the said Canal now passes into and through part of the said parish of Braunston in consequence of which the poor of the said parish have for many years considerably increased and been very burdensome to your petitioners.[63]

Bad characters were also said to 'infest the neighbourhood of the tunnels',[64] and it was only by adopting a system of licensing leggers that it had proved possible 'to prevent the robbery, plunder and disturbances which had previously prevailed'.[65]

### THE FAMILY BOAT

The most important source of recruitment to the crews of the slow-boats, however, came from a source which was to have far-reaching effects on canal life for generations to come. The *wives* of the slow-boat captains began to travel with their husbands, and to assist them in the navigation of these vessels, until 'family' boats were numerous.

Canal historians have recently come to hold the view (in contradiction to Rolt's earlier thesis), that the emergence of the family boat was a phenomenon concurrent with the coming of the railways. Of course, the 'coming of the railways' can embrace a considerable number of years, and much depends upon one's assessment of when the railways become a competitive alternative mode of transport. For Hadfield this seems not to have been before the decade of the 1840s. He commented:

> There were very few family boats till competition with the railways drastically forced down freight rates and with them boatmen's wages. This is borne out by the figures of the 1841 Census. Though the total of 28,166 people in the canal business must be a good deal less than the truth, the figures of 23,226 men and 132 women in England and Wales described as boat and barge men and women make it clear that the family boat was most exceptional.[66]

His deductions are corroborated by Charles Bowling, a factory inspector, who, in 1875, insisted that

> Thirty years ago no women or children lived in canal boats, and that most probably, their doing so has been the result of the competition of the railways, which has compelled canal companies to convey their traffic at a cheaper rate.[67]

However Bowling was wrong and Hadfield was mistaken in his emphasis. There is plenty of evidence to prove that by 1841 the family boat was common and had long been so.

There were clearly very few families on board in 1795, since the registers for the four counties reveal that only thirty-two out of 571 captains lived wholly on board, and even then it is far from certain that their families lived with them.[68] We can be definite only about the presence of one woman on board boats—that of the widowed Hannah Hipkiss. Occasionally the presence of women and children is suggested over the next decade or so. The mother of the unfortunate Owen had been accustomed to go regularly with the boats, and he was described as having been a boatman all his life in 1840, when he was 39 years old.[69] The year 1808 saw an advertisement for the sale of a 'family' boat.[70] There is nothing, unfortunately, to indicate how widespread the practice was. However, by 1819 there are indications that the family boat was a common sight, upon the Grand Junction canal at least. Hassell noted that, as the boats prepared to enter the blackness of Blisworth tunnel, just beyond Stoke Bruerne,

> the men, throwing off their upper garments and lighting up their lantern, gave the helm for steerage to the women, *one or two females generally attending each boat* [my italics].[71]

Canal-boat missionaries referred frequently to boatmen's wives in 1830–1, at Paddington,[72] and by 1832 the practice was well enough established for a member of the Select Committee to enquire, 'They are in the habit of having women on board with them continually are they not?'[73]

Conclusive proof of the practice being both widespread and long-established emerges from a study of the minutes of the 1841 Select Committee on Sunday Trading. Richard Heath, of Stourport, mentioned that, in 'Slow Boats . . . carrying Mineral Products, where Despatch is of little Consequence, then the Man's Wife and Family often live with them'.[74] Nor was it a case of the family accompanying the boatman on an occasional trip, for Mr Bouverie, of the Grand Junction Company, made it clear that

> a great many of the men who navigate on the Canals have no Homes of their own; they have no Homes but their Boats. It is the case with many People engaged in the Coal Trade . . . they carry themselves, their wives and their Children with them.[75]

Joseph Baxendale, a man of the widest knowledge of canal affairs, both geographically and technically, confirmed that it was the general practice for slow-boat men to make the cabin the family home.[76] Hadfield has underestimated the inaccuracy of the 1841 Census.[77]

Since it is often held that it was railway competition that had brought about this development, had this competition already been severe enough by 1841 to bring families in large numbers on to the boats in the years immediately before? This is highly unlikely. Nowhere in the evidence put before the Committee on Sunday Trading is there any reference to the phenomenon of women living on board being a recent one. Surely such a dramatic shift would have been a facet of canal life worthy of mention? It seems to have been rather the opposite which had taken place, according to the Reverend John Davies. He thought that 'of late years that [families living entirely on board] has diminished'.[78] And, if some railways were beginning to make their presence felt by 1841, many still remained to be built, and for many years it was the fly-boat trade—'Goods requiring haste in despatch'—which bore the first onslaught of railway competition, and not the slow trade, where families lived on boats. A specific example confirms that railways had as yet had little to do with the prevalence of the family boat. At Oxford the carrying firm of Henry Ward & Co. employed twelve boatmen. Two of these lived in Oxford with their families, but for the remainder the boat cabin was the only home, for themselves and their families.[79] This was before any railway was built along the line of the Oxford canal.

Thus it was not railway competition which had created the family boat in the first instance, as has been suggested most recently. Nor had it arrived with the first canals, as Rolt had urged originally. It would seem to have emerged at around the turn of the century, and to have been common before the first railway of any significance was built, and long before any *serious* railway competition.

The factors which caused women to take to the boats are not certain. Poverty cannot be ruled out as a reason for the arrival of some women (through unfortunate circumstances or improvidence), but the suggestion that the competitive nature of canal carrying over a period of time forced women and children on to the boats through poverty is belied by the evidence showing the general prosperity of master boatmen. The reasons for a woman joining her husband probably varied from one boat to the next, and they may have been decided as much by sociological as by economic pressures. Many perhaps came to be with their husbands because they might not otherwise see them for weeks on end. Possibly it was only during the summer months that they travelled with them at first, but perhaps they acquired a taste for canal life and stayed. Husbands were probably not blind to the advantages of the saving in rent, fuel, and labour bills if the house on shore was given up. These considerations would still carry weight even if they were already earning a reasonable amount. In real terms it could mean that a man's earnings might be increased by at least 10s [50p] a week by such a decision, at any time in this period. And, of course, there was nothing new or unusual about women working with their husbands. Possibly, too, wives had also 'heard that it is not an uncommon Thing for them to hire females to accompany them on voyages say from London to Manchester',[80] and went to keep an eye on their husbands. The Reverend Davies revealed how 'Often times the Wife goes up with her husband as a sort of Protectress, to keep him from spending his Wages'.[81]

The deterioration in the quality of urban life may have tempted others to take their family on to the boats. Given the overcrowding in both town and country dwellings during this period, to take up permanent residence in the cabin of a canal boat may not have appeared to be such a retrogressive step. There may also be something in John Hemelryk's theory[82] that the numbers of families on the canal tended to fluctuate with good or bad times, rather in the way that a trade slump in the industrial towns forced families to abandon their house and go to share with others, or return to the countryside, until times were better. Thus, in bad times a boatman might take his family with him, but as times improved he again rented a house.

It may well have been that the high prices of some years during the Napoleonic Wars, the bad times of the depressed years immediately afterwards and of other less lengthy recessions, or even a period of protracted frost (of which there were several in the 1820s), brought sufficient short-term hardship for a boatman to take his family on to the canal. It seems clear that, if this was the case, the subsequent waves of prosperity did not seduce as many from the canals as the storms of recession and hardship had flung upon them. If economic considerations were uppermost in forcing families on to the boats, it would probably be during the years 1815–22 that the push was at its strongest, and particularly during 1816–17, when trade was exceptionally bad and competition between canal and other carriers was at its strongest. It was during those same years that the housing shortage was at its most acute, according to the census returns:

*Number of persons to an inhabited house in England and Wales*[83]

| Year | Number | Year | Number |
|------|--------|------|--------|
| 1800 | 5·64   | 1831 | 5·60   |
| 1811 | 5·65   | 1841 | 5·41   |
| 1821 | 5·75   |      |        |

However, it matters not so much why it was so, or even exactly when it was so, but that it was so, for, from the day that women came to live upon canal boats, the links of their husbands and children with some fixed home and community, and with outside society, were cut off, as indeed were their own. The seeds of separation were laid. The most important result of this exodus from the land was that it was to allow children to be born, and to grow up, in a world completely cut off from all but a rudimentary understanding of the rest of society and its standards, and with little opportunity to break out through education and other contacts.

It also meant that, since boys and girls came to grow up in increasing numbers knowing no other life than that of the canals, the main source of recruitment came from within the class itself. By 1841 boating was becoming a self-perpetuating occupation, partly because the supply was available from within, but also because there was an increasing reluctance to enter from outside. The Reverend Frederick Wade demonstrates both points with the following rather tortuous answer:

> I cannot recollect a single Instance [of outside recruitment] and often in my Neighbourhood [Kidsgrove] when the Collieries are not in full Work and Parents are anxious to get their Children into Employment,—(I have never known a Case of the Parents putting their own Children from another Class into the Employment of the Boat People)—they have universally expressed the greatest reluctance to do so . . . . One would think it an easier Life than that of a Collier, but they do not like it.[84]

Recruitment was not yet as restricted as the Reverend Wade made out in 1841, for a glance at the 1851 and 1861 Census books reveals that labour continued to come from outside, usually as boys or young men. Richard Cumberlidge of Rugeley, a 17-year-old boatman in 1861, was the son of an agricultural labourer,[85] as was Thomas, the 19-year-old son of Joseph Bloor, of Cheddleton Heath.[86] Others nearby were the sons of a carpenter, a coal miner, a brass tap founder and a bricklayer.[87]

Many of these were probably pushed on to the canals rather than pulled. William Shaw, born at Upton-upon-Severn in 1841, being frequently and brutally punished by his stepfather for the most trifling offences, left home and eventually took up employment on a canal boat. Possibly he never forgot his short time as a boat boy for, after eighteen years or so of action-packed travel around the world, and on the Mersey as a river policeman, he took up the post of Missioner to Seamen at Runcorn in 1875, where he did much good work for canal boatmen.[88]

Canal recruitment also benefited from the ever widening net thrown out by the Factory Acts, a net of increasingly fine mesh. As more and more industries came under the provisions of the Acts, the number of industries untroubled by inspectors dwindled. Canal boats remained an avenue of escape, according to Inspector Blenkinsopp, a midland factory inspector, for he believed that, 'children are sometimes sent to work in them in order to avoid the Factory and Workshops Acts'.[89]

Adults occasionally came on to the canals in later life, but usually their stay was of limited duration.

LIVING CONDITIONS AND EARNINGS

The arrival of women and children on board the boats in significant numbers was only made possible, of course, by the appearance of decent cabin accommodation on most boats from the 1790s. At the same time, the break with shore life was perhaps not so dramatic as we have presented it. It would seem that, for some boat people at least, the cabin was supplementary to their life on the canals rather than central to it. It was perhaps used for sleeping accommodation when all else failed. For there is evidence that boatmen continued to stay at canal-side inns long after cabins were generally provided. Benjamin Brookshaw, a beerseller of Market Drayton, informed a canal committee in 1841 that he had

> a share in a small Tenement adjoining the Canal and did in consequence of their being no accommodation for the Boatmen and their horses . . . enlarge his house and erect stabling for [their] accommodation,

which was 'much frequented by the men and horses'.[90] In 1840 William Clemson, a boatman from Derby, 'had been residing for the last few days at the Eagle and Child public house at Newcastle'.[91]

At many canal wharves it was forbidden to sleep in or to keep a fire in a boat. Boatmen obviously had to sleep elsewhere if they wanted to tie up by a wharf for the night. And the census enumeration books for 1851 and 1861 show that some boatmen were neither sleeping on their boat nor at home. At Alrewas in 1851 the house of Thomas Langley, cordwainer and grocer, in addition to being the home of himself and his family, was also, that night, the resting place of William Cox, boatman, his wife Nancy, both 64 years old, and their servant William Winfield, 16.[92] James Johnson, a 40-year-old boatman, was staying with a brickmaker's labourer, Robert Till and his family, at Brereton near Rugeley.[93] Similarly, in 1861, George Johnson of Alrewas, hay and corn dealer, was host, with his family, to Charles Febrook, 29, boatman, his wife Sarah, and their servant Charles Russell, 12.[94] Sarah Hill, 34, 'Boatswoman', a native of Manchester, was staying in the household of Thomas Chill, a 44-year-old blacksmith, in Back Lane, Stone.[95] A more intensive search of the census returns, for other areas, would probably reveal that elsewhere some boat people were staying with friends, or relatives, or in cheap lodgings. Large families clearly could not do this and by 1861 most boaters slept every night on the boat, or perhaps occasionally in their own home, if they had one. The examples quoted above perhaps demonstrate how, at one time, many boatmen had had their own special stopping places and used the boat cabin only as a last resort.

The hardships and disadvantages of canal life, however, continued to be compensated for by relatively high earnings, at any rate for master boatmen. The Birmingham steerers previously referred to earned 15s [75p] *a day* in making a trip to the collieries north of Birmingham and back each day, or the very substantial sum of £4 10s [£4·50p] per six-day week, before expenses.[96] In the same year Crowley & Co. were paying 6d [2½p] per mile to their slow-boat steerers which, with an average mileage of fifteen miles a day, would produce £2 5s [£2·25p] for a six-day week before expenses.[97] Boatmen hired for boating on the Coventry canal between 1840 and 1844 were paid 7s [35p] a day, from which they must pay for the horse and hand.[98] Therefore, when Mr Hayes, agent of the Staffordshire and Worcestershire Canal Company suggested in 1841 that a master boatman might earn between 15s [75p] and £1 10s [£1·50p] a week on an average, after paying for the horse, but before paying for hired labour, and depending on the value of the cargo carried, it might not be unreasonable to assume that most captains earned nearer to £1 10s [£1·50p] than to 15s [75p].[99]

Fly-boat captains were very well paid. For the voyage from Manchester to London, which might take up to six days, but more usually five, they would be paid £8 according to Bouverie, from which they had to pay day wages to the other three men and for their feed.[100] Richard Heath's captains were paid £9 for the week's voyage from Stourport to Manchester, in 1841. He was right when he said they got 'a great deal of money'. These two instances may have been exceptional, in that these captains were paid for horsing the boat (which was unusual with fly-boats), but Mr Heath clarified the position by estimating that 'on Average he would earn for himself 30s [£1·50p] a week for his own Labour, after all expenses'.[101] Pickfords' captains seem to have earned even more, since, for a voyage from Manchester to London, they were paid five guineas, from which sum they had to pay the three hands; but the horses were provided by Pickfords.[102]

There is other evidence to testify to the general prosperity of boatmen. Dr Iredale always included the captains of boats in the prosperous class of Barnton,[103] and gives us the specific instance of John Beech (1759–1840), who came to be able to purchase his house and extend it before his death.[104] Isaac Jones, of Lawton, one of Worthington and Gilbert's boatmen, owned at least six houses by the time of his death in 1817.[105]

For the canals were generally prosperous in this period. It is true that during the post-war slump of 1815–22 many canal carriers felt the pinch (especially in 1816 and 1817), not only because of the general stagnation of trade, but also on account of increased competition from coastal shipping and land carriage. Canal carrying remained a competitive business, and there is no reason to amend our earlier view of the difficulties and disasters that a canal trader, and particularly a small trader, was exposed to. None the less, the return of prosperity and the expansion of the economy (which was generally sustained apart from some short periods of slacker trade), meant that transport needs continued to outstrip transport supply. A carrier who was well-established, having adequate capital reserves, perhaps other lines of business and reasonably good luck was, in the 1820s and 1830s, a prosperous man. The diary of G. R. Bird, boatbuilder and carrier of Birmingham, demonstrates this clearly. He dined not infrequently 'with the members of the Bean Club . . . at the Royal Hotel', or entertained other carriers, as they entertained him; and, no doubt in consequence, he complained frequently of the gout. He went on at least two continental holidays during the space of the diary (1820–30). He owned land, a house in Edgbaston, and property at Stourport in addition to his boat-building and carrying business.[106] The prospectus of a proposed Birmingham and London Junction Canal of 1830 listed three midland carriers as substantial shareholders,—John Crowley, John Whitehouse and William Whitehouse.[107]

These were not poor men, and there is no reason to assume that they became wealthy by paying their master boatmen low wages, as Sir George Chetwynd alleged. He may have been referring to the boat hands rather than to the captains who employed them when he said, 'I understand they are very inadequately paid, and therefore they are induced to pilfer and do many Things they would not otherwise do'.[108] Pickfords' hands were earning 8s [40p] and maintenance in 1822,[109] and the hands employed by the captains of Richard Heath's fly-boats received between 7s [35p] and 8s [40p] a week, and their maintenance, in 1841.[110] It would perhaps be foolish to arrive at firm conclusions based on such flimsy evidence, but the suggestion must be that boat hands were little better off in financial terms than agricultural labourers in many parts of the country, and actually worse off than some in others. Taking into account the nature of the work, the rewards were poor, if these examples were typical. The prosperity of canal carriage was not markedly in evidence below the level of captain, but then many of the hands were boys or young men and any hand worth his salt soon became a master, of a slow-boat at least.

CONCLUSION

The Canal Age saw the numbers of canals, boats, and boatmen greatly increased. Boats travelled faster and further, and boatmen were called upon to work more arduously, for which the master boatmen at least were generally well-rewarded financially. This may have been less true of the boat hands. Some of this last group, a large number of whom eventually became boat captains, were not of the best character, because the peculiarities and disadvantages of the work repelled many people. A large number of hands were, of course, young men and boys, and, where such people were in evidence, far from the moderating influences of home and community, mischief could often result. This was particularly true of the fly-boat men, who had to snatch their pleasures as quickly and as intensely as they could. The arrival of wives and families on board slow boats, usually as a substitute for the hired hand(s), meant that the creation of a rootless separate society was assured. This was already clearly distinguishable in the 1830s, if it were not yet as isolated as it was to become. The years of the Canal Age saw the emergence of a society which was different in many respects from the surrounding earthbound English society; different from previous canal populations; increasingly a self-perpetuating society; and there is little reason to suppose that it was a better society than the one that had gone before, or the one around it.

NOTES TO CHAPTER FOUR

[1] Hadfield, *The Canal Age*, p. 208.

[2] OXC 4/80/1, Sherratt to Dunsford, 2 November 1793.

[3] PIC 4/26, 'Copy of a Diary kept by Josiah Baxendale, M.D.', 27 September to 13 October 1821, p. 3, in Short Histories, etc.

[4] H.L.R.O., MS., Mins. of Evid., H.C., 1836, vol. 23, Manchester and Leeds Railway Bill, 20 April 1836, pp. 135–40; M.S., Mins. of Evid., H.L., 1832, London and Birmingham Railway Bill, 2 July 1832, p. 73 (henceforward, London and Birmingham Railway Bill, 1832).

[5] Manchester and Leeds Railway Bill, *op. cit.*, 20 April 1836, pp. 76, 111–14.

[6] *Ibid.*, pp. 73–5.

[7] H.L.R.O., MS., Mins. of Evid., H.C., 1836, vol. 32, North Midland Railway Bill, 17 March 1836, p. 143.

[8] *Ibid.*, p. 147.

[9] H.L.R.O., MS., Mins. of Evid., H.C., 1837, vol. 20, Manchester, Cheshire and Staffordshire Railway Bill, 12 April 1837, p. 122.

[10] H.L.R.O., MS., Mins. of Evid., H.C., 1836, vol. 20, Manchester and Cheshire Railway Bill, 21 March 1836, pp. 32–3.

[11] *Ibid.*, pp. 12–13; MS., Mins. of Evid., H.C., 1836, vol. 21, Manchester and Cheshire Junction Railway, 19 April 1836, p. 426.

[12] It was not thought unreasonable to assume that the difficulties experienced by traders in the 1830s were markedly different from those in the 1790s, except by degree.

[13] BCN 4/372, Houghton to Spooner, 13 April 1816; BCN 4/373, Houghton to Simpson, 8 May 1820.

[14] Boat Register 1795, 74–83, C.R.O; *Report and Evidence of the Select Committee on the Observance of the Sabbath Day*, 1831–2 (697), VIII, qq. 1984, 1988 (henceforward referred to as *S. C. on Observance of the Sabbath*, 1832).

[15] OXC 4/80/3, Twiss to Dunsford, 23 December 1795. Twiss inferred that such boats travelled at night on some canals.

[16] *Ibid.*, 22 March 1799. An entry in the margin reads 'Bache and Co Stage Boats to pass in the night'.

[17] Rees, *op. cit.*, p. 68 (my numbering).

[18] BCN 4/373, Houghton to Pickford & Co., *et al*, 4 September 1818.

[19] BCN 4/372, Houghton to Woodcock, 17 November 1814.

[20] *Ibid.*, Houghton to Whitehouse, 4 October 1816, where he wrote, 'has [*sic*] some have permission the rest seem entitled to it'.

[21] *Ibid.*, 25 May 1816.

[22] *Ibid.*, 4 October 1816.

[23] Mr Turnbull gives some indication of the complicated organisation of the fly-boat trade: 'Pickfords and the canal carrying trade 1780–1850', especially pp. 14–15.

[24] H.L.R.O., MS., Mins. of Evid., H.C., 1836, Birmingham, Derby and Stonebridge Railway Bill, 14 March 1836, pp. 104–7.

[25] London and Birmingham Railway Bill, 29 June 1832, pp. 34, 40–1.

[26] Birmingham, Derby and Stonebridge Railway Bill, *op. cit.*, 14 March 1836, pp. 50–60, gives details of some other routes and the numbers of boats involved.

[27] GJC 1/3, 27 December 1822, p. 161.

[28] GJC 1/6, 30 November 1836, p. 118.

[29] Birmingham Canal Bill, 21 April 1839, pp. 166, 184.

[30] BCN 1/1, 21 September 1770, p. 207.

[31] OXC 4/80/6, Russ to Oxford Canal Company, 7 December 1798.

[32] BCN 1/7A, 2 November 1798.

[33] BCN 4/371B, Houghton to Robinson, 24 July 1802.

34 *S. C. on Observance of the Sabbath*, 1832, qq. 1813–14, 1981.

35 *S. C. on Sunday Trading*, 1841, qq. 29, 146.

36 Boat Register 1795, 74–83, C.R.O.

37 *S. C. on Observance of the Sabbath*, 1832, qq. 1824–5.

38 *S. C. on Sunday Trading*, 1841, q. 1249.

39 *Ibid.*, q. 1160.

40 *Canal Boatmen's Magazine*, February 1832, pp. 15–16, British Museum (henceforward Br. Mus.), PP. 1090 c.

41 *Household Words*, 11 September 1858, p. 292 and 18 September 1858, p. 321.

42 *Staffordshire Advertiser*, 28 March 1840.

43 *Household Words*, 18 September 1858, p. 318.

44 *S. C. on Sunday Trading*, 1841, q. 1254.

45 *Canal Boatmen's Magazine*, February 1832, p. 15; John Hassell, *A Tour of the Grand Junction Canal in 1815* (1819; 1968 ed.), p. 48.

46 GJC 1/2, 9 August 1821, pp. 216–17; GJC 1/3, 27 December 1822, p. 161; GJC 1/5, 5 November 1832, p. 160.

47 GJC 1/6, 26 December 1836, p. 130.

48 Birmingham Canal Bill, 21 April 1839, pp. 27–8.

49 London and Birmingham Railway Bill, 29 June 1832, p. 40.

50 Birmingham Canal Bill, 21 April 1839, p. 175–7.

51 Poor Law Settlement Papers, Shelford, 1 March 1800, N.R.O., P.R. 85.

52 *Ibid.*, 26 March 1810.

53 *Ibid.*, 10 January 1811.

54 Poor Law Settlement Papers, Armitage, 18 February 1801, S.R.O., D. 805/3/3.

55 *Ibid.*, 5 September 1816.

56 PIC 4/1, p. 10, extract from *The Morning Chronicle*, 30 July 1822.

57 Iredale, 'Canal settlement: Barnton, 1775–1845', p. 99.

58 Redford, *Labour Migration in England, 1800–50*, p. 1.

59 *S. C. on Sunday Trading*, 1841, q. 954.

60 *Ibid.*, 22.

61 *First Report of the Commissioners appointed to inquire as to the best means of establishing an Efficient Constabulary Force in the Counties of England and Wales*, 1839 (169), XIX, p. 53 (henceforward *Constabulary Force Report*, 1839).

62 PIC 4/26, pp. 4–5: Baxendale senior gives a description of Braunston in 1821.

63 Petitions and Evidence relative to the Oxford Canal Bill, 1829, Oxfordshire County Record Office, OX vi/ii/i.

64 GJC 1/3, 27 February 1826, p. 18.

65 GJC 1/8, 15 September 1841, p. 84.

66 Hadfield, *British Canals* (1950; 1966 ed.), p. 73. See also his *Canal Age* (1968), p. 151.

67 Report of the *Commission on the Working of the Factory and Workshops Act*, 1876 [C.1443], XXIX (henceforward referred to as *Factory and Workshops Commission*, 1876), vol. 1, appendix C, p. 121.

68 Boat Register, 1795, for Lancashire, Cheshire, Staffordshire and Gloucestershire.

69 *Staffordshire Advertiser*, 28 March 1840. See below p. 71.

70 *Aris's Birmingham Gazette*, 25 April 1808; GEN 4/857/4.

71 Hassell, *A Tour of the Grand Junction Canal in 1819*, p. 45.

72 *Canal Boatmen's Magazine*, May 1830, p. 59, April 1831, p. 45 and October 1831, p. 118, Br. Mus., PP. 1090 c.

73 *S. C. on Observance of the Sabbath*, 1832, q. 1829.

74 *S. C. on Sunday Trading*, 1841, q. 619.

75 *Ibid.*, 1048.

76 *Ibid.*, 1220, 1223.

77 Or rather, as our later studies of the census material reveal, the figures which come closest to

giving us a true picture of the number of women on board boats are not those taken from the 'Occupation Tables', but those showing the number of people sleeping on board during the night of the census. Unfortunately, the 1841 figures do not differentiate between the different types of vessel and for our purposes they are meaningless. See Appendix IV*b* for a discussion of the statistic relating to boatwomen in the 'Occupation Tables'.

[78] *S. C. on Sunday Trading*, 1841, q. 779.

[79] *Ibid.*, qq. 865–7.

[80] *Ibid.*, q. 82.

[81] *Ibid.*, 779.

[82] An ex-boatman.

[83] *Census 1901, General Report*, 1904 [Cd. 2174], table 4, p. 194.

[84] *S. C. on Sunday Trading*, 1841, q. 953.

[85] Census 1861, RG 9, 1978, p. 100, Public Record Office, Portugal Street.

[86] *Ibid.*, RG 9, 1951, p. 50.

[87] Census 1851, HO. 107, 2015, pp. 408, 414, 425; Census 1861, RG 9, 1903, p. 83.

[88] *Seamens Institute, Runcorn* (1906), pp. 2–3, pamphlet at Runcorn Public Library.

[89] *Factory and Workshops Commission*, 1876, vol I, appendix C, p. 133.

[90] BLC 1/2, 10 July 1841, p. 12.

[91] *Staffordshire Advertiser*, 2 May 1840.

[92] Census 1851, HO 107, 2015, p. 45, P.R.O. (Portugal Street).

[93] *Ibid.*, p. 414; see also Henry Smith, *ibid.*, p. 428.

[94] Census 1861, RG 9, 1976, p. 46.

[95] *Ibid.*, 1911, p. 32.

[96] Birmingham Canal Bill, 21 April 1839, p. 176–7. See above p. 52.

[97] *Ibid.*, p. 138.

[98] Coventry Canal Wages Book, 1840–4, at Stoke Bruerne. See Thomas West, (Week 46, 1840, Edward Walker, Week 19, 1841, and Thomas Clarke, Week 24, 1844).

[99] *S. C. on Sunday Trading*, 1841, qq. 216–20.

[100] *Ibid.*, 1053.

[101] *Ibid.*, 625–9.

[102] *Ibid.*, 1163.

[103] Iredale, 'Canal Settlement: Barnton, 1775–1845', pp. 128, 141.

[104] *Ibid.*, p. 77.

[105] Wills at Chester, Isaac Jones, late of Lawton, Boatman, W.S. 20 March 1817, C.R.O.; Boat Register 1795, 3, L.R.O.

[106] 'Diary of G. R. Bird, wharfinger and carrier of Birmingham, including weather reports and their effect upon canal traffic, 1820–30' (henceforward 'Diary of G. R. Bird, 1820–30'), Birmingham Reference Library (Birm. R.L.), 662750.

[107] *Birmingham and London Junction Canal Petitions*, 1830, Birm. R.L. 26200, p. 55.

[108] *S. C. on Sunday Trading*, 1841, qq. 15–16.

[109] PIC 4/1, p. 9, extract from *The News*, 28 July 1822.

[110] *S. C. on Sunday Trading*, 1841, q. 628.

V

# The Styx
## The morality
## of the boating class
## in the Canal Age

FROM AROUND 1800, critics of the boat people came forward in growing number to condemn the life style of the floating population, in ever stronger terms. In that year, Charles Handley had been critical of 'the character of these men in general', but the boatmen had not yet become the 'vile set of rogues' that one critic felt them to be in 1818.[1] By 1829, religious men were speaking of the 'dark and benighted state' in which the boatmen lived; of their 'careless and dissolute practices'; and of their 'decided wickedness'.[2] Men involved in the carrying trade came forward to add their denunciations in 1832. James Panther, a clerk with John Whitehouse and Son, the canal carriers, found them to be 'very bad; I do not know that there is any class of men in this country that is so bad'.[3] Charles Sibley, a warehouse owner, conceived them to be 'very demoralized; they have neither fear of God nor of man'.[4]

Men of a religious nature, as these two were also, were not always the most objective of observers, but their low opinions were more than matched in the torrent of criticism which the events of 1839 brought tumbling down upon the heads of the boatmen. 'They are extremely illiterate, uninstructed and depraved', commented Sir George Chetwynd, of the Trent and Mersey Canal Company.[5] Alexander Hordern, from his viewpoint at Bushbury, on the Staffordshire and Worcester canal, believed them to be 'the most degraded Class of Society, so far as I have seen'.[6] One boatman, in Staffordshire Gaol, was said to have made 'such Disclosures as beggar all Description of the Abominations that are committed on Canals, and the Habits of Boatmen, their pilfering and Habits of horrid Depravity'.[7] The *Chester Courant*, in 1839, claimed that 'The demoralized condition of the men employed on the navigations of this kingdom has long been notorious'.[8]

It was two circumstances occurring in 1839 which brought the existing state of affairs on England's canals to the attention of a shocked public. The first was the report of the Constabulary Force Commissioners, which contained many unfortunate revelations, mainly about the dishonesty of the boatmen.[9] The second concerned the tragic case of Christina Collins. This last resulted in the setting up of a select committee (on Sunday Trading) in 1841, and this unearthed further disturbing information. From these two reports it is possible to paint on history's canvas a picture of dishonesty, violence, cruelty, drunkenness, immorality, ignorance and squalor as representing the general way of life which had emerged upon England's waterways during the Canal Age. Nor is it difficult to find examples, from other sources, to add detail to such a landscape, filled in abundance with all the sin that mankind is heir to.

DISHONESTY

Dishonesty on the part of the boatmen seems to have come in several forms. Firstly there were the depredations committed by the boatmen upon the areas through which they passed. Alexander Hordern revealed that there was

> A good deal of petty Pilfering; cutting Grass, stealing Turnips poaching and breaking into Hen Roosts and Things of that Kind . . . they are generally provided with a Scythe; they can get into a Field, and mow Clover enough for a Horse for two or three Days which is all done in a few minutes.[10]

Francis Wilder was one such boatman who in 1839 at the Town Hall, Burslem

> was charged with entering a field by the canal side, in the parish of Trentham, and cutting a quantity of vetches with a hook. . . [He] was secured with some difficulty, the officer losing his hat in the scuffle.[11]

Mr Kershaw was asked, 'Do not the men steal fowles, and poach and steal sheep even?', and he agreed that 'there have been many complaints of that kind where clothes hung out to dry, poultry and so on have been stolen'. All boatmen, according to Mr Pickford, were 'to a greater or lesser extent poachers', and he had even known deer to be carried off. One 'depredator', J. C., admitted to having 'many a time milked farmers' cows in the night'.[12]

Complaints on this score had been few in the eighteenth century, but in 1798 three of Pickfords' boatmen had perhaps demonstrated the changing order of things when they 'had kild and carried away several Geese'.[13] By 1819, inhabitants close to a canal were clearly mindful of the dangers to which their property was exposed. Hassell came across 'his Lordship's [Earl of Essex] fisherman's cottage, another pretty retreat . . . and an excellent station for checking the depredations of the boatmen'.[14] Such measures were not always successful for in 1832 'There were some men on one line who in the night time got into some gentleman's fishery and took his fish'.[15]

Secondly, the dishonesty of the boatmen extended to the goods they carried, where outrageous felonies were carried out, often speedily detected and clearly proved. One audacious robbery in Staffordshire in 1838 involved the transference of four silk bales, valued at £600, from boat to cart in the middle of the night.

Only half was ever recovered, although the parties concerned were quickly convicted and transported for the offence.[16] Earlier, in 1811,

> The master belonging to one of Mr Pickford's craft on the Paddington canal with four men, were yesterday charged . . . with having stolen a quantity of china etc., the property of their employers. It appeared that a crate of china, etc., was shipped on board the barge for Messrs. Spode, from their manufactury, and on being landed it was discovered to have been opened, and divers articles were missing. The property was found concealed in the cabin of the barge.[17]

Many acts of robbery were carried out under the influence of drink, or drink was at the bottom of them, and consequently they were soon discovered, sometimes dramatically. Turnbull quotes the case, in 1809, where a boat left Paddington with a mixed cargo of goods, including brandy, rum and gunpowder—an explosive mixture. Two of the crew attacked one of the barrels with an axe; their lantern's flickering glow was inadequate as an illuminator, but successful as a detonator, since they chose the wrong barrel, blew up themselves and the boat, and set fire to three haystacks.[18]

According to the Constabulary Force Commissioners, robberies on a grand scale were not a really serious problem, for they concluded that 'the bulk of . . . [the] produce . . . conveyed . . . on canals, is tolerably safe from large or violent robberies', but, 'it was proved at the same time to be subject to systemised petty thefts of great importance in the aggregate'.[19]

There had apparently grown up in the nineteenth century a subtle system of pilferage, involving boatmen, backed by an extensive network of receiving that was peculiar to the waterways. Dowling, the Commissioner of Police at Liverpool, explained how

> Bales are opened, boxes and cases are broken open and plundered, and it is so well done that the discovery is almost a matter of impossibility until they arrive at their destination, because they are addressed by order at Manchester to the parties abroad . . . so that before the return of the loss arrives in England six or eight months may have elapsed.

He had discovered that there were general depots for the reception of goods stolen on the canals not far from each waterway. The same depredations were carried out 'upon every canal'. According to other witnesses the first receiving houses were usually cheap beer houses, which proliferated along the canals following the Beer Act of 1830.[20] Either the proprietor was a 'fence', or such men congregated there.

This subtle pilfering was usually carried out where there were no houses and no persons present except the boatmen, who all shared in the plunder. An undisturbed opportunity to break open boxes and barrels was, however, not enough because the boatmen, especially the master, would have to answer for any obvious disturbances in the cargo. Hence, they developed very skilful techniques, which demanded the use of special 'smuggling' tools. The report is interesting because it gives details of the delicate way in which boats were robbed.

Large heavy bales of cloth were packed so firmly by hydraulic press that the centre formed itself into an arch. The bale was left in the hold, but twine was run through the ends of the pieces by the robbers. To this twine a hook was attached, and then, by means of tackle and windlass fixed to the mast, pieces were drawn out from the centre of the bale, but the arch remained and the bale therefore appeared to be complete. Raw wool and silk were extracted in very small quantities, perhaps two or three ounces, 'and yet of considerable value in the aggregate'. Where larger quantities were extracted water proved a useful substitute and silk was 'very easily weighted with salt, moisture, and other materials'. Messrs Venn and Bull remarked on how,

> if a cargo of ironmongery, or Sheffield goods, is robbed, we cannot discover it, not even by weighing it; they may put in a brick or a stone to make up the weight. We could not discover it until the parties to whom the goods belonged unpacked them, and compared them with the invoice.

By this time the goods might have passed through two or three carriers' hands, and it would be difficult to say whose men were responsible. 'Nails', Messrs Venn and Bull continued, 'is a thing we are continually being plundered of, and we cannot detect it without weighing the bags, which, from the immense quantity that are carried, would be a serious obstruction in the point of time and expense.'

Some packages and cases were sealed for greater security, but the boatmen were not to be so easily kept from their plunder. The knowledgeable Mr Dowling explained how the seal was renewed, using grease on a cork. The captain might even carry a supply of different kinds of twine so that the package would still look exactly the same as before.

Nor were barrels secure from mischievous hands. For extracting sugar and other dry goods, J. C. confessed how he and his accomplices had

> slipped the hoop, made a small hole under it, and introduced the borer, and took what we liked . . . . When we took wine or spirits, we knocked a hoop aside and made a hole on one side for letting out the liquor, and one on the other for letting in air; when we had taken what we wanted, we put water in to make it up, and pegged up the hole and replaced the hoop.

The tools of 'Smugglers' included

> Hammers, in the handle of which were Turnscrews, and everything requisite for breaking open Casks. Then there are Syphons and different sized pumps, some made of Tin; the best are made of Copper, and screw together, so that if found in a Boatman's Pocket you would not know what it was. These being inserted into one of the Casks you may thereby draw off a large quantity of Liquor in a very short time.[21]

The practice of setting aside a part of the boat for such valuable cargoes to be locked up in seems not to have solved the problem. This may have been because the provision of such a separate cargo space was never as widespread as might have been expected. James Panther, in 1832, confirmed that, because of the growing lack of confidence in the boatmen some years before, the boat owners had 'required a quarter of the boat to lock up the spirits, wines, furniture, plate, etc., so that they should be secure, in addition to the locks put on them'.[22] However, it is clear that many fly-boats had no lock-up section. The expense of building these separate cabins (which reduced the overall cargo space and were not always used), probably deterred many companies from equipping their boats with them.

The loading of a canal boat was not always the innocent industrious occupation that it might appear. J. C. revealed how

> The hands loaded their own boats, and . . ., when we got a package we thought we could get anything out of, we stowed it where we could easily get to it. If we got a package we thought we could make nothing of, we put it at the bottom of the boat.

Further facility was afforded by the fact that some canal employees were in league with the boatmen, sometimes actively but more often passively. Sometimes a warehouseman might notice that something had been opened, but 'we tipped him something, and he would say nothing about it'. There were other means of maintaining secrecy, for far from all canal employees were criminals. On 1 September 1815,

> a man named Cotton was charged with a felonious assault with intent to murder the porter of Pickfords Wharf . . . The prisoner was a bargeman . . . and the porter appeared to have excited his emnity as well as that of several of his comrades, in consequence of detecting and putting to an end several of the evil practices of the bargemen. They vowed revenge . . . On Wednesday night the porter and his wife were seen passing along the Edgware road . . . After they had arrived at their home, the bargemen attacked both of them, cutting and beating them dreadfully . . . The porter fastened on the prisoner, and never left him till the cries of 'Murder' brought assistance.[23]

Boatmen usually picked up their criminal ways as boys, and were taught to pilfer by the other boatmen. Once embarked upon a life of crime there were, of course, considerable pressures upon them to continue; pressures which might still be exerted even if a boatman left the canal. J. C. told of how he was left £420 by an uncle.

> I then commenced business in the grocery line at Runcorn, and purchased frequently purloined property from boatmen. Many of the boatmen's wives used my shop, and got greatly in my debt. I durst not compel payment for fear of 'them blowing me'. I was now much given to drink, so was my wife. I failed and had to begin boating again.

Theft was facilitated by '"the easy way of getting shut of things". Whatever part of the road you were in you could find a fence (a receiver)', said J. C. Sometimes these men would take an active part in the robbery.

Thieving was not confined to a boatman's own cargo, but stealing from each other and from the boats of other boatmen also occurred. For this last reason Baxendale dreaded a number of boats being unexpectedly assembled at one point.[24] William Ward, the Oxford carrier, explained how his boatmen were 'obliged to stay to protect their Boats . . . [The fly-boat men] would take Coals or Sacks of

Grain off the Boats.'[25] Boat hands could be very light-fingered. In the space of a
few weeks in 1840 several incidents are recorded in the *Staffordshire Advertiser*,
involving Thomas Underhill in the theft of his captain's trousers;[26] Isaac Raisin in
the disappearance of his captain's watch and purse;[27] and Joseph Hallawell in the
robbery of his captain's flannel coat.[28] Some months before, a theft had involved
Richard Bell, another boat hand. George Corns, a lad on another boat, had witnessed the sale of some garments belonging to Bell's captain, John Higgins, to one
of Pickfords' men. Higgins soon noticed his loss, but it was a week before Corns
explained how they had disappeared. Bell, facetiously, would only admit to
having 'swallowed them'.

### VIOLENCE, DRINK AND SEX

The reason for George Corns' reticence confirms the impression that there were
some rugged characters to be found on the nineteenth-century waterways, for the
boy mentioned that,

> on the same day the . . . robbery was committed the prisoner came out of his boat
> towards him and knocked him down . . . and took from his pocket a shilling; he did
> not name it until a week or two afterwards, Bell having threatened to beat him if he
> did so.[29]

Other examples of violence by individual boatmen are not difficult to find.
One magistrate, a Mr Rose, complained that 'boatmen in general were disorderly
fellows and must be taught how to behave themselves'.[30] On one occasion the
boatmen's propensity to violence led to what amounted to a pitched battle in the
City basin of the Regent's canal. It was in July 1822 that Pickfords had contracted
to convey 800 soldiers from Paddington to Liverpool in twenty-six boats crewed
by 104 men. The largest part of these men were unhappy with the wages that
were to be paid. At the hour when the boats were due to leave the City Road
basin (11·30 p.m.), instead of the boats leaving, Edward Wray sprang from the
darkness shouting, 'Now my boys—this is your time!' Along the length of the
wharf seventy to eighty bargemen emerged from the darkness. Chanting the
battlecry, 'Huzza! Edward Wray for ever!' they quickly seized the beams of the
lock gates to prevent any boats leaving the basin, cut the towing ropes, heaved
two of the horses into the water, and began to search out those blacklegs who
were prepared to work for the wages offered. If they refused to join the rioters,
they were bundled overboard with the horses, and 'nearly met with watery
graves'. By now a party of police from Hatton Garden, the watchmen, and loyal
(or traitorous) bargemen, were advancing upon the dissidents to be met by a hail
of flintstones. Hand to hand fighting soon developed and became 'a most desperate conflict . . . and several were desperately wounded'. However, the police
courageously tackled the conspirators and succeeded in putting them to flight,
capturing six prisoners.[31]

Violence was not restricted to human beings. For many boatmen the horse was the scapegoat for their frustrations. As early as 1783 it was said that

> The boats . . . are each drawn by something like the skeleton of a horse, covered with skin; whether he subsists upon the scent of the water is a doubt; but whether his life is a scene of affliction is not, for the unfeeling driver has no employment but to whip him from one end of the canal to the other.[32]

The only change, by 1841, seems to have been that there were more horses to abuse. 'There are very few Descriptions of Animals treated more cruelly than the Boat Horse', remarked Sir George Chetwynd.[33] Thomas Harrison, of Worcester, complained:

> We have a great deal of Inconvenience on the Worcester and Birmingham from Six on the Sunday morning till late in the Day, some with sharp Instruments, others with big sticks abusing those small Animals [donkeys] till their Rumps were raw.

He agreed that 'They are [frequently of the very poorest description] and Half of them famished to Death'.[34] It was not so surprising that horses frequently fell into the canal, since John Crowley admitted that 'a horse will go fourteen hours a day'.[35]

It was often unwise to reprimand boatmen if they were cruel to their horse, as the report of an incident upon the Paddington canal makes clear.

> On Saturday, *George* and *Rockingham*, the masters of two Paddington canal boats, *Attlebury*, a driver of the towing horses, and *Tibbs, Masters* and *Golding*, three boat-men, were charged with a most brutal assault upon *William Collins* and *William Wal-ters*, belonging to the new police . . . the prisoner, *Attlebury*, was seen beating a bay mare, employed in towing the barges. Sergeant Collins remonstrated with him on his cruelty; the prisoner however beat the animal more cruelly, at the same time swearing at the officer . . . [The officers] asked the prisoner *George* the name of the owner of the mare. The latter replied in the grossest language; and all the prisoners, *Golding* excepted, jumped ashore. Collins was struck a tremendous blow in the face by *George*, and *Walters* at the same time being pierced by a boat-hook through the lip. They were then thrust into the canal, and the prisoners vociferating, 'Drown them!—Murder them!' The policemen now begged for mercy and the prisoners proceeded with their barges. Two gentlemen described the outrage as one of the utmost brutality, and that those who witnessed it were fearful to repel the attack, the desperate temper of the boatmen being too well known.[36]

At the root of much of this kind of behaviour lay the evil of heavy drinking. Surprisingly, before the turn of the century, references to drunken boatmen were few, although there were public houses by the side of the canals, and at least some boatmen must have carried alcoholic refreshment or lock keepers would have been unable to beg drink from them. 1802 seems to have been the first year that drinking attracted the attention of the Birmingham Canal Company. It was then reported that

> Two of Henshall and Co's Boats had an order to pass down the Locks on Sunday the 4th Inst—Dawson the steerer did not follow the Boats before Wednesday. Dawson

got an order sometime ago to pass on the Sunday—he stop'd his Boat a[t] Tyburn and another with him Drank until Monday evening.[37]

By 1841 the number of places tempting boatmen from the straight and narrow had proliferated. 'There are a great Number of Beer-houses on the Line of the Canal; they are put there particularly for the Purposes of the Boatmen', remarked Francis Twemlow.[38] John Crowley begged 'to state the difficulty we have to keep our Men to sober and orderly Conduct in consequence of the Beer shops that are established by the Locks'.[39] And it was drink which was to cause, in large measure, the series of events which were to scandalise public opinion in 1839, even to the extent of arousing it, for a year or two, to making demands for something to be done about the boatmen's condition. Three of the boatmen involved were to regret the day that they had set foot on a canal boat.

Christina Collins was a young woman in her early thirties who, in June 1839, was on her way from Liverpool to join her husband in London. She was to travel by one of Pickfords' London fly-boats, boarding it at Preston Brook. The crew of the boat consisted of the captain, James Owen, 39, 'a bluff middle-aged man'; George Thomas, 27, several years a Pickford boatman, from Wombourne; William Ellis, 28, employed by Owen for about five weeks, coming originally from Brinklow; and a boy William Musson (sometimes Muston), 16, from Chilvers Coton in Warwickshire. As the boat sped down the Trent and Mersey canal the men became more and more drunk, and Mrs Collins became increasingly fearful, until her worst fears were realised when she was raped and murdered and thrown into the canal. The boy was not incriminated, but Owen and Thomas were sent to the gallows, and Ellis, by a last-minute reprieve, was transported for life.

This story of the sad and terrible end of Mrs Collins showed up those concerned with canals in a very poor light. Only the workings of British justice emerged with any credit from the whole sorry affair. Of course, there were other murders in nineteenth-century England, but what was particularly horrifying about this one was that a woman had been attacked and killed in a public conveyance by the very people who should have been ensuring her safety and welfare. It was as if the driver and guard of a stage coach had raped and murdered their only passenger. Even worse was that the people who should have been aware of the dangers, or even knew of the dangers facing this woman (for the crew made no secret of their intentions to passing boatmen), more or less stood indifferently by. It was a sad indictment of the whole canal world.[40]

In this case violence combined with sexual immorality to produce a tragedy unprecedented on the canals. But boat people generally were often criticised for their sexual licence. *The Staffordshire Advertiser* remarked that 'Fornication and adultery are commonly prevalent'.[41] William Ward said, 'They are in the most demoralized State they can be; there are Boys and Girls of Fifteen or Sixteen Years of Age all together; they have lost all sense of Shame'.[42] The Reverend Davies recalled

being much pained at the first child I was called to baptise [at Runcorn]. I was almost horrified when they told me that the mother of the child had been pregnant by her own Brother.[43]

The case of Christina Collins demonstrated that the canals were not always the safest place for women, but there were women of another sort rumoured to be attracted there.[44] And Panther offered the information that 'the men generally in London are drawn into brothels, and associate with females of the worst description'.[45]

We must beware, however, of accepting too readily the evidence of such witnesses. Morality differs from one generation to another and between different cultures. And we must also consider whether boatmen were any worse than their contemporaries in other occupations and classes.

## NOTES TO CHAPTER FIVE

[1] G. L. Turnbull, 'Pickfords and the canal carrying trade 1780–1850, p. 18, quoting Lea to Langton, 22 October 1818. Lea was Pickfords' agent at Braunston.

[2] *Canal Boatmen's Magazine*, vol. 1., supplementary number, 20 May 1829, p. 35, Br. Mus., PP. 1090 c.

[3] *S. C. on the Observance of the Sabbath*, 1832, q. 1827.

[4] *Ibid.*, 1833.

[5] *S. C. on Sunday Trading*, 1841, q. 13.

[6] *Ibid.*, 109.

[7] *Ibid.*, 10.

[8] *Staffordshire Advertiser*, 3 August 1839.

[9] *Constabulary Force Report*, 1839.

[10] *S. C. on Sunday Trading*, 1841, qq. 175–6.

[11] *Staffordshire Advertiser*, 7 September 1839.

[12] *Constabulary Force Report*, 1839, pp. 53–4.

[13] BCN 4/371B, Houghton to Pickford, 15 June 1798.

[14] Hassell, *A Tour of the Grand Junction Canal in 1819*, pp. 11–12.

[15] *S. C. on the Observance of the Sabbath*, 1832, q. 1991.

[16] *Constabulary Force Report*, 1839, p. 50.

[17] PIC 4/1, p. 53, newspaper cutting from *The Star*, 9 July 1811.

[18] Turnbull, *op. cit.*, p. 19, quoting from *The Gentleman's Magazine*, vol. LXXIX (1809), p. 372.

[19] *Constabulary Force Report*, 1839, p. 48. The following details of thefts are drawn from pp. 49–56 of this report, unless otherwise indicated.

[20] 11 Geo. IV and 1 Willm. IV, c. 64.

[21] *S. C. on Sunday Trading*, 1841, q. 39.

[22] *S. C. on the Observance of the Sabbath*, 1832, q. 1807.

[23] PIC 4/1, p. 52, newspaper cutting from *The Star*, 2 September 1815.

[24] *S. C. on Sunday Trading*, 1841, q. 1224.

[25] *Ibid.*, 882.

[26] *Staffordshire Advertiser*, 14 May 1840.

[27] *Ibid.*, 9 May 1840.

[28] *Ibid.*, 18 April 1840.

[29] *Ibid.*, 28 September 1839.

[30] *Ibid.*, 31 August 1839.

[31] PIC 4/1, p. 9, newspaper cutting from *The News*, 28 July 1822.

[32] Hadfield, *British Canals*, p. 59, quoting from W. Hutton, *A History of Birmingham* (1783).

[33] *S. C. on Sunday Trading*, 1841, q. 52.

[34] *Ibid.*, 363, 368.

[35] *Ibid.*, 559.

[36] *Canal Boatmen's Magazine*, January 1830, pp. 11–12, quoting from *The Globe*, 30 November 1829.

[37] BCN 4/371B, Houghton to Robinson, 24 July 1802.

[38] *S. C. on Sunday Trading*, 1841, q. 449.

[39] *Ibid.*, 576.

[40] Details of the Christina Collins incident can be gathered from the reports, comments and letters in the *Staffordshire Advertiser*, and particularly under: 'The inquest', 22 June and 29 June 1839; 'The trial for rape', 27 July 1839; 'The trial for murder', 21 March 1840; 'The condemned boatmen', 28 March 1840; 'The execution', 11 April 1840 (two editions); and further details in the edition of 18 April 1840. Some interesting details of fly-boat working also emerge.

[41] *Staffordshire Advertiser*, 11 April 1840.

[42] *S. C. on Sunday Trading*, 1841, q. 867.

[43] H.L.R.O., MS., Mins. of Evid., H.L. 1840, Weaver Churches Bill, 21 July 1840, p. 205. He did not specifically refer to the boating population in this case, although the rest of his evidence was about boatmen or flatmen.

[44] *S. C. on Sunday Trading*, 1841, q. 82.

[45] *S. C. on the Observance of the Sabbath*, 1832, q. 1829.

# VI

# A balanced view

### FALLIBILITY OF 'COMMITTEE' EVIDENCE

THE PICTURE OF CANAL-BOAT LIFE which emerges most forcibly from a study of the evidence and reports of the committees and commissions which investigated the social aspects of the canals in the 1830s and early 1840s is not a pleasant one. Whether it was altogether a true picture is another matter. Social historians have become increasingly critical of 'committee evidence' in the nineteenth century. Harrison, in his studies of matters relating to drinking and drunkenness, goes furthest not only in casting doubts on the evidence and conclusions of committees, but in demonstrating the grave shortcomings of the actual workings of such committees as well.[1] His criticisms of the 'Drunkenness Committee' of 1834 are relevant, in greater or lesser degree, to other nineteenth-century committees. They were often packed with men of partisan interest, were biased in the selection and questioning of witnesses, and in the interpretation of the evidence thrown up. Committees which sat during June and July were particularly suspect, for it was 'a time when Respectability left London for the country and a time when a zealous few could easily get their way'.[2] Witnesses were invariably middle-class and often of a religious—and particularly of an Evangelical—bias. Employers were usually well-represented. The people who were to be most affected by any decision that the committee might arrive at were frequently absent. No pub-goer was asked his opinion on licensing reform, but temperance men were eagerly listened to. No boatman found his way into the halls of Westminster, but carriers were invited there frequently. Blaug has shown how the evidence in the Poor Law Report of 1834 was an endless recital of ills from squires, magistrates, overseers and clergy, but not from the poor themselves. 'In what age', he wrote, 'would it not be possible to collect complaint from the upper classes about the laziness of workers.' He shows how the evidence and reports of the Commissioners fitted in with their preconceived notions of the Poor Law problem, notions which were wrong and which did not fit in with the facts.[3] It might be advisable to view the evidence of the Police Commissioners of 1839 with an equally jaundiced eye. Similarly, at least some of the criticisms levelled by Harrison and others, against Committees in general, apply to the Select Committee on the Observance of the Sabbath, of 1832, and to the Select Committee on Sunday Trading of 1841; this last being particularly suspect, following as it did on a brutal and well-publicised murder. Perhaps 'momentary passions rather than systematic enquiry lay behind it'.[4]

### MORALITY OF THE BOATING CLASS IN THE CONTEXT OF THE TIMES

The first point to note, then, is that the wickedness (etc.) of the boat population does not stand out in such stark relief, after other committees have been seen to provide a medium for the middle classes to air their views and prejudices about the 'lower orders'. It seems that the 'lower orders' generally (divisions within the working class being rarely recognised), were often seen as a shiftless, drunken, immoral, dishonest lot, into which boatmen would no doubt have merged but for their distinctive occupation. Indeed, carmen, dustmen and labourers at the wharf at Paddington were felt to be in as great a need of salvation as the boatmen,[5] as were all transport men.[6] Years later, Harriet Martineau wrote to Elizabeth Barrett:

> I dare say you need not be told how sensual vice abounds in rural districts. [At Ambleside] it is flagrant beyond anything I ever cd. have looked for: . . . every justice of the peace is filled with disgust, and every clergy[n] with (almost) despair at the drunkenness, quarrelling and extreme licentiousness with women.[7]

Boatmen had no monopoly of sin.

For, although Blaug and Harrison might criticise the conclusions and methods of commissioners and committees, they do not deny the existence of 'indolence and vice', or that there was drunkenness in plenty in the England of the 1830s. To look more closely at drinking, for example, we find that custom still insisted that 'strong drink [was] necessary for strong men and strong work', although some labourers were by then becoming more discerning.[8] Hence, wages were often paid partly in beer. Habits of drinking were induced which could not be laid aside when men were not at work. The inadequate supplies of pure water, the shortage of amusements other than drinking, and the centring of so many aspects of life around the public house, all contributed to drunkenness being a widespread feature of working-class life in the first half of the nineteenth century (although other classes were not without their heavy drinkers as well). It was not only canal carriers who were supposedly suffering on account of the proliferation of beer houses, for, in Leicestershire, the farmers all said, 'the Beer Shop Act has proved a very bad one for this parish'.[9] Transport workers were particularly liable to drunkenness, for public houses played such an important part in the organisation of the transport system.

If the population at large was a drunken one, it was often, also, and partly in consequence, a violent and cruel one. Harrison and Trinder describe how elections, race meetings, wakes and fairs in Banbury (and doubtless elsewhere) were the venue for cruel animal sports and prize fighting, and usually degenerated into orgies of drunken violence.[10] And violence was not restricted to special occasions. The working class were not slow to splash the early nineteenth century with other 'note[s] of vivid colour', as Oscar Wilde was wont to label 'sin'.

But recent studies demonstrate that the committees and commissions, in their eagerness to prove the correctness of their prejudices, and in their anxiety to stir up public opinion, not only exaggerated these existing evils, but they were not above quoting the evils of yesteryear as if they were still widespread, a ploy particularly popular among factory and poor law reformers. They invariably hesitated to mention (or perhaps even grasp) that many of their conclusions and strictures applied only to certain sections of the working class, and to dwindling sections at that.

When viewed in this wider perspective we must ask ourselves how the boatmen, as depicted by commissions and committees, compare with the rest of the working-class population, as depicted by other commissions and committees. Accepting that there were some very real and unpleasant evils—such as excessive drunkenness—in the England of the 1830s, we must also question how far, in fact, such parliamentary investigations give a true picture of the working class in general, and the boating class in particular. In short, was the boating population (real or imagined) any worse than the rest of the population (real or imagined)?

### EVIDENCE CONTRADICTING THE PESSIMISTIC VIEW OF CANAL-BOAT LIFE

It would be wrong to infer, as we have come close to doing, that members of the middle class, without exception, were incapable of being objective and truthful, or that they had no sympathy with or understanding of the working classes. It was not necessary to be a Mayhew to do that.[11] There are thousands of examples who, by thought and deed, have proved false any such suggestion. One 'Tiphys' wrote of how no one reading the Police Commissioners' report, or the comments in the press following the murder of Christina Collins, in 1839,

> would hesitate for a moment in drawing the conclusion that the inland watermen of England, without exception, were individually addicted to murder, lust and rapine; that they were never to be approached but with feelings of horror and never to have anything entrusted to their care but with a certainty of being plundered. Surely the perpetration of the horrid crime alluded to is not to be taken as a proof of the general depravity of boatmen, or of their aptitude to commit offences of equal atrocity; nor are they to be treated as accessories, nor upon the strength of the current of public feeling, which from such an event, has set in strongly against them, to be charged with 'many other enormities of ordinary though unobserved occurrence'. It is but an act of justice due to that libelled class of men to declare, that notwithstanding their acknowledged vices—and that there are many exceptional characters to be found among them—they are not in the estimation of those best capable of judging, considered inferior either in point of honesty or morality to any other class of men moving in the same sphere of life. That their manners and deportment in general are

rough and unpolished every one will admit, but morality and good manners are not synonymous terms, and experience has shown that a person of rough exterior is quite as likely to possess an honest and kind heart as one whose demeanour is more polite and whose manners are better polished.[12]

There were also a few witnesses before the Committee of 1841 whose evidence contradicted that of the majority. Francis Twemlow informed their Lordships:

I have been Chairman of the Staffordshire Quarter Sessions Six Years . . . and during that Time I do not think I have had for Trial more than that Number of Offences against Boatmen for robbing their Cargoes.

He knew of 'no Cases of Murder but the one I mentioned before, nor any of aggravated Assaults',[13] which must cast grave doubt on the claim of the Reverend Davies, that the ranks of the boating class were being constantly 'thinned by Transportation and other Punishments'.[14] Twemlow also thought that 'Boatmen (I allude more particularly to Captains of Boats) are Men of better character than they were formerly'. He was of the opinion that fewer depredations were being committed than in former times, and he contended that the carriers he had spoken to were also of that opinion.[15]

And there were carriers who did not condemn their men universally. Richard Heath, of the carrying firm of Matthew Heath and Sons, Stourport, could say, 'There is a wide Variety of Character; but I should say they are Men whose moral Character has very much improved within the last Ten or Fifteen Years'.[16] John Crowley said, 'Many of them are very trustworthy, honest, moral and sober'.[17] 'I know some of them are very bad but some are very good', Mr Hayes concluded.[18] Baxendale used to think them 'a much more respectable Set of Men than they had Credit for being, and very manageable'.[19] Nor were all the casual boat hands completely condemned. Heath admitted that their character was, in general, worse than those of the captains, 'but a great Number of those Young Men are praiseworthy in their Conduct', he added.[20] The Reverend Davies was happy to be able to draw attention to some boatmen, who were 'Kind Fathers, affectionate Husbands, honest servants and really Ornaments to their Station in Society'.[21]

On the question of dishonesty, evidence from elsewhere gives the report of the Police Commissioners an unnecessarily catastrophic look. It is peculiar, to say the least of it, that in the midst of all this talk of extensive pilferage, those merchants, manufacturers and traders, whose dissatisfaction with the canal system was leading them to support the building of railways, rarely complained of pilferage of their goods, except on the route via the Trent to Hull, and there only because of the transhipment at Shardlow, Gainsborough and Hull, where goods lay exposed to theft on wharves for long periods.[22] Of all the faults of the canals, as recorded in the surviving minutes of evidence taken for railway bills in the 1830s, only one witness, Henry Hemsley of the Union Flint Glass Company, felt that pilferage was a real fault of the canals,[23] but another midland glass (and nail) manufacturer said, 'There is no Complaint of Pilferage'.[24] His grievance, like that of other witnesses in the 1830s, was the slowness of canal transport and, above all, the 'want of

certainty'. Another merchant, also, specifically mentioned that, 'on the Liverpool
and London lines we never suffer loss—In the whole course of my business I never
knew of any pilferage on that line'.[25] At least some of the blame for loss could be
laid at the door of the Grand Junction Canal Company, who had 'a very arbitrary
and unjust way of ascertaining what kinds of Goods are in the Packages'. A hole
was broken into casks, which, in the case of nails, for example, meant that the con-
tents were liable to fall out.[26]

If examples of the dishonesty of boatmen can be found, equally, it is never difficult to find manufacturers who were suffering loss at the hands of their employees.
Embezzlement by clerks, both in the canal world and outside it, was frequent.
Thefts of goods in transit perpetrated by men other than boatmen were not
uncommon, especially as canals attracted many unsavoury elements to their
banks. A shop keeper in Barnton was found to have been stealing from canal boats
in the years after 1815.[27] William Robotham, a clerk to James Shipton, at Wolverhampton, was found guilty in 1839 of stealing stockings while loading a boat, and
was sentenced to twelve months' hard labour.[28] Lock keepers continued to
indulge in illegal transactions with boatmen including the washing of boatmen's
linen by their wives.[29] Examples of the continued carelessness of carriers, especially in the earlier part of the century, in the matter of their declarations, raises the
question of how much was carelessness and how much dishonesty.[30]

While the boatmen were often rough and ready people, at least some of the
violence in which they were involved can be put down to their being unnecessarily impeded. Hence, although Francis Wilbee, a toll clerk at Boxmoor, had
brought a charge of assault against a boatman, it was decided that he had 'by an in-
discreet zeal given provocation to the Boatman'.[31] Joseph Taylor admitted that he
had 'pitched it into' William Bainbridge, but in extenuation he pleaded that the
complainant had stopped his horse, to gauge his boat, a second time.[32] Thus many
of the allegations levelled at the boating class can be qualified, in one way or
another, and it is important to try to present a more balanced view than the one
which parliamentary bodies seemed to hold in the Canal Age.


### THE TRUE SITUATION

It is clear that the character of boating, and of boatmen, changed in the period
from about 1790 to 1840. Existing research points to the earliest boatmen being
generally an honest, respectable and hardworking race, even if they were none
too particular about the way they treated canal property and canal officials causing them undue delay. By the 1790s, it would seem that, because of the increasing
distances and changing modes of operation (in particular the introduction and
growth of fly-boat working), and the growing number of boats, canal boating
generally attracted a lower class of man (or more often boy). Taking to the boats
did often provide a good hiding place for villains. The increasing number of valuable goods carried, and the need for casual labour, brought unsavoury characters

to loiter on the canal banks, in public houses, and in the later beer shops. Kershaw knew of instances

> when men have been discharged from their regular employment, they have gone to those places where these bodies congregate together, and lived there for months and months, without any ostensible means of livelihood. They infest the banks of our canals to a very great extent.[33]

As a result of all these factors there is no doubt that thefts from canal boats did increase. The principal carriers had been forced by events to form an 'Association for Apprehending and prosecuting felons' by 1802, which, by 1804, was offering rewards for information about thefts from boats and wharves.[34] Boatmen were not specifically mentioned as the culprits, but an Act of 1819, which aimed at the easier conviction of felons stealing from boats, makes clear that the boatmen were seen as the chief suspects.[35] It may well have been that they had become generally more dishonest than the population at large. They certainly had more opportunity to apportion goods of value—in tunnels, in rural areas, at night—with less chance of discovery than most others. The dangers of being caught were also slim, since there were few people actively out to catch them.

> While we engaged upon a course of crime there was no hindrance. We never feared anything for there are no constables on the canals. There are a few bank riders . . . but the driver gives us the signal and we get the cloth down and make all right,

said J. C.[36] Often too, the people who sighed over the losses from pilferage were the slowest to do anything about it. The police, where they existed, the manufacturers, the canal companies and the carriers seem to have found it difficult to get together to take effective measures. Some unscrupulous carriers would employ boatmen and their horses at very low rates, lower than anyone else could afford to work, both sides happy in the knowledge that pilfering would make up the difference.[37]

None the less, as we have seen, there is evidence to demonstrate that, by the 1830s, there was, in fact, very little pilfering of cargoes. The catastrophic tales put out by witnesses to the Commission of 1839, and to the Committee of 1841, while interesting in showing how and what went on in the shady corners of the canal transport system, were probably more descriptive of what had gone on in an earlier age (particularly during the bad times 1815–22), and were, perhaps, an exaggerated description at that.

Similarly, suggestions of wickedness, drunkenness and violence (etc.) were probably equally exaggerated. There is no doubt that there were some villainous characters on the canals. Boatmen had to be forceful people to get their boats through. There were many young, undisciplined, unmarried men, cut off from civilising influences, who were to be found letting off steam after five days or more 'on the cut' with little rest, preparing themselves for a similar period of abstinence. Such people often made their presence felt *en masse* in some unexpected place owing to frost, or some other delay. Sometimes local worthies were successful in getting the locks closed on Sunday, or for several hours on that day, but the crowds of bored and frustrated boatmen who were thus detained, to drink and fight and swear, as the citizens wended their righteous and dignified way to the church services, caused swift changes of mind.[38] At Barton Turnings near Burton-on-Trent, for example,

> there was such a Scene of Drunkenness and fighting, and Breaches of the Peace and Riot, that the very individuals who requested the Trent and Mersey Company to stop the trading actually requested us to order the Boats to proceed.[39]

For, while the worthy citizens and clergy were often keen to save the souls of the boatmen, in respect of breaking the commandment, they were usually cooler in welcoming them into their midst. For, lacking any real police force to keep the boatmen in some form of order, given the character of some boatmen, the absence of anything constructive for them to do, coupled with the reluctance to allow them into church or to create some other form of worship or amusement, it is not very surprising that the gathering of large numbers of boatmen led to disorders.

There was a desire among the boating people to be accepted into society, but the rejection by society, real or imagined (usually real), played an important part in creating an inward looking sub-culture, a sense of inferiority, and a sense of abandonment among the boating class, which gave further foundation to society's prejudices. 'I think their Impression now is, that they are a degraded Class of Beings; that they are separated from Society', Chetwynd observed.[40] Twemlow thought that because of 'their Dress and Appearance they consider themselves a marked Class of Persons'.[41]

Looking at the evidence as a whole for this period of the Canal Age, even accepting the very real blemishes in their character, and that there had probably been a deterioration in standards as compared with the earliest boatmen, the most sensible conclusion seems to be that the canal-boat population was neither 'worse' nor 'better' than the working-class population at large, but different. There had been and were mischievous practices and people on the waterways, but in keeping with the rest of the population, these were lessening in numbers over the years. The arrival of women on canal boats may have contributed to this improvement.

## RESULTS OF THE PUBLICITY OF 1839–41

The events and information thrust upon the public in 1839–41 had several results. Firstly, they tended to confirm prejudices about the boating class, which were already firmly established in the public mind. Secondly, a Canal Police Act was passed with great haste, in 1840, which permitted canal companies to set up a police force, with powers extending to half a mile on each side of the canal. Little came of this Act.[42] A third result was that religious organisations came forward with a righteous flourish to bring 'light to the heathen'. Vicars and bishops and canal companies began to fall over themselves to outline their intentions, although we should not ignore the good work previously done by some few clergy and organisations. However, the first flush of reforming zeal evaporated; boatmen were not so keen to be saved; the public lost interest; and many, if not all, of the new ventures faded away.

Canal companies did, however, take a more sustained interest in the welfare of the boaters, after the unsavoury revelations had, perhaps, stirred the consciences of the directors and proprietors. Until this time, concern for the morals and affairs of the boatmen had generally ended when they had no relevance to the structure of the canal, or to the expedition of trade upon it.[43] This was not an unreasonable attitude, except perhaps in circumstances of acute distress, when common humanity demanded that the company, with others, help alleviate suffering.[44] No one, for example, would have considered laying responsibility for the spiritual and moral (or even physical) welfare of the waggoners at the door of the turnpike trusts.

In 1840 the Grand Junction Company, for one, began to exert more of an influence on the lives of the boatmen. On 19 February of that year it was resolved that canal officials should note down the names and details of any boatmen seen to be drunk.[45] The company paid much closer attention to the character of the men taking over canal-side public houses.[46] In 1841 Lord Francis Egerton was in the process of setting up a floating chapel at Runcorn, and already the Bridgewater concern had established a floating chapel at Preston Brook to hold 120 people.[47] The committee of the Staffordshire and Worcestershire canal gave proof of its concern.[48] Minute books everywhere began to record a greater awareness of the existence of canal boatmen, and, of course, canal companies became increasingly concerned with the boating population, as employers, from the mid-1840s.

A fifth result was that the boatmen were almost successful in having Sunday as a day of rest, like other people. Once Sunday working had become accepted, it was difficult to stop it. Market boats had to travel on Sundays to arrive for the Monday market.[49] By 1840 a complicated system of fly-boat services had developed, working to a fairly rigid timetable, and the cessation of work on one day would throw this system into a chaos which would be difficult to rearrange.[50] Most fly-boats started out late on Saturday night, or early on Sunday morning, from the north and midlands, because it was on Saturday night that most goods arrived from the manufacturers.[51] This necessitated a Sunday traffic.

Some carriers saw no point in stopping on the Sunday. John Crowley described how

> the Slow Boats usually work only from Sunrise to Sunset, and they rest every Night; as it regards Sunday, I do not apprehend the Sunday is a necessary Time for resting having that Rest from Labour for the Men every Night.[52]

Again, if one carrier stopped his boats on a Sunday his competitors would be able to take some of his trade.[53] The only way to ensure a day of rest for the boatmen on Sunday—and a petition 'signed by almost all the Boatmen on almost every Canal in the Country'[54] showed, not surprisingly, that they desired it—was if all the canal companies closed their canals on the Sabbath. However, apart from the fact that they would not 'act with anything like Cordiality',[55] it turned out that they had no legal power to close their canals.[56] Where canal companies did close the locks on Sundays (presumably illegally), in response to public opinion, the prohibition did not usually last very long, as we have seen. Some carriers did insist that their men must rest on the sabbath, even though it involved them in loss.[57] Most boatmen, however, were compelled to toil seven days a week unless the legislature could enforce uniform closure of canals on Sunday. Many people were agreed, also, that it was the lack of a day of rest which had led to some of the evils of canal life. Some felt that cutting the boat people off from worship and instruction on the sabbath was responsible. Others were probably more correct in thinking that constant toil, week in and week out, with no rest and little prospect of it, must lead to excesses when any opportunities of distraction from labour arose. Sunday labour also meant that the gap between the land population and the water people had widened, since the latter came to have so little time to spend on land.

Numerous petitions followed on the murder of Christina Collins and the trial of the three boatmen, demanding that there should be a law to prohibit the carriage of goods on canals and railways on Sundays.[58] Lord Hatherton, the chairman of the resulting select committee, which sat from 3 May to 7 June 1841,[59] in presenting the minutes of evidence to Parliament, claimed that 'the Committee were unanimously of opinion, that the evidence taken presented the strongest possible case for legislative interference', and the Government agreed to introduce a Bill.[60]

But the moment was passed. Canal companies and carriers were reluctant to cease work on Sundays unless railways did also. Railways were becoming more important; they were taking up more and more parliamentary time. More members of parliament and the public were coming to own railway shares, and to wish to travel on Sundays. The memory of Christina Collins slipped quietly into history, as her violated body had slipped silently into the canal at Brindley's Bank.[61] Interest in the sins of boatmen faded, as the steam locomotive captured the eye and imagination of the public. The boating population was allowed to return to journeying, generally unseen and unheeded, on the water highways, little the worse and perhaps somewhat improved by their months of publicity. Sunday working continued, generally unabated, until nearer the end of the century.

### NOTES TO CHAPTER SIX

[1] Brian Harrison, 'The Sunday Trading riots of 1855', *Historical Journal*, VIII, 2 (1965), pp. 219–45; 'Two roads to social reform: Francis Place and the "Drunken Committee" of 1834', *Historical Journal*, XI, 2 (1968), pp. 272–300.

[2] *Ibid.* (1968 article), p. 291.

[3] Mark Blaug, 'The myth of the old Poor Law and the making of the new', *Journal of Economic History*, XXIII, 2 (June 1963), pp. 151–84.

[4] Harrison, *op. cit.* (1968 article), p. 295, quoting W. J. Fox.

[5] *Canal Boatmen's Magazine*, November 1829, p. 145, Br. Mus., PP. 1090 c.

[6] *Ibid.*, May 1830, p. 51.

[7] R. K. Webb, *Harriet Martineau: A Radical Victorian* (1960), p. 260.

[8] *Select Committee on Inquiry into Drunkenness*, 1834 (559), VIII, q. 317 (evidence of Edwin Chadwick).

[9] *Report of the Poor Law Commission*, 1834 (11), XXIX, p. 88a; *ibid.*, (20), XXXVIII, p. 87e.

[10] B. Harrison and B. Trinder, 'Drink and sobriety in an early Victorian county town: Banbury 1830–60', *English Historical Review*, supplement 4 (1969), pp. 7–14.

[11] See E. P. Thompson and Eileen Yeo, *The Unknown Mayhew: Selections from the Morning Chronicle, 1849–50* (1971).

[12] *Staffordshire Advertiser*, 17 August 1839.

[13] *S. C. on Sunday Trading*, 1841, qq. 413–14.

[14] *Ibid.*, 740.

[15] *Ibid.*, 396, 411, 503.

[16] *Ibid.*, 612.

[17] *Ibid.*, 577.

[18] *Ibid.*, 212.

[19] *Ibid.*, 1180.

[20] *Ibid.*, 624.

[21] *Ibid.*, 740.

[22] H.L.R.O., MS., Mins. of Evid., H. C., 1836, vol. 1, Birmingham, Derby and Stonebridge Railway Bill, 14 March 1836, pp. 100–1, 107.

[23] London and Birmingham Railway Bill, 2 July 1832, p. 85.

[24] *Ibid.*, 3 July 1832, p. 100.

[25] Birmingham, Derby and Stonebridge Railway Bill, *op. cit.*, 14 March 1836, p. 101.

[26] London and Birmingham Railway Bill, 2 July 1832, p. 87; GJC 1/3, 8 March 1825, p. 338.

[27] Iredale, 'Canal settlement: Barnton, 1775–1845', p. 50.

[28] *Staffordshire Advertiser*, 27 July 1839.

[29] GJC 1/7, 22 January 1840, p. 189 and 22 July 1840, p. 287; GJC 1/8, 28 September 1842, p. 257. In this last instance a lock keeper was discharged for selling vegetables to the boatmen.

[30] GJC 1/1, 27 September 1816, p. 43; GJC 1/1, 1 February 1819, pp. 288–9.

[31] GJC 1/4, 19 January 1828.

[32] *Staffordshire Advertiser*, 28 September 1839.

[33] *Constabulary Force Report*, 1839, p. 54.

[34] *Aris's Birmingham Gazette*, 30 August 1802 and 18 June 1804; GEN 4/857/4.

[35] 59 Geo III, Cap. 27.

[36] *Constabulary Force Report*, 1839, p. 53.

[37] *Ibid.*, p. 50.

[38] *S. C. on Sunday Trading*, 1841, 1114, 1040.

[39] *Ibid.*, 28.

[40] *Ibid.*, 84.

[41] *Ibid.*, 487.

[42] *Ibid.*, 33–8, 1197–9.

[43] See for example GJC 1/2, 20 January 1820; BLC 1/3, 14 January 1836, p. 3.

[44] As in the instance described in BLC 1/3, 18 July 1838, p. 35.

[45] GJC 1/7, 19 February 1840, p. 203.

[46] *Ibid.*, 22 July 1840, p. 288; GJC 1/8, 28 September 1842, p. 260, 12 October 1842, p. 286 and 12 April 1843.

[47] *S. C. on Sunday Trading*, 1841, q. 711.

[48] *Ibid.*, 172.

[49] *Ibid.*, 1043.

[50] *Ibid.*, 574.

[51] *Ibid.*, 149, 571, 672, 822–3, 914.

[52] *Ibid.*, 532.

53 *Ibid.*, 209, 857.

54 *Ibid.*, 548.

55 *Ibid.*, 1154.

56 *Ibid.*, 709.

57 *S. C. on the Observance of the Sabbath*, 1832, qq. 1802–3; *S. C. on Sunday Trading*, 1841, q. 489.

58 *Hansard*, LIV, 12 June 1840, c. 1100; *ibid.*, LVII, 23 April 1841, c. 1018.

59 *S. C. on Sunday Trading*, 1841.

60 *Hansard*, LVIII, 14 June 1841, c. 1486.

61 *Staffordshire Advertiser*, 21 March 1840.

# VII

# Change and decay
## The effect of the railway
## upon canals and canal-boat life
### 1840–1914

### THE IMMEDIATE IMPACT OF RAILWAY COMPETITION 1840–70

THE EFFECT OF THE STEAM LOCOMOTIVE upon the lives of the boating population is shrouded in mystery, and only occasional pieces of evidence enable us to peep through the curtains of obscurity to see something of the feelings and experiences of these people, in those difficult times. Many of our conclusions must be of a tentative nature.

The most recent research suggests that the years after the railway first became a significant competitor were not quite as difficult as has sometimes been thought. The crippling effect of new railway lines upon the weakest, usually southern, rural canals, was often immediate, dramatic and, within a few decades, fatal, leading in practice to their virtual or complete demise before the end of the century.[1] Presumably boatmen must, here, either have taken a reduction in income, left the waterways for work on land, or gone elsewhere on the canals in search of work, if such work were to be had. But on the stronger canals the tonnages carried were generally maintained, and on some they significantly increased, down to the 1860s, at least (see Appendix III). That these increases were often obtained at the expense of formidable reductions in receipts and dividends need not concern us here.

The first impact of this new form of transport upon the stronger canals was, perhaps, not so desperate because, as Hadfield points out, there is a time lag in the change over from one form of transport to another.[2] Until a new system is fully developed the old retains many advantages. The factories and mines which had grown up by the side of the waterways continued, in many instances, to be best served by canal transport. The railway system remained disjointed, certainly before 1850, and for some years afterwards, and Mather has demonstrated how, in consequence, the railway companies often 'depended upon adjacent canals for power to enter into competition for the long-distance traffic'.[3] Nor were railways and canal companies always the implacable enemies that they have been made out to be, since, often, a period of rate war between two such companies would be followed by years of more profitable truce. James Loch, the Superintendent of the Bridgewater Trust (1837–55), looked upon some railways as hostile and others as friendly.[4] In 1845 the Oxford Canal Company was 'Desirous of continuing the friendly feeling with the promoters of the London and South Stafford' Railway'.[5] Competition from the railways in the 1840s was perhaps not as new (in some areas pre-railway transport was already very competitive), nor as persistently severe, as Jackman and Clapham have portrayed.[6] In addition, man's natural conservatism favoured the canals. The coal traders of Banbury memorialised the Oxford Canal Company, in 1850:

> To this perfect disruption and change [using the railway] the undersigned are greatly averse—As proprietors of wharves bordering on the canal, as owners of boats, as employers of boatmen and others, the faithful servants of many years, their interests, habits and prejudices all incline them to pursue the path they have so long been accustomed to.[7]

It was only when a really fine network of railway lines was being completed, thus filling in the gaps that had continued to be the preserves of many canals, that even the strongest began to feel the pinch. Branch lines began to be built to the mines and factories previously served by waterways. New factories were being attracted to the railway rather than to the canal. Railway companies, by amalgamation, came increasingly to have a regional monopoly, and could no longer be played off against each other by canal companies. Railway men no longer looked to the canals for help in breaking into and carrying on trade, as they developed their own collection and distribution systems, as they increased their warehouse capacities and their track mileage. Hence, by the time the economy was again beginning to experience more protracted trade slumps in the 1870s, 1880s and early 1890s, the railway companies were in a position to be less tolerant of canal competition, and less keen to keep rate-fixing agreements. None the less, it seems fair to assume that before the 1870s the stronger canals remained reasonably successful, sometimes, it is true, because of the railways rather than in spite of them. Such inadequate statistics as there are suggest that maintained and increased tonnages on many canals would guarantee adequate employment for most boatmen during this first period of railway competition.

Unfortunately, there were several factors which adversely affected boatmen's employment other than the difficulties of a few minor, and rather inconsequential, canals. The growing tonnages were being carried over shorter distances, and hence any increased demand for the services of boatmen was at least partly offset by the fact that fewer were needed to move a given tonnage of goods (see tables 2, 3 and 4).

On other canals the through trade was declining; dramatically on the Kennet and Avon canal, after the opening of the Great Western Railway from Bristol to London in 1841;[8] more slowly on such canals as the Oxford and the Birmingham canals.[9] Above all, it was the higher-value type of goods, which had made up an important part of the through trade of most canals, which was being lost to the

TABLE 2    *Trade navigated on the Grand Junction canal, 1833–52 (annual averages, over four years, in tons)*

| Years | Through trade | Local trade | Entire trade |
|---|---|---|---|
| 1833–36 | 190,521 | 627,015 | 817,561 |
| 1837–40 | 218,903 | 769,551 | 988,452 |
| 1841–44 | 249,377 | 777,454 | 1,026,831 |
| 1845–48 | 251,104 | 855,045 | 1,106,149 |
| 1849–52 | 219,266 | 843,094 | 1,062,710 |

*Source* Adapted from *Second and Third Reports of the S.C. on Railway and Canal Bills, 1852–3* (79, 170, 246, 736) (henceforward referred to as *S. C. on Railway and Canal Bills, 1852–3*), appendix I, p. 143.

TABLE 3    *Down coal boats passing through Farmers Bridge locks, Birmingham, per year*

| Year | Birmingham coal boats | Distance coal boats |
|---|---|---|
| 1844 | 8,687 | 5,974 |
| 1855 | 11,001 | 1,129 |

*Source*   BCN 4/181.

TABLE 4    *Coal carried to London (tons)*

| Year | By sea | By rail | By canal |
|---|---|---|---|
| 1852 | 3,330,000 | 317,000 | 23,000 |
| 1882 | 3,826,000 | 6,750,000 | 8,000 |

*Source*   S. C. on Canals, 1883 (252), qq. 1533–6.

railways. They had already captured a great deal of this trade from the Bridgewater canal in 1839,[10] and the 1840s saw more and more of the transfer of such goods from water transport to the more rapid means of locomotion. Presumably fewer fly-boats were needed and fewer fly-boat crews. As Joseph Baxendale pointed out in 1841, 'If the trade becomes a Slow Trade instead of a Fly Trade there will be only Two Men instead of Four Men in a Boat; that must make a very material difference'.[11]

Not only were canal carriers cutting down on their fly-boats and fly-boat crews, they were actually abandoning the canals altogether, sometimes to retire from trading completely, but more often because they were seduced on to the railway.[12] According to George Loch of the Bridgewater concern, one by one the carriers had been driven off, because they were 'unable to face the competition, or the inducements held out to them by the railway companies to give up their trade'.[13] The experience of the Worcester and Birmingham Canal Company in 1848 further illustrates the nationwide sequence of events in the 1840s, as new lines opened.

Since the opening of the Bristol and Birmingham Railway many offers have been made to Traders on the Canal to induce them to remove their business from the Canal to the Railroad, and one after another they have yielded to the temptation thus offered and in September last Messrs. Pickford and Co. [gave] . . . notice that . . . on the 25th March next they would give up possession of the warehouses.[14]

Pickfords had begun to transfer their large canal traffic on to the railways in 1838, and the number of boats had been reduced by 25 per cent by 1841.[15] The process was virtually completed in the years 1845–8.[16] Throughout the country, carriers, and particularly fly-boat operators, were leaving the canals.[17] What happened to all these fly-boat men thus thrown out of work? Pickfords, for example, had employed in the region of 500 men and boys on their boats around 1838.[18] By 1849 this company had only a few boats[19] engaged in collection and distribution (boatage), for the railways, in and around Birmingham. Where had all their boatmen gone?

Other events could throw boatmen out of work. The Birmingham and Liverpool Junction Canal Company (soon to become a part of the Shropshire Union Railways and Canal Company) decided in 1843 to play the railways at their own game. This company began to use steam tugs to draw trains of boats, from eight to twelve in number, containing 160 to 240 tons of goods, along the canal from Autherley and from Ellesmere Port.[20] Even though such a system saved goods from being lost to the railway, many boatmen were obviously thrown out of work, for these trains seem to have been managed by only three men on the tug, plus one or two to assist at the locks, these last being stationed there.[21] Eighty boats[22] were engaged in this trade between Wolverhampton and Ellesmere Port and, whereas previously the boats had been taken separately all the way, boatmen were now merely concerned with collection and distribution between Wolverhampton and Autherley Junction. This fact must have made serious inroads into the employment of the upwards of 600 persons employed as boatmen in 1841 upon the Birmingham and Liverpool canal.[23]

On another occasion, according to a Mr Burchell, the opening of the Grand Junction Railway Company's Madeley station in 1846 diverted, almost overnight, the very considerable export trade of porcelain and earthenware which, in passing down the Trent and Mersey canal from the Potteries to Liverpool, had been a principal source of income for the company and had created considerable employment for boatmen.[24] Of course, such trades, which had disappeared so dramatically, often came back, in part at least, to the canals. The train system on the Birmingham and Liverpool canal did not, in fact, last very long and had probably been abandoned by 1846, with a return to the old system of horse haulage. However, if many boatmen got their jobs back, or increased their employment as a result, they had, no doubt, suffered a period of unemployment and uncertainty paralleled elsewhere. The boatmen of Banbury were perhaps typical of many others in the 1840s and 1850s, in their reluctance to leave a life-long occupation. In 1850, it was said, many of these men have been, and are still keeping themselves and their horses, some without any and others with insufficient employment hoping (perhaps against hope) that some equitable arrangement might be made to avoid their being driven from their old pursuit.[25]

On the other hand, it would almost certainly be wrong to create a picture of the canal scene in the 1840s and 1850s as one where boatmen were to be found in sullen groups at every turn on the 'cut', tightening their belts and watching their horses starve before sad and despairing eyes. References to such a state of affairs, if they exist, are hard to find.

Certainly, the 1840s were years of uncertainty and dislocation for many involved with canals. Mr Easton's remark in 1844, that 'few if any Boats [have] been built for several years',[26] generates no great atmosphere of confidence, but there is no evidence of mass unemployment of boatmen, of savage wage reductions, or of other examples of all but the most temporary distress. For new jobs were being created by the canal companies, as they themselves went into the carrying business, on their own and other waterways, to replace the deserting private carriers. The Bridgewater Trustees expanded the range and size of their carrying interests in the 1840s. The Shropshire Union Company, on its formation in 1845, took over the carrying business of its predecessor (the Birmingham and Liverpool Canal Company), and the older establishment of the Ellesmere and Chester Company.[27] The Leeds and Liverpool Company[28] and the Grand Junction Company both began carrying in 1848.[29] By 1853 this last company was said to be the largest canal carrier in the country, having taken over much of the country's long-distance canal trade.[30] The trade carried on was that taken over from the independent carriers, whose boats and horses the canal company had bought.[31] It would seem reasonable to assume that the boatmen of the original carriers transferred, with the boats and horses, to work for the Grand Junction Company. One boatman at least had done this, for Captain Randle, who had been with Pickfords since 1808, took over a Grand Junction fly-boat in 1848.[32] Elsewhere, other canal companies were taking over the stock, and presumably the boatmen, of other carriers. George Mellish, a director of the Grand Junction Company, claimed in 1853 that his company had lost little of the fly-boat trade to the railways, and it may well have been that, in the 1840s at least, a rough balance was almost achieved between the number of boatmen being thrown out of work and the number of new jobs being created.[33]

However, it may also have been that this equilibrium was maintained because some boatmen left the canals, with their employers, to become involved in carting and handling for those carriers who transferred their trade on to the railways, sometimes to become closely concerned with their working. For example, Captain Laws offered to allow McKay, a canal carrier, to farm the Lancashire and Yorkshire Railway Company's station at Ashton (ie. to find clerks, porters and carts at so much per ton), if he would carry by rail.[34] Pickfords, who became deeply involved in railway carriage, had, when their boat trade was finally broken up in 1848, offered Captain Randle a position as a porter on the railway.[35] Although he had turned it down, no doubt others among their boating staff received similar offers and accepted them. Unfortunately, this view of the 1840s is mainly conjecture. From 1851, the more reliable census material allows a more definite appraisal of events, as they affected the boatmen, to be made.[36]

There was a decline in the number of boatmen from 1851 to 1911 of 14·5 per cent, which is not a very dramatic fall, over sixty years, in a supposedly decaying industry.[37] None the less, the general impression must be (since boatmen were leaving the waterways), that there was a decline in the amount of work to be done, which was reflected in reduced earnings, which induced men to leave.

Most of the decline in numbers came in the 1850s and 1860s. The changes in the age structure of the boating force give us some clue as to the kinds of men who were leaving the waterways then. The most marked decline shows itself in the younger age-groups. The age range 15 to 25 showed a decline of 18·6 per cent, and that of 25 to 35, 16·5 per cent, in the 1850s. This suggests that not only had recruitment fallen off but that also some of those boatmen who had been between 10 and 25 in 1851 had either lost their jobs, or left the waterways, before 1861, in greater numbers than older boatmen. The fact that losses in the next decade—the 1860s—evened out, roughly, over all the age-groups (apart from a significant fall in the recruitment age-groups) suggests that a great many of the lost jobs in the 1850s were among fly-boat crews, which had previously been made up principally of young men and boys. The significant fall in the number of men sleeping on board in the 1850s confirms this (see Appendix IV*d*). Other evidence shows that the optimism of George Mellish, in asserting that canals could continue to compete with railways in the long-distance fly-trade, was not justified, for by 1855 the Grand Junction Company was thinking of relinquishing the carrying trade because of its unprofitable nature.[38] By 1883 the fly-boat was becoming a rather obsolete and unwanted object, although much depended on how prosperous times were. Fellows Morton and Clayton & Co. were then running such boats purely as a service to their customers, at a loss of £100 to £150 per year.[39] None the less, fly-boats continued in operation until after the First World War.

These changes had resulted in boatmen becoming, on average, rather older as an occupational group—in 1851, 44·8 per cent had been over 35; in 1861, 47·6 per cent fell into that category—but little further change seems to have occurred before the 1890s. As a rough indication of the rate at which an industry is decaying, we can perhaps confirm, by this evidence, that the decline was not quite so rapid as has sometimes been supposed.

Further evidence of falling earnings might be thought to be provided by the increase in the number of females sleeping on board in the 1850s, as indicated by the statistics given in Appendix IV*d*. These figures would certainly seem, at first glance, to confirm the view, now widely held, that railway competition 'drastically forced down freight rates and with them boatmen's wages', hence forcing the boatmen to take their wives and children on board with them.[40] Moreover, one gets the impression, from reading the most recent canal studies, that this movement of women and children on to canal boats was a continuous and increasing process down to 1914. The census material does not confirm this impression, since, in fact, it shows a decline in the number of females on board, from 1861, except for a slight increase (2·9 per cent) during a decade (the 1880s) which included several economically very depressed years.

Of course, it is dangerous to draw firm conclusions based on statistics representing only one day in isolated years, especially as we shall see later that the number of women and children on board could fluctuate markedly in the space of a few months. There were also to be influences at work other than economic ones, in persuading women to leave the boats. None the less, even if we cannot insist that the trend was firmly for families to leave the boats as the nineteenth century wore on, grave doubts must be thrown upon the accepted view that poverty compelled them to take to the boats more and more. We have already seen how men continued to leave the canals in the 1860s, inferring reduced incomes, but women did not increase in number then. In 1875 Pamphilon[41] had made the statement that

> during the last few years owing to the severe competition between railway and water, the rates have gone down and the canal carriers have a difficulty in competing with the railways, and they cut down the bargemen's wages, who as a necessary consequence are not able to support a man, and they bring in their wives and children.[42]

Yet the end of the decade revealed a substantial decline in the number of females, not all of it due to the rather ineffective Canal Boats Act of 1877.

Family boats were extremely numerous long before 1841 even, and although there was a very definite increase in their numbers in the 1850s, at least a part of the explanation for this could be that many fly-boat captains must need now have become slow-boat captains, if they were to stay as boatmen. It is true that by so doing they probably took a drop in income, but it is unlikely that they were thrust into such financial straits that they had to take their family to save on labour. They took their family with them because it had long been the tradition for slow-boat men to have their wives and children with them, although some slow-boats were worked by all-male crews.

Hence, it was railway competition which had reduced the income of some boatmen, and it was railway competition which had been instrumental in increasing the number of family boats in the 1850s (and possibly in the 1840s as well), but the idea that railway competition produced such drastic and continuing cuts in the boatmen's earnings that poverty forced them to take their dependants with them to save on labour, rent, etc., is not proved. Indeed, the view that the standard of living of the boating class was savagely reduced must also be open to criticism.

THE IMPACT OF RAILWAY COMPETITION UPON THE EARNINGS OF CANAL BOATMEN BY
THE 1870S AND 1880S

In fact, it may well have been that by the 1870s and 1880s there was a shortage of

TABLE 5 *Some weekly earnings on narrow boats[a] in the 1870s and 1880s*

| Year | Master (after paying for horse, etc., but before paying for hired labour) | Hand | Derivation | Source |
|---|---|---|---|---|
| 1875 | £1 9s 6d [£1·47½p] £2 2s 6d [£2·12½p] £1 12s 6d [£1·62½p] £1 13s 6d [£1·67½p] £1 7s 6d [£1·37½p] | Mostly family boats | Actual net weekly earnings seen by Commander May, a north-west midland factory inspector. | *Factory and Workshops Commission, 1876,* vol. II, qq. 11274–82. |
| 1875 | approx. £2 3s od [£2·15p] | £1 1s 6d [£1·7½p] if an all-male boat. | Actual average weekly earnings paid by the Bridgewater Co. in May. Evidence of Saunders, the company's agent. 'They resemble those of other canals,' he added. | *Ibid.,* qq. 10786–93. |
| 1883 | approx. £2 8s od [£2·40p] *(my estimate)* | ? | Narrow-boat labour estimated at 8s [40p] per day[b]. Evidence of J. S. Watson. | *S. C. on Canals,* 1883, appendix 9, p. 230. |
| Early 1890s | ? | ? | Piece rate of 10d [4p] per mile per boat full, 5d [2p] empty, in common usage (before expenses). | *Royal Commission on Canals and Inland Navigation in the United Kingdom, 1906–9* (henceforward referred to as *R. C. on Canals, 1906–9),* vol. I, 1906 [Cd. 3183–4], XXXII, qq. 2458, 2517[c]. |

*Notes*

[a] Boatmen on broad boats continued to be well paid and generally better off than narrow boatmen. See *Factory and Workshops Commission,* 1876, vol. II, q. 10795 for wages paid on the Bridgewater canal, and *Royal Commission on Labour,* vol. III, group B (*Transport and Agriculture*), 1893–4 [C. 6894–VIII], XXXIII (henceforward referred to as *R. C. on Labour* (group B), 1893–4), qq. 17175–82, 17246–52, for wages paid on the Yorkshire waterways.

[b] All calculations throughout this study have been based on the six-day week. Many boatmen worked seven days a week down to 1914. Their earnings were possibly higher than we have often calculated.

[c] Phillipps, general manager of the North Staffordshire Railway Company and the Trent and Mersey Canal Company reckoned that those were the rates paid when his company were carriers; *R. C. on Canals*, vol. I, 1906 [Cd. 3183–4], XXXII, q. 2517. The North Staffordshire Company ceased to act as canal carriers on 31 December 1894; B.T.H.R., NS 1/20, North Staffordshire Railway Traffic and Finance Minute Book, 13 November 1894, minute 16632, 22 January 1895, 16705.

TABLE 6   *Average net weekly earnings per year of narrow-boat masters and hands, 1875–84*

| Year | Master's average net weekly earnings after all expenses | Slow or fly-boat | Hand |
|------|--------------------------------------------|--------------|------|
| 1875[a] | £1–£1 5s [£1·25p] | Slow | — |
| 1875[b] | £1 5s [£1·25p]–£1 10s [£1·50p] | Slow | — |
| 1875[a] | £1 17s 6d [£1·87½p] | Fly | £1 (each of three hands) |
| 1879–80[c] | – | Slow | approx. 18s [90p] |
| 1884[d] | £1–£1 10s [£1·50p] | Slow | — |
| 1884[e] | £1 12s [£1·60p] | Slow | — |

*Notes*
[a] *Factory and Workshops Commission*, 1876, vol. I, appendix C, p. 123 (Bowling, Birmingham factory inspector).
[b] George Smith, *Our Canal Population: The Sad Condition of the Women and Children – with Remedy* (1875), p. 81.
[c] Smith, *Canal Adventures by Moonlight* (1881), p. 183.
[d] *S. C. on Canal Boats*, 1884, q. 1136 (Hales, manager of Shropshire Union Company).
[e] *Ibid.*, 542 (Mr George, district agent of Worcester, Birmingham and Droitwich canals, etc.).

boatmen, which kept wage rates up, even in the period of the most severe competition. Pamphilon admitted, rather inconsistently, that there was a 'dearth of labour' in 1875,[43] and Saunders, of the Bridgewater concern, mentioned how 'we have difficulty in obtaining this class of labour'.[44] There was, of course, the long-standing tradition of waterway life among those who had lived permanently for generations upon the canals, tending to keep boaters there, even if wages sank very low. They were often reluctant to leave such a way of life, as much from a fear of the unknown world beyond the towing path as from the attractions of their known world. Hence it was that carrying companies, even though they might have the interests of their employees at heart, were always fearful that reforming legislation might result in this section of the boat population being rapidly depleted. As Mr Hales, of the Shropshire Union Company, freely admitted,

> Our fear is that if anything was done to take certain classes of boat people out of the boats, we should have a difficulty in replacing them; they are a class by themselves.[45]

None the less, even if some boatmen were reluctant to leave the waterways altogether, they had no qualms about leaving to work for another carrier. 'We should at once, if our wages were much higher than theirs, obtain their labour', Saunders explained.[46] Employers of boatmen had to keep an eye on the wage rates paid by their competitors.

For actual wage rates (see tables 5 and 6) we must rely largely upon the opinions of the men giving evidence to the various committees; men who were not always as objective as they might have been in their assessments, some being eager to prove that boatmen could afford to rent houses and hire labour other than their families, and others being anxious to show the opposite.

Estimates of average net weekly incomes over the year were variously given as in table 6.

One of the lowest earnings mentioned was that of the master boatmen engaged on the brick boats, coming into London from the brick works to the north of that city and returning with manure or breeze. Some of these master boatmen worked at a fixed rate of 18s [90p] per week. Others, paid by freight, would earn more, but their income would be more irregular. The living conditions on such boats were worse than on most.[47]

It would seem that, depending upon the region, the more prosperous slow-boat captains, working with their families, if they were hard working and efficient, might average £1 10s [£1·50p] net a week over the year in the period 1875–84, especially when they were carrying goods that paid higher rates. At the bottom of the scale those family-boat men involved in carrying very low-value cargoes like stone, manure and fluxingstone might average only 18s [90p]–£1. The majority of the family-boat men were probably earning something in between, averaging in the region of £1 5s [£1·25p] a week net through the year. In the case of the family boat, of course, where the boat was the permanent home, as observers were quick to point out, there would be no rent or rates to pay and, often, no fuel bills either. Looked at in this way the amounts earned compared very favourably with those outside the canals, even at the lowest level.[48] The wage rates confirm Commander May's opinion in 1875 that there was no 'case of poverty proved as regards the boatmen; on the contrary I think they are people who are earning very fair wages'.[49] Pamphilon, too, in the same year had made the point that boatmen's wages had been reduced, but he had also replied to the question, 'Are the wages high in this business?', 'They are very fair'.[50] And still in 1886 an independent observer could comment that boatmen's earnings '. . . generally speaking are considerably more than the ordinary wages of most labouring men . . . Boatmen are always well clothed and well shod, and they feed equally well.'[51]

Where there were two men on board with, perhaps, a family on shore, it is difficult to assess their average weekly earnings. They were perhaps paid more between them than the family-boat men, but less individually. That is, the master of an all-male boat received more, but in paying his hand his net income was lower than that of the captain of a family boat. In other words, family boatmen were undercutting the wages paid to all-male, slow-boat crews. However, this was not yet apparently a serious difficulty, for all-male crews tended to be found on boats carrying the more valuable and hence more remunerative cargoes and, as Inspector Johnson pointed out, 'Considering the large number of boats navigated at present by men only, this financial difficulty can hardly be so great as is represented'.[52]

On the whole, it seems quite clear that despite the difficulties of adapting to the new competitive form of transportation, master boatmen had remained prosperous people. Indeed, there is no real evidence to suggest that all boatmen, like the rest of the working population did not make significant *advances* in their *real* incomes in the second half of the nineteenth century. G. H. Wood calculated that

> The Standard of Comfort of the British wage-earner is now [by 1904] on the average, not less than 50 per cent and probably nearer 80 per cent higher than that of his predecessor in 1850 . . .[53]

And already by 1875 boatmen appear to have been no worse off and perhaps better off as compared with the early days of the railways. In 1841 fly-boat captains were said to earn £1 10s [£1·50p] a week on average, but by 1875 they were making £1 17s 6d [£1·87½p].[54] Both slow and fly-boat hands had advanced from around 8s [40p] with maintenance to about £1 a week.[55] According to the Rousseaux indices, prices were lower in 1875 than they had been in 1841.[56] Admittedly they were only 4 per cent lower, and the imperfections of price indices, especially in the early years, are well known. Moreover, the comparisons are between isolated examples of wages paid and doubtful estimates. However, prices were substantially lower by 1883[57] when it is again possible to compare the 8s [40p] a day said to be the standard rate for narrow-boat labour alone (i.e. employer's horse) with the 7s [35p] a day (including payment for the boatman's horse) paid by the Coventry Canal Company between 1840 and 1844.[58] The fall in prices was even more marked by the early 1890s[59] when it is again possible to compare the rate of 10d [4p] per mile per boat full, 5d [2p] empty, then in common usage, with the 6d [2½p] per mile paid to Crowley's slow-boat steerers in 1839.[60]

Of course, there are many pitfalls in making such comparisons and any conclusions must be extremely tentative. But the available evidence does tend to indicate that there had been an increase in money wages and most certainly in real incomes by the last quarter of the century as compared with the 1830s and early 1840s, and such evidence casts serious doubt upon the idea of drastic and continuing cuts in the boatmen's earnings stemming from railway competition, a doubt not denied (if not confirmed) by a comparison of the rather wide-ranging estimates of slow-boat masters' year round earnings.[61]

It appears, in fact, that boatmen's real earnings followed the general pattern in this period. Wood concluded his summary with the statement that 'of this advance more than one-half has been obtained during the past quarter of a century',[62] and it is now accepted that it was especially during the misnamed period of the 'Great Depression' (1873–96) that the working class made the greatest advance in terms of real income. For while on the whole money wages remained stable (tending to fall at the beginning, then stabilising and rising in later years), living costs (especially food prices) fell substantially.[63]

There were indeed reductions in the money incomes of the boatmen in the early years,[64] and these have often been quoted to confirm the declining fortunes of the boaters, but the later advances, especially in the years 1889–91, have attracted less attention.[65] Were these advances large enough to compensate for previous losses sufficient to maintain the boatmen's standard of living? The example of the Aire and Calder Company's fly-boat men (admittedly working on barges and not narrow boats) suggests that they were. These men had been forced to accept a 12·5 per cent cut in pay in 1878, but from October 1889 their wages rose swiftly until by the end of 1891 they stood at about 1 per cent below the 1878 level.[66] During those fourteen years prices had fallen by about 15 per cent and food prices by about 20 per cent.[67] Clearly the real income of these men had increased substantially and there is no reason to suppose that other boatmen had not made similar gains. Unemployment among boatmen may have been greater and their advances in real income may not have been as large as those of others, but the idea that railway competition brought a continuing deterioration in the boat people's standard of living in the nineteenth century (or at least before about 1896) is evidently a myth.

COMBINATION AMONG CANAL BOATMEN IN THE NINETEENTH CENTURY

It is widely believed that one reason why the working man, and in particular the skilled working man, came to make a significant advance in real income during the period 1873–96 was that, by trade union activity, he was able to resist the downward pressure on his wage. Prices fell further than wages. Broadbridge found little evidence of union activity or combination among the boatmen, and he quotes evidence from the Commission of 1876.[68] Lord Balfour had enquired if there were any trade unions on the canals. 'No,' Pamphilon replied, 'they have shown a[69] little inclination that way lately; they threatened to strike some time ago, and we thought they were so low in the scale that we would not allow them to descend to striking and we met them.'[70]

However, this is a clear indication that boatmen did sometimes combine together, and that such combinations might meet with success. On the face of it, canal boating might appear to be too dispersed an occupation to lend itself to such activity, and formal organisation did remain weak,[71] but the evidence of one company shows that boatmen did unite to resist wage cuts or to make demands.

On 7 December 1860 the Shropshire Union Company received 'A memorial from the Canal Boatmen as to their wages'.[72] In 1864 steerers refused to go up light from Ellesmere Port to Wolverhampton, and the company forced Bishton, the haulage contractor, to pay the boatmen revised rates.[73] A strike of the Staffordshire boatmen in 1871 led to a rearrangement of the rates of haulage.[74] In 1872 they again appeared to win some concessions, or to resist (partially) attempts to push down the rates of pay, after a nine-day strike.[75] In 1873 some slow-boat steerers had threatened to strike, and others actually did so in 1876.[76] Who won in this instance, when the company dug in its heels, is not clear. Nor was it known whether the steerers in the fluxingstone trade submitted quietly to the reductions of 1882 and 1885, but their application for an advance, in May 1890, met with success.[77] The years around 1890 were, in some respects, especially favourable to boatmen, when their services were much in demand. In 1889, the Shropshire Union Company was having considerable difficulty in finding steerers for the fluxingstone trade,[78] and in 1891 competition for steerers between companies was strong. Hales reported that the steerers employed by the North Staffordshire and Anderton companies had been awarded an increase in the rates of pay, and he was ordered to negotiate terms with his own steerers lest they defected.[79] It is clear, from the experience of the Shropshire Union Company, that boatmen were neither docile nor powerless when it came to combining to resist pay cuts and demanding pay rises. Such action was not restricted to the employees of this company, nor to the later nineteenth century.[80]

### DECLINE

From the mid-1890s on, however, the standard of living of boatmen probably began to deteriorate. Although the evidence of actual incomes remains extremely sparse the undeniable fact of a significant exodus from the waterways seems to support such a suggestion. It was perhaps not so much that piece-rates were reduced—such evidence as exists suggests that they remained much the same down to 1906 at least[81]—but there were significantly fewer tons to be carried, as shown by the following figures.

*Tonnage carried over canals in England and Wales*[82]

| | |
|---|---|
| 1888 | 33,123,666 |
| 1898 | 34,022,493 |
| 1905 | 32,340,264 |

This could have reduced incomes and almost certainly inhibited increases. On balance actual weekly money incomes probably changed little in the years before the First World War—narrow boatmen's earnings were estimated at £1 10s [£1·50p], including lodgings, in 1906[83]—but of course prices and the money wages of others were rising.[84] At a time when most of the working classes were finding difficulty in maintaining their standard of living,[85] boatmen appear to have fared comparatively badly.

It was the masters who insisted on leaving their wives at home who suffered the most serious decline. It became increasingly difficult for them to get the labour to crew their boats at the wages that they could offer and yet still compete for work with the family-boat men, who could afford to accept less.[86] Bitterness that the men of all-male boats felt for the family-boat men became increasingly acidic, as the latter were accused of keeping wage rates down.[87] Such men did not generally respond by taking their own families on board, as perhaps some had done temporarily during the bad times of the 1880s, but rather they abandoned the waterways. One boatman, for example, John Dallow, had finally wearied of working for very long hours, to earn no more than £1 4s [£1·20p] a week, and in 1913 he emigrated.[88] Both groups of census figures show that, from 1891, more and more people were leaving the canals, but men without their dependants were leaving more rapidly; for in spite of other pressures on them to leave, the family-boat men were still generally prosperous individuals, as later evidence will show, whereas the men without their wives (except where they were carrying higher-value goods), were slipping into the earnings group of the labouring class. The percentage of men over 35 years of age rose from 47·7 per cent in 1891 to 55·7 per cent in 1911.[89] The number of new boats registered each year was generally declining, and particularly from 1900 (see figure 2). By 1914 canal boating as an industry had

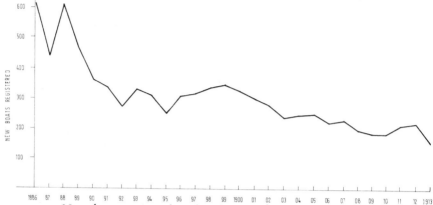

FIGURE 2 New boats registered under the Canal Boat Acts, 1877 and 1884 (1886–1913). Compiled from statistics in the annual reports of the Local Government Board, 1887–1914

begun the real slide into decline, soon to be perceptibly quickened by the First World War, the motor lorry, and the inter-war slump in the industries which were its biggest users. Only the introduction of motor boats, probably, enabled it to survive until recent times.

### SOME COMPENSATIONS

We should, none the less, draw attention to the fact that company boatmen were being compensated in other directions. They had obtained greater assistance in finding horses. Over the question of stoppages through frost, etc., there was probably a change to benefit the boatmen. Although it is not clear what had happened in the days before canal companies became much more directly concerned, it seems unlikely that boatmen were paid during such stoppages. An 1838 resolution that 'the charge incurred for soup to the boatmen during the frost be allowed', perhaps indicates that their means of subsistence were extremely limited.[90] Similarly, in 1861, the Grand Junction Canal Company, which had never received charitable requests with much sympathy, had decided that

> the Bill amounting to £6 8s 0d [£6·40p] paid by Mr Norman for Bread and Soup distributed to Boatmen and their families by order of the Committee during the late severe Frost be allowed.[91]

In the last quarter of the nineteenth century it became increasingly the practice to make advances, which had to be repaid, to the boatmen during times of stoppage.[92] In January 1879 £444 had been advanced in frost money to Shropshire Union steerers, rising to £785 by 26 February.[93] During the prolonged frost of 1895 Leeds and Liverpool Canal Company boatmen were put on half pay,[94] and by 1904 the Shropshire Union Company seems to have adopted the same practice.[95]

On 25 February 1891 it was agreed to allow the steerers of this company's boats to join the Provident and Pension Fund of the London & North Western Railway Company, and retired steerers began to enjoy the advantage of a 5s [25p] pension, although some pensions had been allowed before this time.[96]

Boatmen also began to be helped more through times of sickness and injury, though whether this was due to the benefits of the Provident Society, the Employers' Liability Act of 1880, or the greater humanity of the company, is not clear, for there were cases before the 1891 decision which allowed steerers to join the Provident Society, although such outright payments became more numerous from that year. No doubt the Workmen's Compensation Act of 1897 accounted for a further increase in such cases of compensation.[97]

## CONCLUSION

By way of forming a tentative conclusion we can perhaps assert, with some confidence, that, in the 1840s, 1850s and 1860s, employment opportunities were reduced. There was a reduction in the number of fly-boat men as carriers left the waterways. Where fly-boat captains became masters of the increasing number of slow-boats, their earnings must have fallen. On the other hand, unemployment and reductions in earnings were perhaps offset by the new jobs created by canal companies; by the increasing number of slow and local boats; by a voluntary exodus of boatmen in the wake of their employers on to the railways; by the increasing attractiveness of other jobs in a booming economy (in other words there was probably as much pull as push in the waterway exodus); and, partly for the same reason, the falling off in recruitment from outside the canal labour force. Hence, although there were times and places where boatmen experienced dislocation, unemployment and hardship, it was usually only of a temporary nature. There is no evidence of widespread or continuing unemployment, or of swingeing reductions in earnings among them. The steam locomotive did not do to the canal boatmen what the power loom had done to the hand-loom weavers.

The evidence thrown up by the rather questionable wage statistics, fortunately backed up by other material, does, perhaps, indicate that by the 1870s and early 1880s matters had improved somewhat. Paradoxically, at a time when railway competition was increasing in severity, real incomes seem to have advanced as prices fell. Earnings still compared favourably with those of the labouring classes generally, and the family-boat man's particularly so. The master of an all-male slow-boat continued to be well remunerated, because such boats usually carried higher-value goods. Boat people probably fell into the income range of the lower skilled workers, although there were, of course, degrees of prosperity on the canals. Boatmen as a class were not slow to combine together to maintain, or even increase, their standard of living.

Our conclusion of the continued prosperity of canal boatmen generally, in conjunction with other evidence spotlighted in this and a previous chapter, throws grave doubts on the accepted assumption that poverty, induced by railway competition, forced more and more families on board boats in the second half of the nineteenth century.

The recovery from the severe slump of the mid-1880s was not as sustained as it had been from previous depressions. The decline in the industry became more marked in the twenty years or so before the First World War. The all-male boat master found times increasingly hard, as the carriage of the more remunerative goods diminished, and as he found himself increasingly competing for work with the family-boat man. Higher wages on land attracted both him and his hands. Family boaters were declining in number as well, but much more slowly, since they, as yet, were still relatively prosperous people.

### NOTES TO CHAPTER SEVEN

[1] Hadfield, *The Canal Age*, p. 161; Vine, *London's Lost Route to Basingstoke; London's Lost Route to the Sea*; Kenneth R. Clew, *The Kennet and Avon Canal* (1968), pp. 94 and 118 in particular; *The Somersetshire Coal Canal* (1970); Household, *Thames and Severn Canal*; Peter Stevenson, *The Nutbrook Canal: Derbyshire* (1970).

[2] Hadfield, *British Canals* (1966), p. 212.

[3] Mather, *After the Canal Duke* (1970), p. 141.

[4] *Ibid.*, p. 351.

[5] OXC 4/53, Durrell to G. C. Glynn, 19 June 1845.

[6] Mather, *op. cit.*, pp. 120–33.

[7] OXC 4/110, 'Memorial from coal traders of Banbury to Oxford Canal Company', in Oxford Canal Guard Book, 1 July 1850, p. 57.

[8] Clew, *Kennet and Avon Canal* (1968), p. 94.

[9] Hadfield, *British Canals* (1966), pp. 215, 208–10.

[10] Mather, *op. cit.*, p. 136.

[11] *S. C. on Sunday Trading*, 1841, q. 1256.

[12] Mather, *op. cit.*, p. 217; Hadfield and Biddle, *The Canals of North West England*, vol. II, pp. 287–9. Both give examples of some carriers involved.

[13] *S. C. on Railway and Canal Bills*, 1852–3, q. 1688.

[14] WOBC 1/2, 4 January 1848.

[15] *S. C. on Sunday Trading*, 1841, q. 1226.

[16] Turnbull, 'Pickfords and the canal carrying trade, 1780–1850', pp. 24–5.

[17] See *ibid.*, quoting from PFC 1/4, 30 January 1839 (Bache & Co. and others); Mather, *op. cit.*, pp. 136, 146 (Worthington), pp. 137, 141 (Hargreaves); *S. C. on Railway and Canal Bills*, 1852–3, qq. 295, 315 (Kenworthy).

[18] *S. C. on Sunday Trading*, 1841, q. 1249.

[19] Turnbull, *op. cit.*, p. 20.

[20] BLC 1/2, Birmingham and Liverpool Junction Canal Committee Minute Book, 1840–4, 21 December 1843, pp. 25–7.

21  *Ibid.*, minutes of the Select Committee, letter: Joseph Cubitt to Earl of Powis, 11 May 1843.

22  *Ibid.*, 25 April 1844, p. 29.

23  *S. C. on Sunday Trading*, 1841, q. 543.

24  *S. C. on Canals*, 1883, appendix 22, p. 293.

25  OXC 4/110, 'Memorial from coal traders of Banbury to Oxford Canal Co.', in Oxford Canal Guard Book, 1 July 1850, p. 57.

26  BLC 1/2, 25 April 1844, p. 29.

27  Hadfield, *Canals of the West Midlands* (1966).

28  Hadfield and Biddle, *op. cit.*, vol. II, p. 399.

29  The actual decision to start carrying was taken on 16 August 1847; GJC 1/10, pp. 167–9.

30  *S. C. on Railway and Canal Bills*, 1852–3, qq. 1540, 1621.

31  The names and details of the carrying firms approached, and taken over (the second did not always follow from the first), are to be found in GJC 1/10, 11 to 18 July 1848, pp. 378–84; GJC 1/11, 8 August 1848, pp. 3, 6–7; 29 September 1848, p. 31, 34–5, 37; 4 October 1848, 27 November 1848, p. 59; 9 January 1849, p. 77; 2 May 1849, p. 119; 19 July 1849, p. 140.

32  *Household Words*, 18 September 1858, p. 321.

33  *S. C. on Railway and Canal Bills*, 1852–3, q. 1540.

34  Mather, *op. cit.*, p. 217.

35  *Household Words*, 18 September 1858, p. 321.

36  See Appendix IVa for a discussion of the accuracy of the 1841 Census, and Appendix IVc for the numbers, ages, etc. of boatmen, 1851–1911.

37  Of course, if there were a large increase in the number of watermen and lightermen over these years, this could distort the decline in the numbers of canal boatmen, but this is unlikely. See Appendix IVa.

38  GJC 1/14, 5 October 1855, p. 41.

39  *S. C. on Canals*, 1883, qq. 2666–7.

40  See above, p. 54 (Hadfield).

41  Goods and canal manager of the North Staffordshire railway, owners of the Trent and Mersey canal.

42  *Factory and Workshop Commission*, 1876, vol. II, qq. 10522–3.

43  *Ibid.*, 10513; see above p. 91.

44  *Ibid.*, 10794.

45  *S. C. on the Canal Boats Act, 1877 (Amendment Bill)*, 1884 (263), VIII (henceforward *S. C. on Canal Boats*, 1884), q. 1213.

46  *Factory and Workshops Commission*, 1876, vol. II, q. 10794.

47  *Ibid.*, vol. I, p. 129.

48  Some wage rates for comparison are given in *Returns of Wages published between 1830 and 1886*, 1887 [C. 5172], *Manchester District*: labourers (1877): 18s [90p]; carters (1880): 19s [95p]; joiners (1880): £1 5s 9d [£1·29p] (p. 182); colliers (1883): £1 7s 5d [£1·37p] (p. 134). *Birmingham District*: labourers (1883): 17s 6d [87½p]–19s 6d [97½p]; carters (1883): 18s [90p]–£1; smiths (1883): £1 14s [£1·70p]–£1 16s [£1·80p] (p. 185).
Bowley's *Estimated Adult Men's Wages for a Full Normal Week, United Kingdom* for 1880 show roughly how boatmen, and especially many family-boat men and fly-boat captains (even after possible substantial cuts in their 1875 pay), were well placed in comparison with their fellows:

|                | s  | d | [£ p]    |
|----------------|----|---|----------|
| Lowest decile  | 16 | 0 | [80]     |
| Lower quartile | 20 | 0 | [1·00]   |
| Median         | 24 | 3 | [1·21]   |
| Upper quartile | 28 | 0 | [1·40]   |
| Highest decile | 36 | 6 | [1·82½]  |

(A. L. Bowley, *Wages and Income in the United Kingdom since 1860* (1937), p. 46.)

49  *Factory and Workshops Commission*, 1876, vol. II, q. 11274.

[50] *Ibid.*, 10498.

[51] Extract from *The Mail* (probably the *Birmingham Daily Mail*), 8 February 1886, 'Maritime Birmingham', in Newspaper Cuttings Relating to Canals, collected by G. H. Osborne, Birm. R.L. 243972.

[52] *Factory and Workshops Commission*, 1876, vol. I, appendix C, p. 119.

[53] G. H. Wood, 'Real wages and the standard of comfort since 1850', *Journal of the Royal Statistical Society*, vol. LXXII, 1909, p. 101.

[54] Compare above, p. 59 and table 6.

[55] Cf. p. 60 and tables 5 and 6.

[56] B. R. Mitchell and P. Deane, *Abstract of British Historical Statistics* (1962; 1971 ed.), pp. 471–2.

[57] By 20 per cent 1841–75 according to the Rousseaux indices, *ibid.*

[58] Cf. p. 59 and table 5.

[59] The Rousseaux indices show a fall of 44 per cent from 1839 to 1891, and 57 per cent by 1895; Mitchell and Deane, *op. cit.*, pp. 471–2.

[60] Cf. p. 59 and table 5.

[61] Cf. p. 59 and table 6.

[62] G. H. Wood, *op. cit.*, p. 101.

[63] Evidence of falling prices, wage movements and consequent increases in the standard of living are to be found in the various indices listed in Mitchell and Deane, *op. cit.*, pp. 343–58, 471–6, 488–9, 498.

[64] See above, p. 91 (Pamphilon) and below, p. 96, and see also *S. C. on Canal Boats*, 1884, q. 277 (John Corbett, M.P.).

[65] See below.

[66] *R. C. on Labour (group B)*, 1893–4, qq. 17233, 17259.

[67] In Mitchell and Deane, *op. cit.*, the Rousseaux indices show a fall in the overall price index of 15 per cent between 1878 and 1891 and a fall of 18 per cent in the total agricultural products index; p. 472; the Sauerbeck–*Statist* indices show a fall of 15 per cent (overall index) and 19 per cent (food index); p. 474. The Board of Trade Wholesale Price indices show a fall of 24 per cent (overall index) and 28 per cent (food and drink index); p. 476.

[68] S. R. Broadbridge, 'Living conditions on midland canal boats', *Transport History*, vol. III, 1970, p. 41.

[69] Mr Broadbridge appears to have omitted this *a*.

[70] *Factory and Workshops Commission*, 1876, q. 10527.

[71] John Noble, the boatman president of the Leeds-based Watermen and Riverside Labourers Union, complained that the boatmen of the Aire and Calder Navigation and Leeds and Liverpool canal were difficult to organise; *R. C. on Labour (group B)*, q. 17104.

[72] SURC 1/12, 7 December 1860, minute 3279.

[73] SURC 1/13, 25 May and 29 June 1864, 4718, 4764.

[74] SURC 1/16, 27 December 1871, 8412.

[75] *Ibid.*, 27 October 1872, 9175.

[76] SURC 1/17, 28 May 1873, 9553; SURC 1/18, 29 March 1876, 11201.

[77] SURC 1/23, 28 May 1890, 18187.

[78] SURC 1/22, 23 January 1889, 17675.

[79] SURC 1/23, 25 February 1891, 18482.

[80] See for example GJC 1/1, 22–23 October 1818, pp. 264, 266; see above, p. 69 (strike of Pickfords' men at Paddington in 1822); GJC 1/13, 5–9 August 1853, pp. 41, 43; 26 May 1854, p. 200; 2 June 1854, p. 204; 16 June and 14 July 1854, p. 229 (strikes and threats of strikes by Grand Junction Company's boatmen); *R. C. on Labour (group B)*, 1893–4, qq. 17211–5, 17266 (successful four-week strike of Aire and Calder fly-boat men, in 1891).

[81] The rate of 10*d* [4p] per mile full, 5*d* [2p] empty quoted above in table 5 seems to have continued to be in operation in 1906; *R. C. on Canals*, vol. I, 1906 [Cd. 3183–4], XXXII, qq. 2458, 4404.

[82] *Ibid.*, vol. VIII, 1910 [Cd. 5204], XII, appendix 4, table 11, p. 23.

[83] *Ibid.*, vol. I, 1906 [Cd. 3183–4], XXXII, appendix 10, statement 3, p. 31.

[84] In Mitchell and Deane, *op. cit.*, the Rousseaux indices show a rise in the overall price index of 21 per cent from 1895 to 1906 and 34 per cent from 1895 to 1913; the Sauerbeck–*Statist* indices show a rise of 15 per cent and 23 per cent; the Board of Trade Wholesale Price indices rose by 10 per cent and 16 per cent; pp. 472–6.

[85] In Mitchell and Deane an adaptation of Wood's index shows a rise in money wages (not allowing for unemployment) from 1895 to 1906 of 19 per cent and from 1895 to 1910 of 25 per cent; Bowley's index showed a rise of 18 per cent in money wages from 1895 to 1906 and 16 per cent from 1895 to 1913, but real wages fell by 2 per cent (1895–1906) and by 3 per cent (1895–1913); pp. 343–4.

[86] *30th Annual Report of the Local Government Board* (henceforward L.G.B.) *for 1900* (1901), p. 217.

[87] *32nd Annual Report of the L. G. B. for 1902* (1903), p. 211. It was apparently trade union pressure, emanating from the crews of all-male boats, which was instrumental in getting a committee set up to look into the question of living in on canal boats, for this reason, in 1920. See Ministry of Health, *Report of the Departmental Committee Appointed to Inquire into the Practice of Living-in on Canal Boats in England and Wales . . .* (1921), p. 3 (henceforward *Committee on Living-in* (Report), 1921).

[88] Extract from *Birmingham Post*, 31 May 1968, in Birmingham Newspaper Cuttings: Canals and Waterways (1946), p. 85. Birm. R. L., 662820.

[89] See Appendix IVc and IVd.

[90] BLC 1/3, 18 July 1838, p. 35.

[91] GJC 1/16, 15 February 1861, p. 70.

[92] *Factory and Workshops Commission*, 1876, vol. II, qq. 10864–5 for evidence that the Bridgewater Navigation Company paid frost money.

[93] SURC 1/19, 29 January and 26 February 1879, 12669, 12731.

[94] Hadfield and Biddle, *op. cit.*, vol. II, p. 407.

[95] SURC 1/25, 17 January 1900–18 October 1905. Note the lower amount of steerers' debts outstanding from 16 December 1903; minute 22122.

[96] SURC 1/23, 14 January 1891, minute 18445, Minutes of Officers' Conference (16922); SURC 1/20, 27 July 1882, 14639.

[97] For some examples see SURC 1/22, 14 November 1888, 17606 (15812); *ibid.*, 26 March 1890, 18140 (16429); SURC 1/23, 28 July 1891, 18717 (17160); *ibid.*, 16 November 1892, 19190 (17687, 17690, 17693); SURC 1/24, 13 May 1896, 20130, (18429); *ibid.*, 19 October 1898, 20788. See SURC 1/25–1/27 for further numerous examples.

# VIII

# The 'Number One'
## Canal-boat
## ownership
## 1800–1914

IN THE FIRST FORTY YEARS or so of canal development we saw how small men, in the financial sense, had had a relatively insignificant role to play in the ownership of boats and the transportation of England's goods.[1] It is true that in 1795 as many as 40 per cent of the boats registered, in the counties studied, were owned by men who had fewer than six boats, but many of these were shown to have been substantial mill-owners and manufacturers, landowners, merchants of salt and other goods, coal-mine owners, ironfounders and canal officials, most of them using boats in connection with their business. There seem to have been relatively few small professional carriers, even fewer who had risen from humble beginnings, and fewer still who had emerged from the boating class. Although we found specific examples of boatmen who had come to acquire their own boat, through a partnership or by dint of hard work and hard saving, the most convincing statistic of all to emerge from the registers of 1795 was that fewer than 4 per cent of the boats were owned by their steerers, accounting for a mere 6 per cent of the masters.

### OWNER-BOATMEN IN THE CANAL AGE

However, it may well have been that the owner-boatman and the financially small operator came to carve out a greater slice of canal trade for themselves in the generally prosperous years after 1795 (acknowledging of course that there were some years of bad trade). Joseph Baxendale, in 1841, did mention that 'Some of the Slow Boats are navigated by the Men who own them'. It would seem that it was the dream of every boatman, and particularly of the fly-boat captain, to own his own boat, and some of them did achieve their ambition. Baxendale explained that, on leaving Pickfords' fly service, 'Many of them bought a Boat for themselves'.[2]

Slow-boat men, too, continued to be able to acquire ownership of their own boat. Richard Widdowson had been a mere farm labourer in his youth, and a rather itinerant one at that, but from taking up boating as a hand, in 1796, he had by 1823 come to own his own boat taking coal from the Birchwood pits (five miles up the Cromford canal) to Newark, where he lived with his wife and children. In that year he was 45 years old and he had acquired the boat at some time in the years after 1810.[3] Samuel Parkes had worked as a boatman for others for ten years before he set up as a coal dealer in about 1818, presumably with his own boat. By 1839 he owned nine boats, bringing coal to his wharf at Bordesley Street, Birmingham. He had been one of the first to move there, in 1819, but by 1839 forty or more coal traders had become installed. He revealed that the price paid to a steerer for a voyage from the colliery to the wharf had fallen from £1 4s [£1·20p] gross through £1 to 15s [75p] as improvements to the canal had been made, thereby speeding up voyage times. As a round trip to the Wednesbury, Oldbury, West Bromwich and Bilston Collieries took no more than two days, and could often be done in one long day, it is more than possible that others among these forty dealers had emerged from being hard-working men in the boating class.[4]

Other factors were favouring the small man. The boatman's biggest problem, that of raising the necessary capital to acquire a boat, was solved by the appearance of building clubs. Just as primitive house-building societies were beginning to feature in working-class life by the end of the eighteenth century, so *boat* building societies were being formed, by the more dynamic and prosperous of the boating class.

Hence, in February 1808, the Jones Birmingham Boat Society was formed, 'for the purpose of raising a fund for building as many new Boats as this Society shall consist of members'. For every share (i.e. prospective boat) that a member possessed, he had to pay 6s [30p], at each fortnightly meeting, held at the Waggon and Horses, Summer Row, Birmingham. An additional 3d [1p] was collected to provide alcoholic refreshment. A further guinea [£1·5p] was demanded at every quarterly meeting. When £40 had been paid to the Treasurer (John Jones, the publican), a draw was made for the first boat, and the lucky winner was then expected to arrange for the building of his boat with James Taylor of Birmingham Heath, who was to build all the boats for £86 each. Until all the boats were completed they remained the property of the society and bore the initials J.B.B.S.[5]

Hence it is possible that small and humble men were increasing in importance, both numerically and proportionally, but it is difficult to assess the relative part played by such men as compared with an earlier period, and as compared with other types of carriers.

The Cromford canal permit books throw a glimmer of light on to this problem (see table 7).

Of course, the inadequacy of such small numbers, over such short periods of time, and in such a limited area, must make any conclusions extremely hazardous ones, but it does seem that, in this area at least, the 'number one' played a not insignificant role.[6]

Alexander Hordern supported such a suggestion, when he explained that 'Most

TABLE 7   *Boats passing on to or off the Cromford canal, Derbyshire, 1817–41*

| Dates | Total number of boats | Owner-steered boats | |
| --- | --- | --- | --- |
| | | Number | % |
| 12 June 1817 | 19 | 1 | 5 |
| 3 July 1817[a] | 18 | 7 | 39 |
| 25 April to 2 May 1820[b] | 154[c] | 51 | 33 |
| 25 March to 1 April 1823[b] | 122 | 27 | 22 |
| 18 May to 25 May 1841[b] | 128 | 29 | 23 |

*Notes*
[a]  Only two full days available in 1817.
[b]  Seven full days excluding Sunday.
[c]  There were more than 154 vessels, but throughout this table boats with the same steerer, passing more than once, have been excluded.

*Source*   Cromford Canal Permit Books at D.R.O. numbered in date order: 367–385, 691–708, in 501/B/B1 (for 1817); 1591–1746, 501 B/B2 (1820); 862–985, 501 B/B4 (1823); 2383–2501, 501 B/B45 (1841).

of these Men own the Boats, and they hire themselves out for the Voyage'.[7] He was, presumably, speaking of the boatmen on the Staffordshire and Worcestershire, and Birmingham canals with which he had connections. Unfortunately, it was in the same month that Sir George Chetwynd, one-time chairman of the Trent and Mersey canal, answered the question 'Are any of these Boatmen Owners or Part Owners of the Boats?', 'Very few I think.'[8] Hence, we have evidence to suggest that there were by 1841 large numbers of owner-boatmen and evidence to suggest that there were very few. What was the true situation?

Without comprehensive statistics it is difficult to be definite. It seems unlikely that 'number ones' were expanding into the trade of the large professional carriers, who were not only involved in the growing fly-trade, but often in the slow-boat trade as well. Such firms grew in size and number in the Canal Age, this last fact being best demonstrated by Pickfords' growth. Many others were known to have a substantial number of boats. Crowley & Co. were employing between four and five hundred boatmen by 1841.[9] As we have shown, in Chapter II, anything but the simplest of trades in terms of organisation, finance, value, and probably distance was beyond the capabilities of small operators.

It is a remarkable feature of all but one or two of the owner-operated boats seen passing on the Cromford canal in the three weeks and two days listed in table 7 that they were all carrying coal. Coal was a very suitable cargo for the 'number one' to carry, for, once a trade had become established, it was merely a question of maintaining a conveyor belt system of boats, during the season, from A to B; or several systems from the collieries around A to points B, C, D and E. The small men merely became a part of the moving belt. And for them the carriage of coal was a bread and butter business, nearly always available. There was scope for an increase in the number of small carriers and owner-boatmen here and in the transportation of other low-value goods.

However, evidence for this period of the Canal Age as regards ownership is inconclusive. It is possible, but not certain, that the 'number one' and the small operator generally increased in number, but there is no definite evidence to suggest or reason to suppose that the number of boats owned by them came to be proportionately more important over the country as a whole to any significant degree. The bulk of the trade, and the most valuable part of it, continued to be conveyed by the large carrier.

## OWNER-BOATMEN IN THE RAILWAY AGE

Evidence thrown up at a later period may help to add weight to or detract from such assumptions. As carriers left the waterways, or went bankrupt, in the 1840s and 1850s, they no doubt left a vacuum in the carriage of certain goods, over certain routes, not immediately, and never entirely, filled by the canal company taking over. This vacuum may have been filled temporarily, or permanently, by men hiring or buying, at reduced rates, the boats of their previous employers. In 1853, a Grand Junction Canal Company director said:

> The trade which . . . [is] not carried by us, is usually a heavy trade which is carried, not by general carriers, but carried by men who own a boat and horse. They come with a particular cargo, but are not general traders on a large scale. That, no doubt is a very cheap mode of carrying very heavy traffic.

Whether this was a recent development is not clear, but it is apparent that owner-boatmen were trading in significant numbers. They were, perhaps, not so important as they appear to be at first sight, for only one quarter of the traffic on that canal was carried by independent carriers as opposed to the canal company, and some of this quarter was carried by one large independent.[10]

That men continued to be anxious to own their own boat is clear, as, also, is the continuing availability of capital to procure them through building clubs. The year 1856 saw the formation of yet another of these societies, in Netherton—the Hope Iron Boat Club—which was organised on lines similar to the club of 1808, and was formed by boatmen to raise money to buy iron boats for its members in agreement with two boat builders of Dudley at a cost of £120 each.[11]

One might also have expected that the numbers of owner-operated boats would increase in the second half of the nineteenth century, to carry the growing tonnage of low-value and often local cargoes (for which they were particularly suited), as higher-value goods came to be moved increasingly by rail. Such expectations are borne out by George Smith, who in 1884 insisted that 'The men who navigate their own boats would be, I think, half or two-thirds of the whole of the men navigating boats in the country'.[12]

On the other hand there is plenty of evidence to prove Smith wrong, as usual. Thomas Hales, traffic manager of the Shropshire Union Company, was equally insistent, in 1884: 'Certainly the great bulk of the boats belong to the canal companies or their larger traders'.[13] Pamphilon, in 1875, answered, 'Yes, there is a class of men owning their own boats. They are few in number'.[14] Commander May, a factory inspector for north Staffordshire and north Cheshire, felt that 'the number of men owning their boats is comparatively small'.[15] Factory inspector Henderson noted that 'few of the barges on the Grand Junction canal are owned by the men who navigate them. They are in the hands of the canal companies, brick manufacturers or contractors'.[16]

We can go some way towards confirming some of these opinions. In the latter case, for example, of the 164 boats registered at Paddington between 1879 and 1884 (inclusive), only 9·1 per cent of the boats were steered by their owners, and subsequent registrations showed little change down to 1914.[17] Hale's evidence is born out by the fact that the registrations at Chester (1879–84) show that not one 'number one' boat was registered there out of 326 registrations, and the percentage of boats registered by the Shropshire Union Company amounted to 97 per cent, with, again, little significant change down to 1914.[18]

Similarly, on the Leeds and Liverpool canal, such evidence as has survived indicates that 'number ones' were few in number. At Burnley, not one boat of the fifty-one registered was steered by its owner, the bulk of the boats being owned by collieries, especially by the executors of John Hargreaves, of the Bank Hall Colliery, who owned twenty-nine.[19] The situation at Wigan was much the same, with only 1·8 per cent of the 167 boats registered being owner-steered, the rest being, again, principally owned by colliery owners, the largest being the Wigan Coal and Iron Co. with sixty-one boats,[20] with again, at both places, little change taking place over the years. At Nottingham 9·5 per cent of the boats registered were owner-operated.[21]

The Coventry figure of 17·7 per cent does, however, show a higher registration of owner-steerers, if hardly a dramatic one.[22] And there does seem to have been a greater number of small independents in the midland area. It is particularly unfortunate that the registration records of the most important area, Birmingham, give only the name of the owner and not the master. That there were owner-boatmen in the Birmingham area is clear. Saunders, of the Bridgewater Company, mentioned in 1875 that

> A short time ago we had some extra assistance to bring the potters' material from the port of Runcorn and I sent the agent into the Birmingham and Wolverhampton district to pick up some bye boats,

by which he clearly meant the boats of 'number ones'.[23] Also, an unusually high number of boats, 38 per cent (173 out of 449) were owned by owners of two or fewer boats in Birmingham, although of course many were not owned by their steerers;[24] 25·5 per cent of the boats (115 of 449) were owned by people who owned only one boat.[25]

It does seem that in and around the Birmingham area there were some trades particularly suited to small men, possibly because canal companies were not them-

selves carriers, or larger carrying companies did not venture there, perhaps because the toll policy of the company was discouraging, or the cargoes considered
unremunerative. Hay and straw were possibly two such cargoes, unpopular with
railway and canal-carrying companies alike. But to small men they were lucrative
cargoes.

> A great many of the men who navigate the Worcester Canal bring cargoes of hay
> and straw [in their own boats] which are entirely their own venture. They buy it
> themselves —bring it to Birmingham and sell it; and take back with them a cargo of
> coal from the Black Country in return,[26]

it was recorded in 1886. Such an account is partly substantiated by Sub-Inspector
Johnson's earlier remark that 'the boatmen of the Worcester and Warwick Canals
seem respectable people . . . . Many of them own or hire boats, and trade partly
on their own account.'[27] Mr George, the agent for the Worcester and Birmingham canal, knew of some forty or fifty men, in 1884, who owned their own boats,
some owning two.[28]

On the Oxford canal also, where again the canal company did not carry, the
percentage of 'number ones' was much higher, for 33·3 per cent of the boats registered at Oxford (1879–84) were owned by owner-boatmen bringing coal from
the collieries on the Ashby de la Zouch canal and from around Coventry.[29] At
Hinckley, actually on the Ashby canal, 25 per cent of the boats registered were
steered by this class, carrying coal from the Moira collieries.[30] In another coal-
mining area, at Ilkeston, 25 per cent of the boats were owner-steered.[31] Tring and
Daventry on the Grand Junction Canal, with 39·5 per cent and 31·8 per cent,
were also high.[32]

However, if, on some canals, the percentages of owner-boatmen were high,
and remained largely so down to 1914, they never rose to the proportions claimed
by George Smith, even in those areas mentioned above. And, of course, local percentages give a completely distorted picture to the national scene. It may have
been that George Smith was more conversant with the areas where owner-
boatmen were more numerous, which might explain his exaggeration in part, but
a glance at the numerical importance of the registration districts shows how
unfounded his claims were (see table 8).

What the figures do perhaps demonstrate is that 'number ones' could only survive in certain areas, where there were profitable trades which they could carry
on with little interference, for one reason or another, from the large carrying
companies. It may well have been that these regional patterns of ownership had
been established long before. For example, it is quite possible that the Trent and
Mersey Canal Company, involved as it was with carrying in its own boats, had
from the earliest days resisted any incursions into its territory by bye-traders. The
company was said by some in 1795, to have as

> its object the establishment of a monopoly by enabling the Company so to molest and
> harrass all their competitors as to secure to themselves all the profit of the Carrying
> trade and its attendant advantages.[33]

TABLE 8  *Incidence of owner-steered boats in areas where registers of canal boats survive,*
*1879–1884*

| | Total number of boats registered, 1879–84 | Owner-steered boats | |
|---|---|---|---|
| | | Number | % |
| Chester | 326 | 0 | 0·0 |
| Wigan | 167 | 3 | 1·8 |
| Paddington | 164 | 15 | 9·1 |
| Coventry | 163 | 29 | 17·7 |
| Hinckley | 52 | 13 | 25·0 |
| Burnley | 51 | 0 | 0·0 |
| Oxford | 51 | 17 | 33·3 |
| Daventry | 44 | 14 | 31·8 |
| Nottingham | 42 | 4 | 9·5 |
| Tring | 33 | 13 | 39·5 |
| Ilkeston | 32 | 8 | 25·0 |
| Total | 1125 | 116 | 10 |

Similarly, on the Bridgewater canal, those involved in carrying over it had been, from the first, substantial businesses; and where small men might have infiltrated into the local short-distance trade the duke's policy of demanding a toll of 2s 6d [12½p] for any distance travelled on the canal discouraged their participation and kept such trade for his own boats.[34]

It was probably for such reasons as these that owner-boatmen seemed to have little place in the mainstream of canal activity. Taking the country as a whole, it seems clear that most of the canal transportation in the second half of the nineteenth century was carried on by boatmen who worked for large carrying companies, such as the Grand Junction, the Shropshire Union, the Leeds and Liverpool canal companies; the Trent Navigation Company; the Bridgewater Trustees (later the Bridgewater Navigation Company); the North Staffordshire Railway and Canal Company, the carrying businesses of these last two being absorbed later by the Anderton Company.[35] The Kennet and Avon was another canal company involved for some time in carrying.[36] In addition, and more important, there were the carrying businesses of the Aire and Calder Navigation Company and the Rochdale Canal Company, this last being set up in 1888 when the company was again free of the railways.[37]

Of the independent carrying companies, Fellows Morton and Clayton became the largest in the last quarter of the nineteenth century. Industrialists continued to own large numbers of boats. There was John Corbett, M.P., the salt manufacturer of Stoke Prior, and Chance Brothers of Oldbury, the glass firm. One witness before the 1876 Commission agreed that there was 'a very large number' of boats belonging to large iron companies plying on the canals.[38] Many of the boats going up the Trent and Mersey canal were said to have the names of Messrs. Foster, 'the great ironmasters on them'.[39] By the beginning of the new century two firms among many were singled out for illustration. It was said that,

Brunner Mond and Co. [later to become I.C.I.] have a very large fleet of boats, which ply regularly between our quarries at Froghall and their works at Sandbach; and the Salt Union also have a very large fleet of boats.[40]

There remained also the small industrial firm which owned a few boats to carry its raw materials and finished products, of which there were several examples.[41]

In fact the pattern of ownership was probably much as it had always been, except that the larger carrying companies generally became bigger in the second half of the nineteenth century, absorbing as they did many of the smaller companies of pre-railway days. Hales remarked in 1884 that

> The small bye traders on the canal are less in number than they were years ago. The bulk of the trade now passing over the different canal systems, belongs to the canal owners who are carriers, and also to the large traders; and the difficulties that arise in competing with the railways are such that the small people are not able now to continue working on the canal to a very large extent.[42]

'Number ones' were probably included in this decline. Fred Morton, in the year before, had made his observation that

> a large number of what are technically known as owners or bye-boats, have ceased to exist. These are boats either owned by or hired by the steerers themselves, who work them for their own profit by means of their families. A few years ago these were very numerous on the canals.[43]

The figures of boatmen described as 'working on their own account' in the Census for 1891, 1901 and 1911, standing at 5·9 per cent, 6·1 per cent and 4·7 per cent respectively, show clearly that owner-boatmen remained very few at the end of the century.[44] And although such men had declined in number, these statistics are also probably an indication of how limited a part they had always played in canal transport. Since the total number of boatmen had fallen too, it would appear that over the nineteenth century as a whole the proportion of such men had changed very little.

### SPHERES OF INFLUENCE

From the 1840s the canal scene resolved itself more and more into 'spheres of influence', where, in general, the small independent trader, including the 'number one', had increasingly little place in the scheme of things. Such seemingly independent carriers as remained were often, in fact, very much under the thumb of the canal companies which carried. The Bridgewater Trustees, for example, in order to protect the tolls on their canals, were reluctantly compelled to extend operations in their own boats; to take over competitors who took trade away from their line of canal; and also to take independent carriers under their wing, lest they went bankrupt, or deserted to the railways.[45] By this last arrangement, in 1849, nine of these firms were to become commission agents for the Trustees, theoretically hiring out their boats and plant to them for a commission. This arrangement was to last for six years initially.[46] It is not always clear how long these various arrangements lasted, but the Bridgewater organisation, in the early 1870s, was still carrying under several names.[47]

The Shropshire Union Company, like the Bridgewater Trustees, seems at first to have engaged in the carrying business with reluctance. Soon after the company's formation the carrying trade on the northern and western portions of the canal had been leased to Messrs. Tilston, Smith & Co.,[48] and when this arrangement ended an agreement was entered into with a Mr Bishton whereby the haulage of many of the Company's boats (i.e. the provision of men and horses) was put in to his hands, an arrangement which lasted until March 1866.[49] Circumstances forced the company to control its carrying trade more and more, and to develop its 'sphere of influence', by taking over and discriminating against independent traders, to an even greater and lasting degree than the Trustees had done. In 1849 the company bought the establishment and carrying stock of Messrs Tilston Smith & Co., the boats being valued at £3,111.[50] Other independents followed, including on 1 September 1873, the once proud firm of Crowley & Co., which seems to have been reduced to providing boatage facilities for the London and North Western Railway Company in South Staffordshire. The boating staff, and boats valued at £7,000, were transferred to the Shropshire Union Company.[51] By 1884 the Company owned the largest number of narrow canal boats (400) of any carriers in the country.[52] Consolidation was still taking place in 1901 when it was proposed to take over the remnants (twenty-four boats) of the once mighty Pickford fleet.[53] By 1902 the company owned 450 narrow boats,[54] and in 1907 was employing 586 boatmen and hands (excluding wives and children under 14), on the canal boats.[55]

The Grand Junction Canal Company, when it had entered the carrying trade in 1848, had probably taken over more independent carriers and their stock than even the Shropshire Union had done,[56] but it was not to be so long-lasting for, following the financial disaster of the Regent's Canal explosion in 1874, the company abandoned the business on 1 July 1876.[57] Most of the trade and the boats seem to have been taken over by two large companies, the London and Midland Counties Carrying Co., formed by three men, of whom two had been agents of the Grand Junction Co.,[58] and the London and Staffordshire Carrying Co. This second company appears to have been a forerunner of Fellows Morton and Clayton, being a partnership of Mr J. Fellows and Messrs Holcroft and Hughes.[59]

This firm of Fellows Morton and Clayton Co. Ltd. grew by amalgamations and absorptions to have its own dominating influence in the later part of the nineteenth and in the twentieth centuries. It is not certain when Fellows and Morton joined forces, although the title Fellows Morton & Co. appears in registers in 1882. Already by 1883 Frederick Morton could claim that the company carried 'over a greater extent of country than any other carriers by canal in the Kingdom'.[60] On 3 July 1889 the firm of Fellows Morton and Clayton was incorporated, the Clayton being Thomas Clayton of Saltley and elsewhere. Confusingly, immediately before incorporation, the firm had taken over the important business of William Clayton of Saltley.[61] The company soon came to own the largest number of boats of any private canal trader. From 1885 the boats registered at Birmingham by the company and its immediate derivatives amounted to 379, or about 47 per cent of the total registrations down to 1914.[62] The actual number of boats owned by the firm in 1905 was 219, of which twenty were steamers.[63]

Where these giants operated, small traders were generally discouraged from trading. In 1855, Mr Skey, of the Shropshire Union Company, wrote:

> the rates of tonnage are to be raised so as to exclude the private Trader from entering into competition with the Companies—in fact the existence of the Agreement is incompatible with that of the independent Carrier,[64]

and it seems to have been a policy generally adhered to. If bye-traders became too numerous and competitive, as in 1884,[65] agreements were soon made with other north-west midland canal companies and large carriers, as in 1885, to freeze them out.[66]

Similar pressure on bye-traders had been exerted on other canals where the company was a carrier. On the Leeds and Liverpool canal attempts were made to drive off the bye-traders, although not with complete success, and some toleration of them was allowed on shorter voyages, which the canal company found uneconomic.[67] The Aire and Calder Navigation Company had also developed its 'sphere of influence', and although Bartholomew claimed on its behalf that 'We encourage private carriers',[68] one of them, at least, did not agree.[69]

By the beginning of the twentieth century the atmosphere of canal trading seems to have been one of gentlemanly decadence, where each carrier lorded it over his own territory. 'Is there much competition between your firm and any other firms?' Frederick Morton was asked.

> Not a great deal . . . we each of us have what I may call our sphere of influence. We do not as a rule interfere with each other; . . . for instance from Liverpool we should never think of competing with the Anderton Company for trade between Liverpool and the Potteries; if anyone asked us for a rate we should refer them to the Anderton Company. If anyone asked the Anderton Company for a rate from Liverpool to South Staffordshire, they would refer him to Fellows Morton.

He assured the Commission that they were 'generally very good friends with each other'.[70] The railways usually entered into the spirit of things and allowed the carrying canal companies to fix their rates at 10 per cent below that of the railways. They were all members of a conference.[71] Presumably if any bye-trader began to expand his trade too vigorously, or if too many 'number ones' began to appear where they were unwanted, united action soon drove them away.

### SURVIVAL UNDER DIFFICULTIES

The lot of the small operator had always been a precarious one and many of the difficulties he faced have been outlined in a previous chapter. And, of course, as trade became gradually harder to come by, as it became more difficult to get a fully-loaded boat over the canal, as voyage times increased, the owner-operator was able to build up less substantial reserves against disaster. He became less able to survive a long period of trade depression or bad weather conditions, and a relatively minor accident to his boat, or the loss of his horse, could put a man out of business. Deaths of horses were particularly frequent in and around Birmingham in the early years of the nineteenth century, in consequence of the rickety bridges thrown over the entrances to the proliferating side-cuts. Those 'Miserable make-shifts' had resulted in 'accidents which in some cases have ruined Families and thrown them upon their parishes for support'.[72] If accidents lessened here, as more substantial structures were built, the mortality of canal-boat horses, mainly through falling into the canal, generally remained high throughout the nineteenth century.

Owner-boatmen hired by the Bridgewater Navigation Company, in 1875, were paid £4 a week for the boat, the crew and the horse, and Saunders considered that that would be the usual income of the 'number one' if he was 'making a fair trade and an average amount of earnings'. This does not seem to be a very substantial sum with which to buy a horse (at up to £25), and keep it; perhaps to contemplate buying a new boat (at up to £150), or see to the maintenance of an existing one. It was this last particular which often proved to be the downfall of many an owner-boatman, according to Williams.

> The bye-boatman would, in round figures, be in a little better position than the ordinary boatman, but he soon gets into difficulty because they do not spend money in repairing the boats.[73]

Some trades may have proved more lucrative. It is possible to work out that in the 1880s an owner-boatman could make about £6 10s [£6·50p] in bringing a boat load of timber, or grain, the seventy-seven miles from Sharpness to Birmingham, in a thirty to thirty-five ton boat.[74] A round trip could be done in a week, but of course much depended on the time taken to load and unload.

Some owner-boatmen (and boatmen) remained prosperous by working two boats, especially if they had a large family, one of them perhaps being hired, one horse usually pulling the two boats. John Wain, who contracted for the Shropshire Union's Wolverhampton boatage department with two boats, was put down for a payment of £9 a week.[75] It was sometimes convenient for a boatman to steer the boat of a boat-owner and to take his own boat along with it. For instance, John Wright was the boatman named both for John Corbett's boat *Integrity* and his own *Hebe*, both registered on 6 May 1879 as bringing salt from the Stoke Prior works to London.[76] John Bryan was another.[77]

Being restricted neither by home nor employer, 'number ones' were free to roam at will in search of a cargo, and many did. 'They go anywhere', admitted Frederick Morton.[78] Many, however, appear to have operated mainly in certain definite areas. W. H. King, a narrow-boat owner, was doubtless the type of owner-boatman who was most commonly to be found. His diary reveals that he travelled with two boats, one of them his own.[79] The other, *The Four Brothers*, was the property of a relation, Edward King, who was perhaps his brother.[80] Their business lay mostly at the southern end of the Grand Junction canal, and the bulk of the cargoes carried were bricks and other building materials, brought from the brick and cement works north-west of London into the centre of that city. They returned with breeze and ashes to be used for the making of bricks. When they ventured beyond Braunston with (and sometimes without) building materials, they loaded and returned with coal from Wash Lane Colliery, probably near Coventry. They rarely travelled off the line between there and Paddington, although they had no set route on that line, and rarely was anything other than coal or building materials carried. The two boatmen were possibly untypical in that they never stirred upon the Sunday.

'Number ones' found themselves at a growing disadvantage *vis-à-vis* the benefits that company boatmen came to have. For example, advances and then half-pay increasingly reduced the hardship brought by a long hard frost. George Smith gave some little insight into the distress which could result from a severe cold spell. In 1878 on the Grand Junction canal he came across a boatman and his family

> living in their boat on a short branch of the main canal. On account of the frost they had not done any work for some weeks. They looked a picture of starvation. A fire-less stove and an empty locker in a cabin on a wet cold wintry day are not pleasant companions for a man, wife and three children. Their fast had not been broken for twenty hours.[81]

In 1895 King's cryptic entry of 31 January suggests similar suffering. It read: 'lay at Berkhamsted—froze up till the 1st of March'.

### INDIAN SUMMER OF THE 'NUMBER ONE'

Owner-boatmen were a dying breed in the years before the First World War. That conflict and the motor lorry may have been expected to have continued their decline in number and importance. The dislocations brought by the war had by 1918 reduced the amount carried over British canals to 21·6 million tons compared with 31·6 in 1913, despite government control. The growing use of the motor lorry and the collapse of the post-war boom in 1921 were to deplete the figure further; to 17 million tons by 1924. The return of the controlled companies and carriers to private enterprise on 31 August 1920 effectively ended government subsidisation of the canal industry,[82] and in the following year several canal companies abandoned their large carrying concerns. In fact in the short-term this may have reversed the decline of the 'number one', for it not only put a supply of cheap boats on to the market but also once again left a vacuum in the carriage of goods which could be filled by the small operator. Hence the Wigan register shows an increase in owner-boatmen in the 1920s, some of them working in boats lately owned by the Leeds and Liverpool Canal Company.[83] The Rochdale Canal Company ceased trading in 1921, but a 1922 report read: 'the discharged boatmen who hire our boats are doing a nice little business; they work all the hours they can'.[84] The Shropshire Union also stopped trading in 1921.

It was no doubt for these reasons that, as compared with the 4·7 per cent of boatmen who in 1911 were described as 'working on their own account', there were 11 per cent in 1921,[85] and 9 per cent in 1931.[86] Rolt may have been misled by this increase in the proportion of 'number ones', to a somewhat higher level than before the war; by the subsequent fall in the 1920s and 1930s; and by the fact that he spent much of his journey, in 1939–40, travelling on waterways where owner-boatmen had been traditionally more numerous. In consequence, he perhaps came to believe that these small men had been much more important and numerous, nationally, than they actually had been.

Equally, Rolt generally made much of the sterling qualities of these owner-operators. He waxed eloquent over their beautiful and spotless cabins and so on, but, again, he may only have been seeing the best in these people in that many of the worst had left the waterways, or great improvements had taken place. In 1875 Beddows, the Bridgewater Navigation Company's agent at Runcorn, answered a query with:

> On the whole [our boatmen live decent lives]; we cannot say the same of those living on bye-boats, which are the boats belonging to the men who work them; they are of a lower class; their wages are not so good, because the employment is not so regular and they are not superintended in the way that our boats are.[87]

His colleague, Williams, also considered that 'men in the stated employment of a company with regular work are a superior class of men to outsiders [bye-boat men]'.[88] And there is no doubt that it was this class of owner-boatmen which was to give the most trouble to the inspectors of canal boats, the school attendance officers and the medical officers of health in the years down to 1914.

### CONCLUSION

We can state conclusively that owner-boatmen were numerically unimportant, both at the beginning of the nineteenth century and at the end. They were roughly of the same order of magnitude at both times. It is unfortunate that evidence for the intervening years is so sparse, and particularly for the years of the Canal Age. None the less, considering all the difficulties under which the small man laboured, even before the more meagre years of the later nineteenth century, and considering also the complexities of canal trading, reason, if not firm evidence, must indicate that the role of such men was never anything other than a peripheral one. Certainly such assumptions as 'Originally most craft were owned by the boatmen themselves' or 'In the past the bulk of the canal traffic was handled by these independents [owner-boatmen]', are not justified.[89] Owner-boatmen and small operators lived in a perpetually precarious situation. They were usually restricted to the least profitable of all goods; they were subject to discrimination by canal companies; they often had to rely upon hirings from the larger carriers to exist and they were the first to be cast off in times of slump; they were restricted to the crumbs which fell from the tables of canal giants, even though, in some areas, these crumbs might be substantial ones; and, at the same time, anything from a horse's broken leg to a protracted frost could bring speedy ruin.

Equally, the sterling qualities of the owner-boatmen, whatever they may have been in 1939, were perhaps less in evidence in the years before 1914.

### NOTES TO CHAPTER EIGHT

[1] See Chapter II.

[2] *S. C. on Sunday Trading*, 1841, q. 1167, 1170.

[3] See above, p. 52; Cromford Canal Permit Book, 25 March 1823, at Derbyshire County Record Office (D.R.O.), 501 B/B4; Poor Law Settlement Papers, Shelford, 26 March 1810, N.R.O., P.R. 85.

[4] Birmingham Canal Bill, 21 April 1839, pp. 164–205.

[5] *Articles of Agreement made between the Members of a Society who have agreed to meet at the House of Mr John Jones . . .* (1808), Birm. R.L. 72294.

[6] A detailed study of these permit books over an extended period would decide the matter beyond any doubt.

[7] *S.C. on Sunday Trading*, 1841, q. 163.

[8] *Ibid.*, 64.

[9] *Ibid.*, 549.

[10] *S. C. on Railway and Canal Bills*, 1852–3, q. 1596.

[11] *Hope Iron Boat Club, Rules and Regulations* (1856), Birm. R.L., 72220.

[12] *S. C. on Canal Boats*, 1884, q. 918.

[13] *Ibid.*, 1146.

[14] *Factory and Workshops Commission*, 1876, vol II, q. 10538.

[15] *Ibid.*, 11282.

[16] *Ibid.*, vol I, appendix C, p. 129.

[17] Registers of Canal Boats, 1879–1914, Public Health Department, Paddington Town Hall. In the collection of these and subsequent figures the years 1879–84 have been used (although none were registered in 1884 in this instance), firstly in order to amass a meaningful sample and secondly because boats were not always registered immediately after the 1877 Act came into operation.

[18] Registers of Canal Boats, 1879–1914, Chester City Record Office.

[19] *Ibid.*, Burnley Public Health Department. None were registered 1882, 1883, 1884.

[20] *Ibid.*, Wigan Public Health Department.

[21] *Ibid.*, Nottingham Public Health Department.

[22] *Ibid.*, Coventry City Record Office.

[23] *Factory and Workshops Commission*, 1876, vol. II, qq. 10819–20.

[24] Register of Canal Boats, 1879–84, Birmingham Public Health Department (at Erdington).

[25] This does not in itself mean that there must have been fewer than 25 per cent of the boats owner-steered (although the fact that many of these boats would probably not be owned by their masters would imply that it must be so), because in registers elsewhere there were boatmen registered as owning and steering two and even three boats. These must obviously be classed as owner-steered boats.

[26] Extract from *The Mail*, 8 February 1886, 'Maritime Birmingham' in Newspaper Cuttings relating to Canals, collected by G. H. Osborne (henceforward 'Maritime Birmingham'), Birm. R.L., 243972.

[27] *Factory and Workshops Commission*, 1876, vol I, appendix C, p. 119.

[28] *S. C. on Canal Boats*, 1884, qq. 411–13.

[29] Register of Canal Boats, 1879–1914, Local History Library, Oxford.

[30] *Ibid.*, Hinckley Public Health Department.

31 *Ibid.*, Ilkeston Library, MUS 346. None were registered 1882, 1883, 1884.

32 *Ibid.*, Tring and Daventry (Rural) Public Health Departments.

33 OXC 4/80/3, *A Bill for making a Navigable Communication between the Trent and Mersey Canal and the Burton Canal at Shobnall . . . And observations upon the same*, p. 3, attached to the letter, John Twiss jnr. to Oxford Canal Company, 23 December 1795.

34 Hadfield and Biddle, *The Canals of North West England*, vol. I, pp. 91–2.

35 *R. C. on Canals*, vol. I, 1906 [Cd. 3183–4], XXXII, q. 4405. Or at least part of the Bridgewater Navigation Company's trade was taken over by this company, but part of it was taken over by what was to become Fellows Morton and Clayton Co. Ltd.

36 Clew, *The Kennet and Avon Canal* (1968), pp. 108, 115.

37 *R. C. on Canals*, vol. I, 1906 [Cd. 3183–4], XXXII, q. 4797.

38 *Factory and Workshops Commission*, 1876, vol. II q. 10851.

39 *Ibid.*, 10439.

40 *R. C. on Canals*, vol. I, 1906 [Cd. 3183–4], XXXII, q. 2438 (evidence of W. D. Phillipps, General Manager of the North Staffordshire Railway Company).

41 See Register of Canal Boats, 5 August 1891, 208, Wigan Public Health Department for one example.

42 *S. C. on Canal Boats*, 1884, q. 1287. Rolt in *Narrow Boat*, p. 202, defines bye-trader as 'any trader on a canal other than the canal company itself when carriers', which of course includes 'number ones'. Sometimes, however, the expression bye-trader was used exclusively to describe owner-boatmen.

43 *S. C. on Canals*, 1883, q. 2631.

44 *Census of England and Wales 1891*, vol. III, *Ages, Conditions as to Marriage, Occupation, Birthplaces and Infirmities*, 1893 [C. 7058], p. xii; *ibid., 1901; Summary Tables*, 1903 [Cd. 1523], table XXXV, p. 118; *ibid., 1911*, vol. X, part 1, 1914 [Cd. 7018], table 3, p. 14.

45 Mather, *After the Canal Duke* (1970), pp. 145, 162–3, 167, 169, 202; *S. C. on Railway and Canal Bills*, 1852–3, qq. 1643, 1684–5, 1693.

46 Mather, *op. cit.*, pp. 199–200.

47 Hadfield and Biddle, *op. cit.*, vol. II, p. 366.

48 SURC 1/37, 4 August 1847.

49 SURC 1/13, 6 December 1865, minute 5433.

50 SURC 1/10, 24 May 1849.

51 SURC 1/17, 27 August 1873, minute 9723 and appendix. Some of Crowley's stock had been taken over by the Grand Junction Canal Company much earlier; GJC 1/11, 27 November 1848, p. 59, and 9 July 1850, p. 282.

52 *S. C. on Canal Boats*, 1884, qq. 1124–5.

53 SURC 1/25, 7 August 1901, minute 21574.

54 *Ibid.*, 19 March 1902, 21741.

55 SURC 1/26, 19 June 1907, 22876.

56 See above, Chapter VII, note 31.

57 GJC 1/20, 14 June 1876, pp. 276–7.

58 *Ibid.*, 12 April 1876, pp. 261, 316.

59 GJC 1/20, 26 July 1876, p. 300; 1 August 1877, p. 10.

60 *S. C. on Canals*, 1883, q. 2615. Details of the origins of the two branches of the company are also given.

61 *Memorandum of Association of Fellows Morton and Clayton Limited* (1889); and *Fellows Morton and Clayton Directors' Report* (1890), numbered respectively at Birm. R.L. as 663022 and 663023.

62 Register of Canal Boats, Birmingham Public Health Department.

63 *R. C. on Canals*, vol. I, 1906 [Cd. 3183–4], XXXII, qq. 4278–9.

64 SURC 1/11, 23 February 1855, minute 1681.

65 SURC 1/21, 25 March 1884, 15683.

66 *Ibid.*, 30 September 1885, 16335; SURC 1/22, 24 February 1886, 16537; *ibid.*, 23 February 1887, 16933.

[67] Hadfield and Biddle, *op. cit.*, vol. II, p. 400.

[68] *S. C. on Canals*, 1883, q. 857.

[69] *Ibid.*, q. 2891 (John Hunt, a Leeds canal carrier).

[70] *R. C. on Canals*, vol. I, 1906 [Cd. 3183–4], XXXII, qq. 4429, 4635–6.

[71] *Ibid.*, qq. 5098, 5102 (evidence of C. R. Dykes, Manager of the Rochdale Canal Company).

[72] BCN 4/372, Houghton to Turton, 8 December 1813.

[73] *Factory and Workshops Commission*, 1876, vol. II, qq. 10819–20.

[74] *S. C. on Canals*, 1883, q. 2058; 'Birmingham and Bristol Channel improved navigation', p. 10, paper given at the Fourth International Congress on Inland Navigation, Manchester (1890).

[75] SURC 15/2, Staff Register 1879–97, p. 250.

[76] Register of Canal Boats, 3–4, Paddington Public Health Department.

[77] *Ibid.*, 6 and 20 May 1879, 6–7.

[78] *R. C. on Canals*, vol. I, 1906 [Cd. 3183–4], XXXII, q. 4436.

[79] Diary of W. H. King, canal contractor, 1895, St. Br.

[80] Register of Canal Boats, 17 June 1887, 171, Paddington Public Health Department.

[81] Smith, *Canal Adventures by Moonlight* (1881), p. 60.

[82] Hadfield, *British Canals*, pp. 257–60, 266.

[83] Register of Canal Boats, vol. II, Wigan Public Health Department.

[84] Hadfield and Biddle, *op. cit.*, vol. II, p. 437.

[85] *Census of England and Wales 1921; Occupation Tables*, 1924, table 1, p. 16.

[86] *Ibid.*, 1931, 1934, table 1, p. 10.

[87] *Factory and Workshops Commission*, 1876, vol. II, q. 10815.

[88] *Ibid.*, 10854.

[89] See above p. 16.

# IX

# 'Our Canal Population'
## The social condition
## of the boating class
## in the 1870s and 1880s

### GEORGE SMITH OF COALVILLE (1831–95)

THAT THE CANAL-BOAT PEOPLE again came under the glare of public scrutiny in the 1870s after being allowed, more or less, to return to the quiet oblivion which had characterised their calling before the scandals of thirty years before was due, in large measure, to the dedicated efforts of one man—George Smith, 'a remarkable man who did a remarkable work in a remarkable manner'.[1]

George Smith of Coalville (as he insisted on being referred to) had both the appearance and personality of an eccentric.[2] Rising from extremely humble beginnings, and notwithstanding his poor education, he succeeded, by his hurried but able pen and by his earnest, if uncultured, voice, in arousing intense interest, firstly in the fate of children in brickyards and subsequently in the canal-boat and gypsy populations. His philanthropy resulted in loss of employment and deep poverty for himself and his family; it led to hatred and abuse and even physical violence against him; and it led to his eventual expulsion from Coalville, where he had at one time been the manager of a brick and drainpipe yard at £450 a year. He was, then, not a man lacking in physical or mental courage, and, for a reformer who suffered great privation in the furtherance of his causes, he was obviously not without sincerity.

No doubt his origins and subsequent tribulations played a large part in the moulding of his peculiar personality. According to his biographer, Edwin Hodder, he was a nervous, highly-wrought, impressionable man. He had visions and dreamed dreams, but he often failed to distinguish between his dreams and reality. His zeal and his single-mindedness led him to much exaggeration. He heard the voice of God, and, being chosen by God, was convinced that his way was the right and only way. The fame and success in which his campaigns resulted went to his head, cementing his belief that he was always right and inflating his already substantial ego. God was not alone in taking a keen interest in his every move, for Smith was convinced that the Queen herself followed his campaigns closely. He sent long letters to Her Majesty. On one occasion he wrote of 'A letter from the

Queen which carries a lot with it'. The letter actually read, 'General Sir Henry F. Ponsonby is commanded by the Queen to thank Mr George Smith for his letter of the 29th May'.[3] He was also, apparently, quite without a sense of humour. A joke in a newspaper had caught his eye. 'Speaking of sausages,' it read, 'Mr Smith passed the pork shop the other day. Mr Smith whistled. The moment he did this every sausage wagged its tail.' By the side George Smith had written, 'I did not think that anybody saw me at the pork shop. They must have had sharp eyes!'[4] With God and the Queen supporting him, the eyes of the nation were upon George Smith (of Coalville)!

### THE ALLEGATIONS

This, then, was the reformer, who in October 1873 began his crusade against the evils that he saw upon the English canals.[5] He favoured the London and provincial press with a letter, and he added fuel to the subsequent debate with an article in the *Fortnightly Review* in the following year. He described the gross immorality on board the barges, the drinking and fighting habits of parents, encouraged among children, the indescribable state of filth in which many of the barges were to be found, the prevalence of disease and its rapid propagation, and the utter neglect of all education for the children.[6] He was soon able to put a number to the men, women and children who were 'living and floating on our canals and rivers in a state of wretchedness, misery, immorality, cruelty and evil training that carries peril with it'. There were 'over 100,000'.[7] Some of the evils were quantifiable to a remarkable degree. 95 per cent could not read or write; 90 per cent were drunkards—'swearing blasphemy and oaths are their common conversation'—2 per cent were members of a Christian church; 60 per cent lived as men and wives in an unmarried state.[8]

Admitting his difficulty in being able adequately to describe this veritable Hades, his righteous pen yet seemed always ready to make another attempt. In describing the canal-boat cabin the *furor scribendi* was once more upon him. Where others saw beauty and charm he wrote of 'those hot, damp, close, stuffy, buggy, filthy and stinking holes, commonly called boat cabins'.[9] In these 'hell holes' he told of how 'people of all ages live day and night . . . In these places girls of seventeen give birth to children, the fathers of which are members of their own family'.[10] And in like manner he scribbled on incessantly, startling an unsuspecting English public.

At the same time there were others who expressed their concern at the condition of the people on the boats. The Governor of the county prison at Stafford also wished 'to draw the attention of the charitable and Christian world of England and, if possible, the Government to the state of the canal boat population generally'.[11] Captains May and Baker, factory inspectors, were earnest supporters of George Smith. H. J. Bignold, responsible for factories in north Cheshire and north Wales, observed that 'The education of the children is entirely neglected and a low moral standard prevails among the entire canal boat population'.[12] Pamphilon was clearly of the same opinion, declaring that, the condition of the canal people is a crying evil'.[13] Others joined in the chorus of protest, some of them having heard of rather than seen the evils to which they alluded.

THE DENIALS

On the other hand there were those who felt able to comment favourably on boatmen. Mr Beddows, for example, said, 'Speaking from experience as to the persons employed on our boats, the morals on the whole are quite as good as the morals of any other working class of people'.[14] Fred Morton thought that, 'comparing them with the working classes of south Staffordshire they are far before them speaking generally'.[15] Mr George, with knowledge of the canals to the south and west of Birmingham, felt that, 'the [boat] people generally have risen in the social scale with others'.[16]

Such favourable opinions noticeably stemmed from men involved in the employment of boatmen, from men who clearly had the most knowledge of boaters and their way of life, but equally, they were men unlikely to advertise any evils which might result in interference. None the less, there were what must be considered independent witnesses who supported their claims. Striedinger, factory inspector in the south and west midlands, made clear what he thought of George Smith and his campaign.

> I cannot refrain, in spite of the sensationalism with which 'our floating population' has been treated of late by a few well-intentioned philanthropists, to record, as the result of my experience . . . that, not only in physique, but in morals and intellect too, the much abused canal boat population compare favourably both with the agricultural and with the lower stratum of the manufacturing population.[17]

Another factory inspector in that area, Sub-Inspector Fitton, found them to be 'much less uncouth and rough in their language and demeanour than barge people are generally reputed to be'.[18] Sub-Inspector Bowling, whose district included Birmingham, remarked,

> The cabins on the whole are kept fairly clean, some remarkably so, and among some of the younger and steady boatmen, there seems to be an emulation to make their cabins as clean and smart as possible.[19]

Sub-Inspector Osborne, a Lancashire inspector, commented,

> In these districts the Staffordshire barge[e] is reputed the roughest of his genus, but the boatmen generally are by the canal authorities accounted to have a considerable regard for the law and to be for all practical purposes a very manageable class.[20]

What, then, was the real situation on England's inland waterways? How true were Smith's allegations?

NUMBERS

The method by which Smith arrived at the numbers involved was hardly scientific.

> I took one of the most thickly populated canals [the Grand Junction], and then I took another, about the same length, very thinly populated [the Chesterfield], and arrived at the average in that way, taking into consideration at the same time the many miles that I had walked along the canals, and observed the number of boats from time to time.[21]

On his own admission he had revised his estimate to 80,000–90,000 by 1875, but he invariably, and conveniently, omitted to utilise his new calculation in further letters and articles, and before parliamentary committees.[22]

There are statistics available of the numbers of the boating population, but the very nature of this wandering occupation make such figures susceptible to error. Also, each group of statistics demands numerous qualifications. It should be made clear, at the outset, that boats were manned differently from region to region and within the same region. Boat crews might be made up of:

I    Day-boat men, almost exclusively male, who worked short distances and who returned to their homes every night. Most of the Thames lightermen and watermen and those of other rivers would fall into this category, as would those boatmen who, for example, delivered coal to the canal-side factories of, say, Manchester and Birmingham, and of course the men involved in canal maintenance.
II   All-male crews who had homes on shore, but who frequently slept away from home in the boat, fly-boat men being one example of this type.
III  All-male crews who lived permanently on board, which might again include some fly-boat men.
IV   Men, with their wives and families, who had homes on shore, which they visited periodically, living the rest of the time in the boat.
V    Men, and their wives and families, who lived permanently on board.

The Census of 1871 numbered 29,487 men and 206 women as 'Bargemen, Watermen and Lightermen' in England and Wales, and that of 1881, 29,870 men and 354 women.[23] These figures almost certainly exclude many females who the census elsewhere reveals were sleeping on board that night. In 1871 there were 3,360 and in 1881, 2,753.[24] This means that in 1871 there would be 33,053, and in 1881, 32,977 men, women and children employed in, or involved with, non-seagoing boats in England and Wales, probably excluding male children under five years of age and some women and children at home on the night of the census. Allowing for these people, and for a generous margin of error, perhaps 40,000 might be taken as a figure representative of the upper limits of the total number of people involved.

There were about 6,000 lightermen and watermen working on the Thames in 1891.[25] There were many others similarly occupied on other rivers in England. It would be surprising if the subtraction of such people, principally men, working, but not living, on river boats did not immediately reduce the number to at least 30,000. The elimination of maintenance and day-boat men, on the canals, might reduce the figure even further to around 26,000–27,000 men, women and children who were to be found living upon canal boats and upon a few river boats.

It is significant that another return, prepared in 1884 by the Canal Association, which excluded the main rivers (and some minor canals) found 22,561 boat people upon 1,830 miles of main waterway out of a possible 2,437 miles. There were 13,489 men, 3,297 women over 16, and 5,775 children under 16, of whom 4,033 were under 13. Day-boat men and maintenance men on the canals were included.[26]

Proof that we have roughly the right order of magnitude comes with a return of 1883, from the seventy-six registration authorities set up under the Canal Boats Act of 1877, which showed that boats had been registered to accommodate 33,795 people since 1878.[27] Many of the boats on the register had been broken up by 1883. Mr George put the number of such boats at about 1,000 a year later, which would immediately reduce the number of people involved by 5,000.[28] At the same time, owners of boats always, obviously, registered their boats for the maximum number of people, regardless of whether that number lived on board. Many boats were, in fact, found not to be full. This would again reduce the number very significantly. Day-boat men and maintenance men would not be included in these figures. We can perhaps conclude that the numbers of men, women and children, living, or working (or both), on board *canal* boats was in the region of 20,000–30,000 people. If day-boat men and maintenance boatmen are included the final figure might be nearer 30,000; if not it would be nearer 20,000.

Clearly, from the first two returns (the census and that of the Canal Association), most boats on the inland waterways of England and Wales were handled by men only, and most of them would fall into our first two categories. But, of course, this fact masks regional and local differences. It is significant that in the second return, which is more canal-orientated, the ratio of men to women is much smaller. River boats were usually crewed by men. In some canal areas it was traditional practice for most boats to be manned by men. Fly-boats were exclusively handled by men. It follows that the slow-boat, in certain areas, was much more commonly a family boat. A factory inspector in 1876 estimated that about two-thirds of the boats passing through Sheffield would be family boats.[29] The lock keepers on the Birmingham and south midland canals calculated that between half and two-thirds of the vessels which passed them would be such boats.[30] Two-thirds of the 350 boats travelling northward from the Potteries would house the family, according to Pamphilon.[31]

Not all these families lived permanently on board, having no other home. The Sheffield factory inspector tentatively suggested that only an eighth would do so.[32] At Liverpool, registration returns in 1884 show that only a tenth of the boats were being used as permanent dwellings by the families of the boatmen.[33] Very few families were thought to live permanently on board boats in Nottinghamshire, Derbyshire and Lincolnshire, except sometimes for a few months in the summer.[34] The lock keepers of the south midlands and Birmingham felt that only a small proportion lived permanently on the boats.[35]

On the other hand, only about half of the people on the boats passing through Worcester, between Gloucester and Birmingham, were thought to have homes on shore.[36] And of the hundred narrow boats of the Bridgewater Navigation Company, half were thought to be permanently occupied.[37] Pamphilon seemed to suggest that all the family boats which he mentioned were used permanently as dwellings.[38]

At a national level the 1881 Census found 6,225 males and 2,753 females sleeping on board boats and barges on that night.[39] Some of this number would have homes on shore, but would not on that night be sleeping in them. This must mean that fewer than 8,978 people lived permanently on board boats, having no other home, if the census is correct—which is, of course, open to some doubt. However, this figure is in some way substantiated by the fact that the Canal Association in 1884 found that only 6,645 people of the 22,561 lived wholly on board.[40]

To summarise then, we might tentatively suggest that 40,000 would represent the total number of all kinds of inland watermen, women and children at the outside, which is much below even the revised estimate of 80,000–90,000 of George Smith. His criticisms were levelled mainly at family boats, but these, in fact, were probably occupied by fewer than 26,000–27,000 people, although it is true that these boats were probably concentrated in the midlands and possibly in parts of Yorkshire. The number living permanently on boats, which he considered the most deplorable state of things, was, in fact relatively small, amounting to between 7,000 and 9,000 people only, although again these were probably concentrated in particular areas, and especially in the north-west midlands.

These estimates are of course open to a degree of error, but clearly the error would have to be gigantic to approach Smith's figures. Significantly, by 1892, he had again revised his total estimate to between 17,000 and 20,000 men, 4,000–5,000 women, 9,000–10,000 children of school age, a maximum figure of 35,000.[41] Whatever evils were to be found upon canals, the numbers of people involved in them were not dramatically large.

### OVERCROWDING

The cabin of the 'narrow boat' was approximately $8\frac{1}{2}$ ft long, 5 ft high and $6\frac{3}{4}$ ft wide (see figure 3). The Local Government Board regulations, resulting from the Act of 1877, laid down a fixed number of people who could legally occupy such a cabin, depending upon the amount of air space in it.[42] In practice this usually meant that on a boat built prior to 30 June 1878 a man, his wife and three children under twelve could sleep in the cabin, and that for a boat built after that date a man, his wife and two children might do so.[43] George Smith was not alone in remarking on the overcrowded conditions in these cabins. In 1875 several people testified to having often seen or heard of boats having a man, his wife and four or five children sleeping in the cabin, and sometimes, if the children were young, a 'chap' might live there too. As many as nine children, with their parents, had been known to occupy such a space, which also included all the family possessions if it was a permanent home.[44]

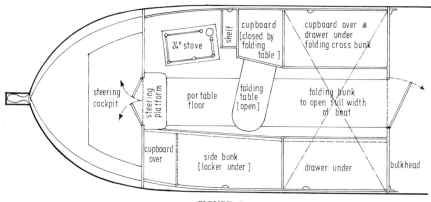

FIGURE 3

The 1871 Census reveals that Smith and the other observers were right, for there were such boats in a grossly overcrowded state. Of the eleven boats tied up at the Crescent Wharf in Birmingham on that night, five of them might be said to house families in excessively overcrowded conditions. Of the worst, the *Joseph* held Charles Sheppard, his wife and their six children and James Knight, aged 24. On another boat there was Henry Chatten, his wife and their six children. *The Mary and Ann* was inhabited by Henry Webb, his wife, their four children and the 14-year-old Harriet Lloyd.[45]

Enough, surely, to justify George Smith's claims, but, at the same time, it is difficult to insist that such a gathering would be typical. In the morning, the 'impromptu hamlet would separate, house by house, to the four winds',[46] and the pattern of boats and occupants which might assemble on the next and subsequent nights would be completely different. It must be noted that at other stopping places the proportion of overcrowded boats was much less. Of the 91 boats discovered with difficulty and haphazardly among the enumeration books for 1871, only 22 per cent could be said to be physically overcrowded, although of the family boats 29 per cent could be so described. There seems to have been nothing new in this phenomenon, for in 1861, of the 109 boats found, 21 per cent were overcrowded and 33·7 per cent of the family boats.[47] On the Grand Junction canal in 1858 children were to be found on boats 'varying in number from two to ten and in ages from three weeks to twelve years'.[48]

George Smith was partially right. There were many boating families living in overcrowded conditions, and had been for many years. Equally, even if the statistics drawn from the census are not representative, there were many families who did not live in such conditions. There is some evidence to show that, among the more respectable (and perhaps better off) boating class, as the family increased in numbers, the wife and children went to live permanently on shore. To quote one example, the wife and children of Joseph Richards would seem to have accompanied him upon the boat until the birth of the fourth child, for the first son, Thomas, had been born at Ellesmere Port, the second, John (12 years old in 1871) at Manchester, Elizabeth (11) at Chirk, but the next three (7, 4 and 2) were all born at Nantwich, and, following their removal to a cottage by the canal side in Chester, the last child was born there. By now, no doubt, the 14-year-old Thomas, described as an assistant boatman, travelled with his father. It is possible, of course, that the whole family were merely visiting their land home, but the description of most of the children as 'scholars' probably rules this out.[49] However, even if Smith gave the impression that the problem was more widespread than it actually was, there was none the less a measure of truth in his assertions.


IMMORALITY

With this difficult question, also, there was probably some truth in Smith's allegations, even if his exaggeration was at times ridiculous. He certainly seems to have been a sensationalist in his assessment of the numbers who lived together, unmarried, as man and wife,[50] and in the way he bandied around the figure of '40,000 illegitimate children'. He claimed that 60 per cent were not married, but, in fact, the census shows that such people were very few. Of course, boat people may have hidden the truth from the enumerator, but in 1890 it was reported that

> The Lichfield Diocesan Barge Missionary . . . has stated that he has worked among these people for six years, and only remembers one unmarried couple in his district who live together as man and wife.[51]

Thomas Hales agreed that cases where the boatmen and women were not married were 'quite exceptional'.[52] It seems unlikely that the Act of 1877 would encourage 60 per cent to tie the nuptial knot by 1884.

However, the problem of numerous people indecently occupying boat cabins seems to have been a very real one. By the definition of the Local Government Board Regulations of 1878,[53] 28·5 per cent of the boats culled from the 1871 Census, and 37·6 per cent of the family boats, could be said to be indecently occupied, when viewed in the best possible light. Whether the matter is viewed in the best, or worst, light depends upon the provision of a movable screen of wood in a cabin occupied by a man and his wife, and any other male over the age of 14 years. Many cabins, before the Act, did have a lace partition in the cabin, but, strictly speaking, this would be illegal. Presuming none of the cabins to have such wooden partitions, 39·5 per cent of all the boats, and 52 per cent of the family boats, might be said to be indecently occupied in 1871. In 1861 an optimistic view would find 22 per cent of all the boats and 35·3 per cent of the family boats indecently occupied, a pessimistic view would find 31·2 per cent and 50 per cent.[54]

It is clear that Smith's fears were not ill founded. There was indecent overcrowding, and he quoted, almost gleefully, examples of immorality, one of which, it was said, 'revealed a very low state of morality amongst our canal population'.[55] But the possibilities of immorality do not necessarily prove the reality of it, nor occasional examples its ubiquitous nature, and no doubt many boaters justifiably resented his allegations. Equally, there were large numbers of boats where there could be no suggestion of indecent occupation, the problem being partly overcome, as we have seen, by the wife and children taking a permanent home on land as the family grew up, or by the more dubious expedient of the elder children being 'pushed out of the nest'.[56] Again, the reformers (with the exception of Captain May) chose to ignore that many similar situations of 'indecent occupation' might be found in the homes of many of the working class on land. For instance, one half of the labouring population of London was said to be forced to live in single rooms, and, according to Lord Shaftesbury,

> the one-room system always leads, as far as I have seen, to the one-bed system . . . [and] you generally find one bed occupied by the whole family, in many of these cases consisting of father, mother and son, or of father and daughters, or brothers and sisters. It is impossible to say how fatal the result of that is.

Seven and eight people were known to live in rooms 6 ft by 8 ft.[57]

None the less, if immorality is not clearly proved among some sections of the boating population, Smith had certainly brought to light the possibility of it. And John Brydone, returning from his first tour of the canals, as Chief Inspector of Canal Boats, in 1884, while he did not wish to 'reiterate what has been so often said of the vice and immorality which pervade this class of people', he had to admit 'It exists! I have found it to be the case.'[58]

### DRINKING

Brydone again seems to have confirmed Smith's allegations, and to have substantiated other evidence, in suggesting that boatmen had remained generally inebriate, as the rest of the population had moved markedly towards a greater state of sobriety. In 1884, he remarked,

> The one great cause underlying the whole of the matter is the old, old story, drink. The lingering about for hours at a time, day after day, in the public house, spending money, time and energy, soon induces poverty, strife, blasphemy, vice, squalor and misery, besides cruelty of many sad descriptions.[59]

The London factory inspector painted a grim picture.

> The social life of the barge population is most degraded. Both men and women drink frequently to excess . . . At Bull's Bridge in Middlesex . . . I have been informed the most disgraceful drunken orgies may frequently be witnessed.[60]

That there might be a good deal of drinking would be readily understandable, for numerous reasons. Being cut off from those influences which had reduced the part alcohol had to play in the everyday life of the working population, drink was still an important facet of the boatman's life. Changes in the transport world, where drunkenness had always been high, had reduced its prevalence to some extent. Railways had produced, of necessity, a more sober body of men working them, and they had also drastically reduced the numbers of men involved in long-distance road haulage. Improved water supplies, which had done much to displace beer as an integral part of the working man's diet, had not found their way on to the canal. Brydone observed,

> A supply of good drinking water is much clamoured for by the boat people, and it is much to be regretted that pure drinking water should be so difficult to be obtained by them, with the result that beer, being always procurable, is made a substitute.[61]

The conditons under which some of the boat people lived, in filth and squalor and grossly overcrowded conditions, played its part in filling the public houses. 'It often drives the men into beerhouses so as to get away from their poor cabins full of squalling children', Pamphilon commented, for when 'a man comes in tired and finds the wife and six or seven children there . . . he is glad to get to the beerhouse'.[62] Delays, at wharves, at locks, through repairs and unfavourable weather conditions, again caused much drinking.

Above all, however, the main reason for excessive drinking probably resulted from the extremely narrow life which work upon the canals entailed. The wandering life of a section of the boatpeople, with few community roots and little real relaxation from toil, precluded them from many of the diversions which the rest of the population could increasingly turn to. For many the only diversion would be the canal-side public houses, 'nasty suspicious dens to say the least of it',[63] where each night they stabled their horse and created their own amusements, or 'what for lack of knowledge they regarded as jollity'.[64] The 'special commissioner' found

> the grimiest of low-ceilinged taproom, a truly savage and barbaric 'tap' wherein is dispensed the thinnest and flattest beer I have ever yet come across. This is the 'bargee's' usual tipple, for rum is only a special drink for great occasions. Greasy wooden 'settles' and battered wooden tables furnish the apartment, and there come the 'jolly bargemen' to make merry. The walls have two distinct and clearly defined rows of black lines, indicating the presence of greasy backs and heads, and when the boatmen have mustered 'harmony reigns' . . . The ballads peculiar to the boatmen possess either the humour of the not specially decorous country ditty, or the sentimentality of the Holywell-Street 'lay' . . . The singer having duly rammed his hands into his breeches pocket, leans his head against the wall, fixes his eyes on the ceiling, assumes a most serious and dismal countenance, and goes to work with the air of a man doing penance for his sins. The choruses are frequent and tremendous. The 'harmony' is often relieved by a little step dancing, in which strange to say, the boatman is an adept; the big burly men are wonderfully light of foot and keep time accurately. The orchestra is usually composed of a fearfully dilapidated old man, operating feebly on the last remains of an ancient fiddle, and extracting thence wheezing old jigs and ghostly strains of nigger 'breakdowns'.[65]

One could hardly use the cliché that boatmen were addicted to strong drink, for Hollingshead had also commented on the 'very thin and sour ale' sold at canal-side taverns.[66] However, it seems clear that boatmen, as a class, drank too much and more than was good for them, as the returns of the Registrar General for the years 1890–2 clearly demonstrate.

*Mortality from alcoholism among occupied transport workers, 1890–2*[67]

| | |
|---|---:|
| All occupied males | 100 |
| Transport service | 162 |
| Railway engine drivers, etc. | 15 |
| Railway guards, etc. | 38 |
| Cabmen, etc. | 215 |
| Carmen, carriers | 131 |
| *Bargemen*, etc. | 131 |
| Seamen | 162 |
| Dock labour, etc. | 400 |
| Messengers, porters. | 115 |

It can be seen that, even at a time when a marked improvement was already visible in the drinking habits of boatmen, deaths from that cause were still well above the national average, though well below that of some other transport workers, especially dockers.[68]

We might be forgiven, then, if we were to fall in with the view, generally held by an ignorant public, that the canal world embraced 'drunken brawls, improper language, constant fights, danger to life and property, [and] hordes of licensed ruffians beyond the pale of law and order', a view which Smith did his best to confirm. However, Hollingshead found in 1858 that such prejudices were 'all proved false before the experience of a few hours, and shamefully false before the further experience of a few days'. He found that tea 'was the favourite and only drink, night and day—except water—not only of our own sturdy boatmen, but of all other sturdy boatmen, as far as my observations went'.[69] If he had made the same journey in 1878 he would probably have expressed a similar view. He had clearly been impressed by the good things of canal-boat life.

Mr Clarke, for many years a missionary to the boating population, enables us to see the situation in its true perspective (and firmly put George Smith into his place in doing so), writing in 1914:

> There was a statement in circulation many years ago . . . that 90 per cent of the boatmen and women on our canals were drunkards . . . this statement was made by an ill-informed and prejudiced writer who made other rash statements about boat people at that time, none of which he could prove, and which contained not a shred of truth that would satisfy a candid enquirer.
>
> That boatmen and boatwomen drank; that a number of them drank far too much and spent time and money in canal-side and way-side public houses they could ill afford was a fact. Yes, alas! I frequently saw in my rambles on the towing path men 'drunk and incapable',

but he estimated that 'at least 70 per cent of the boatmen and women were just moderate drinkers who had only a "little" daily and were never "the worse for drink", while many others were total abstainers'.[70] The reporter of *The Mail* had also judged that 'Comparatively speaking, he [the boatman] is a sober man'.[71]

### HEALTH

Smith insisted that infectious and contagious diseases were rife in canal-boat cabins, to a far greater extent than would be found on shore, and worse, canal boats were the main agents in the transmission of disease from town to town. His stubbornness on this first point was all the more remarkable when, almost universally, friend and foe of George Smith concurred in the view that the canal-boat population was one of the healthiest in England.

In fact, Smith's assertions appeared to be confirmed, for in the *Annual Report of the Local Government Board for 1885* it was recorded:

> The floating population might be expected to be a healthy class, since they live much in the open air, are forced to take a reasonable amount of exercise and earn wages sufficient to procure a proper supply of food. But from a recently published Report of the Registrar General, it would appear that the mortality among them is higher than that of all but a very few classes of the community. Among 'Bargemen, Watermen and Lightermen', between the ages of 25 and 65, the death rate is nearly twice as high as among agricultural labourers.[72]

For there was much that seemed unhealthy about canal-boat life. Drinking water was sometimes taken from the canal, since water points were few and far between, and not all boats carried facilities for storing sufficient quantities of water before the Act of 1884 became fully effective.[73]

Sanitary facilities were very limited. Temple Thurston found it to be so when, as late as 1911, he made delicate enquiries.

> I spoke of this matter one day to Eynsham Harry—I spoke of it with some reserve yet spoke of it because I wished to know. 'What do the women of the barge do in such cases,' I asked, 'when they are miles from any cottage or place of habitation?' 'Do?' said he. 'Why look you, sur—that hedge which runs along by every tow-path. If nature couldn't grow enough leaves on that hedge to hide a sparrow's nest, it ain't no good to God, man nor beast.'[74]

Brydone confirmed that boat people had for long used 'the other side of the hedge'.[75]

Which may have served tolerably well as a convenience, and from a health point of view, in the countryside, but in towns it was a different matter. In Birmingham, for example, toilets by the canal were few in 1921. One witness remarked: 'I have gone on the towpath from Farmers Bridge to Worcester Bar, and I had to put my handkerchief to my nose as the stench was so bad'. In another part of Birmingham the canal company had to clean a part of the tow-path from time to time with chloride of lime.[76] Inadequate sanitary facilities had probably always caused problems where canal boats stopped in towns.

Smith claimed that

> Their habits are filthy and disgusting beyond conception. I have frequently seen
> women in a half nude state washing over the sides of the boat as it was moving along,
> out of the water of the canal, upon the top of which had been floating all manner of
> filth. They wash their clothes—those that do wash—out of the canal water and
> instead of their being white, or near to it, they look as if they had been drawn
> through a mud hole, wrung and hung out upon the boat line to dry.[77]

Boats were often used to transport all kinds of obnoxious substances, particularly from large towns, such as night soil and London slops, usually with little
consideration being paid to the occupants of the cabin. Some of the boats which
the inspectors came across, even after the Acts had laid down tighter regulations
for such vessels, throw light on conditions which must have been more common
before. In 1887,

> Two boats met with carrying offensive cargoes and having no double bulkheads had
> been engaged in carrying bones. The after cabins swarmed with maggots to such an
> extent that they were in a fearful condition and not at all fit for habitation.[78]

Such boats were usually in the last years of their life, being too old, or out-of-
condition, for use with a better class of traffic. The barges employed in bringing
bricks to London, and returning with manure or breeze (refuse from London's
ash-pits), were usually of this type. They were described by Henderson as having
only

> A thin wooden partition, the seams of which are frequently gaping, [as] the only
> division between such a cargo and the cabin which is used as the dwelling-house. The
> filthy condition of the latter . . . is at times therefore indescribable. The cabin indeed
> would become quite uninhabitable if its inmates did not now and again rid them-
> selves of the vermin which overruns them by closing all the apertures and fumigating
> the interior.[79]

Boats which carried other low-value goods were often equally decrepit. Those
involved in the carriage of ironstone, in Staffordshire and Warwickshire, were
'scarcely fit to be used; old and worn out, leaky and therefore very damp, never
painted or well cleaned for years . . . and consequently filthy beyond description'.[80] Here, too, the inhabitants had to resort to fumigation, known technically
as 'smoking them out', or 'bug driving', which consisted of

> stopping up the chimney with a large turf, and all other cracks and openings with soft
> clay, and then burning brimstone inside until the number of their unpleasant com-
> panions is reduced by suffocation. This may be seen any day along the canals.[81]

Under such conditions it would not be surprising to find a high incidence of
disease, and the fears expressed by some medical officers of health (following
Smith's exposures), that diseases were imported into towns by canal boats, would
appear not to be groundless.

In fact, however, the information thrown up by the enforcement of the Canal

Boats Acts does not confirm such suspicions, but, on the contrary, seems to verify the opinions of the largely casual observers that the boat people were a particularly healthy class of people, at least in so far as the great killer diseases of the nineteenth century left them largely unscathed. Whether this was due to a strong resistance to such diseases, or because of a relative isolation from them, is not clear. Cases of infectious diseases notified among boat people were few.[82] Brydone constantly repeated his opinion, after his appointment in 1884, that boat people were remarkably free from infectious diseases.

Of course, such a state of affairs might have been expected to result from the operation of the Acts (by reducing overcrowding and improving sanitary conditions), and probably did so to some extent, but other evidence suggests that boat people had always enjoyed such immunity. In 1885, the Medical Officer of Health and Examining Officer under the Acts at Chesterfield stated that in twelve years' experience he had never known or heard of the occurrence of such diseases on the canal passing through that district.[83] The same authority which had drawn attention to the high death rate among boatmen was, by the following year, expressing a revised opinion.

> Infectious diseases appear to have been of very rare occurrence among the boatmen or their families . . . It would seem indeed that such diseases are less common on canal boats than has been supposed; and the Leeds Urban Sanitary Authority, who have to deal with a large traffic on the waterways in their district, state that only two cases of infectious diseases have been known to them since the date at which the Act of 1877 came into operation.[84]

That the boating population had always been a robust one is suggested by the description of Pickfords' boatmen, who were charged in 1822 with combination and riot.

> The prisoners were all youths between seventeen and twenty years of age, but their robust and manly appearance excited the attention of the magistrates, who could not help remarking the contrast between them and the generality of the London prisoners brought before them.[85]

Nor does there seem to have been any real truth in the assertion that canal boats transmitted diseases, especially in times of epidemic. In his report for 1887 John Brydone wrote, 'It is gratifying to know that, although smallpox has been epidemic in Sheffield, Leeds and neighbourhood, no cases are traceable either from or to canal boats'.[86] He was able to point to a similar escape from a further wave of infectious diseases in 1892.[87]

It seems clear that canal boats were not significant carriers of such diseases. Macleod, from a study of the *Lancet* over this period, observed that, although some sections of the medical profession in the 1870s had feared the spread of infectious diseases through the canal routes, after 1885 their interest waned when it was found to be an unjustified fear.[88]

The point is, of course, that men are not carried away by infectious diseases alone. The reason for a high death rate among the water people becomes clear from the Registrar General's report for the years 1890–2 (see table 9). Unfortunately causes of death were not given in the previous report for 1880–2.

TABLE 9  *Mortality from several causes among occupied bargemen, watermen and lightermen and occupied males in the transport service, as compared with average mortality among all occupied males (the latter being taken as 100 for each medical condition), 1890–2*

|  | Transport service | Bargemen, etc. |
|---|---|---|
| All causes | 128 | 126 |
| Influenza | 109 | 97 |
| Alcoholism | 102 | 131 |
| Rheumatic fever | 100 | 57 |
| Gout | 150 | 0 |
| Cancer | 120 | 102 |
| Phthisis | 116 | 90 |
| Diabetes | 71 | 29 |
| Disorders of nervous system | 113 | 120 |
| Disorders of circulatory system | 130 | 150 |
| Disorders of respiratory system | 147 | 112 |
| Disorders of the liver | 100 | 93 |
| Other disorders of digestive system | 111 | 104 |
| Disorders of urinary system | 120 | 98 |
| Accident | 214 | 393[a] |
| Suicide | 107 | 50 |
| All other causes | 120 | 109 |

*Note*
[a]  Seamen 354.

*Source*  *55th Report of Registrar General (Supplement)*, 1897, p. xxvii, which also gives details of all transport workers.

Nearly all transport workers were exposed to greater risks of accident than the rest of the population, but boatmen were the most accident-prone of all transport men, the dangers even exceeding those of that most hazardous of callings, the sea. Drowning of course was a significant cause of death. The Registrar General's figures included the river men, where the risk of drowning was greater than on the canals, but drownings and other accidents were frequent here also. In 1904 Llewellyn was referring to canals when he remarked, 'Unfortunately the number of deaths from drowning is very large'.[89]

Discounting deaths from accidents, it would probably be found that the health of boatmen, overall, varied little from the norm one way or the other, although, in addition to deaths from accident, boatmen were significantly, and inexplicably, more prone to circulatory diseases, and to the alcoholism already mentioned.

CONCLUSION

The truth about canal-boat life seems to have been that the boats were populated, like the rest of the country, by different types of people, on different kinds of boats, in different circumstances and with different incomes. Probably much of the evidence and many of the conflicting opinions offered were substantially true as far as any one section of the boat population might be concerned.

On the wide northern canals, where the 'narrow boat' was less common, such as on the Rochdale, Leeds and Liverpool, Lancaster, and Bridgewater canals, and on the Yorkshire waterways, where the pay was higher and the living space larger, the people appear on the whole to have been hard-working, decent and respectable people. Of the canal boats on the Leeds and Liverpool canal, in and near Wigan, not one could have been described as being physically overcrowded or indecently occupied, assuming each boat had two cabins, which appears to have been common practice.[90] Very few of the boats registered at Wigan and Burnley between 1879 and 1884 had only one cabin.[91] A similar state of affairs probably prevailed on such broad southern canals as the Kennet and Avon and the Thames and Severn canals, where the boating population was already extremely sparse. At Reading, at the end of the Kennet and Avon canal, only two boats had been registered as dwellings by 1885, and sixteen by 1890.[92]

Many boats were handled by men, and, where such boats were used as dwellings, they were considered to be of a more elevated standard than family boats. Brydone reported, 'I found the cleanest kept boats were almost invariably those on which there was no woman but worked entirely by men'.[93] This was particularly true of fly-boats.[94]

The greatest social problems were to be found among the slow family narrow boats. George Smith was justified in drawing attention to the overcrowding, indecency and squalor in some of these boats and to the indiscipline of some of their occupants. Almost certainly the worst aspects of canal-boat life were found on narrow boats carrying low-value and obnoxious cargoes, paying an insufficient return for a man to be able to afford to keep a house on shore, and leading to a vicious circle of social evils, but even on such boats respectable and hard-working people were often to be found. Such conditions seemed to be most prevalent in Staffordshire and along the southern end of the Grand Junction canal. Inspector Johnson fancied that

> the Worcester and Warwick Canals are favourable specimens; for complaints were made to me by Worcester boatmen that on the Shropshire Union and other canals in the black country the men are very rough in their manners.[95]

If the census reveals that some narrow boats were overcrowded and indecently occupied, it also confirms that more were not. Many boats carried valuable cargoes, and conditions on such boats reflected the greater wealth of their occupants. Drunkenness, while it existed, was far from being the widespread evil that Smith had tried to make out. He had not only exaggerated the incidence of evils, but he had also wilfully exaggerated the numbers involved. He insisted that what was true of the waterway slums was typical of all the boating class, although on one occasion he did admit 'There are many kind-hearted, clean and respectable people amongst them'.[96]

None the less, there were real evils on the canals and it is fair to conclude with the assessment of George Smith by the man who came to hold the position of Canal Boats Inspector that Smith had himself coveted. John Brydone wrote of him:

> However mistaken may have been some of his views and however exaggerated may have been some of the statements his enthusiasm led him to make, still, to him must be accorded the merit of having aroused the attention of parliament to the necessity of legislating for the peculiar conditions of this people and thus to him the canal boat population owe a debt of obligation the full benefit of which they do not give him credit for.[7]

### NOTES TO CHAPTER NINE

[1] Edwin Hodder, *George Smith [of Coalville]; The Story of an Enthusiast* (1896), p. 5.

[2] *Ibid.*, pp. 157–8.

[3] *Ibid.*, p. 255.

[4] *Ibid.*, p. 266.

[5] For full details of this campaign in the country and in Parliament, which resulted in the passing of the Canal Boats Acts of 1877 and 1884, see Macleod, 'Social policy and the "Floating Population". The administration of the Canal Boats Acts, 1877–99', *Past and Present*, 1966; Hodder, *op. cit.*; Smith's own published works.

[6] *Fortnightly Review*, February 1874, reprinted in George Smith, *Our Canal Population: A Cry from the Boat Cabins—With Remedy* (1875; 1879 ed.).

[7] Smith, *Our Canal Population*, p. 9.

[8] *Ibid.*, p. 13.

[9] *Ibid.*, p. 16.

[10] *Ibid.*, pp. 10–11.

[11] *Staffordshire Advertiser*, 18 December 1875, p. 3.

[12] *Factory and Workshops Commission*, 1876, vol. I, appendix C, p. 116.

[13] *Ibid.*, vol. II, q. 10500.

[14] *Ibid.*, 10,814.

[15] *S. C. on Canals*, 1883, q. 2811.

[16] *S. C. on Canal Boats*, 1884, q. 503.

[17] *Factory and Workshops Commission*, 1876, vol. I, appendix C, p. 131.

[18] *Ibid.*, p. 121.

[19] *Ibid.*, p. 124.

[20] *Ibid.*, pp. 130–1.

[21] *S. C. on Canal Boats*, 1884, qq. 615–19.

[22] *Ibid.*, 641, 812–16.

[23] *Census of England and Wales 1871* (henceforward *Census 1871*); vol. IV, *General Report*, 1873 [C. 872–1], p. 94; *ibid.*, 1881, vol. III, *Ages, Conditions as to Marriage, Occupations and Birthplaces*, 1883 [C. 3722], p. xi.

[24] *Census, 1871*, vol. I, *Population Tables: Area, Houses Inhabitants*, 1872, table XII, p. xl, *Census 1881*, vol. II, *Area, Houses and Population*, 1883 [C. 3563], table IV, p. xix.

[25] *R. C. on Labour (group B)*, 1893–4, q. 16897.

[26] *S. C. on Canal Boats*, 1884, appendix 1, p. 75.

[27] *Ibid.*, qq. 46–8.

[28] *Ibid.*, 376.

[29] *Factory and Workshops Commission*, vol. I, 1876, appendix C, p. 136.

[30] *Ibid.*, vol. I, appendix C, p. 118.

[31] *Ibid.*, vol. II, qq. 10503.

[32] *Ibid.*, vol. I, appendix C, p. 136.

[33] *S. C. on Canal Boats*, 1884, q. 186.

[34] *Factory and Workshops Commission*, 1876, vol. I, appendix C, p. 117. No families were known to live on board on the Kennet and Avon canals, although there were a few on the Wiltshire and Berkshire canal; *ibid.*, vol. II, qq. 14206–7.

[35] *Ibid.*, vol. I, appendix C, p. 118.

[36] *Ibid.*, p. 122.

[37] *Ibid.*, vol. II, q. 10,803.

[38] *Ibid.*, 10,479.

[39] *Census 1881*, vol. II, 1883 [C. 3563], table IV, p. xix.

[40] *S. C. on Canal Boats*, 1884, appendix 1, p. 75.

[41] *R. C. on Labour (group B)*, 1893–4, qq. 28386–8.

[42] *Regulations by the Local Government Board under the Canal Boats Act of 1877*, 1878 (103), LXIV.

[43] See Appendix V*a* for other details of the regulations.

[44] *Factory and Workshops Commission*, 1876, vol. I, pp. 121, 126, 128–9; *ibid.*, vol. II, q. 10492.

[45] 1871 Census, RG 10, 3089, Enumeration District 1, pp. 26–7, P.R.O.

[46] R. L. Stevenson, *An Inland Voyage* (1919 ed.), p. 76.

[47] See appendices V*b* and V*d*.

[48] *Household Words*, 18 September 1858, p. 322.

[49] 1871 Census, RG 10, 3722, Enumeration District 6, p. 52, P.R.O.

[50] *S. C. on Canal Boats*, 1884, qq. 856–62.

[51] *20th L. G. B. Report for 1890* (1891), p. 323.

[52] *S. C. on Canal Boats*, 1884, q. 1217.

[53] See Appendix V*a*.

[54] See Appendices V*b* and V*d*.

[55] This particular example, concerning the 18-year-old Phoebe Pearsall, was discussed in the *Coventry Standard*, 22 October 1875, and reprinted in Smith's *Our Canal Population* (1875 ed.), p. 106.

[56] Smith, *Our Canal Population* (1879 ed.), p. 39; *Factory and Workshops Commission*, 1876, vol. II, q. 10834.

[57] *Royal Commission on the Housing of the Working Classes*, 1884, vol. II, 1885 [C. 4402–I], qq. 19, 78, 1467.
19, 78, 1467.

[58] *14th Report of the L. G. B. for 1884* (1885), p. 74.

[59] *Ibid.*

[60] *Factory and Workshops Commission*, vol. I, appendix C, p. 129; see also *ibid.*, p. 119.

[61] *21st L. G. B. Report for 1891* (1892), p. 212.

[62] *Factory and Workshops Commission*, 1876, vol. II, qq. 10504, 10528.

[63] *Birmingham Daily Mail*, 12 March 1875, reprinted in Smith, *Our Canal Population* (1879 ed.), p. 78.

[64] Edwin Hodder, *George Smith [of Coalville]* (1896), pp. 70–1.

[65] *Birmingham Daily Mail*, 12 March 1875, in Smith, *Our Canal Population* (1879 ed.), p. 77.

[66] *Household Words*, 25 September 1858, pp. 356–7.

[67] *Supplement to the 55th Annual Report of the Registrar General . . .*, part II, 1897 [C. 8503], XXI (abbreviated to *55th Report of Registrar General (Supplement)*, 1897, p. xxviii.

[68] However, the high rate of deaths from alcoholism among cabmen and dock labourers can be partly explained by the fact that working as a cabman or as a casual labourer at the docks was the last resort for many alcoholics.

[69] *Household Words*, 18 September 1858, p. 319.

[70] *The Waterman*, April 1914, pp. 38–9.

[71] Extract from *The Mail*, 8 February 1886, 'Maritime Birmingham', in Newspaper Cuttings Relating to Canals, collected by G. H. Osborne, Birm. R. L., 243972.

[72] *15th L. G. B. Report for 1885* (1886), p. civ.

73  *Ibid.*, p. 69.

74  E. Temple Thurston, *The Flower of Gloster* (1911; 1968 ed.) pp. 61–2.

75  MH 25/106, Letter from C. E. de Rance to Local Government Board and subsequent memo, September 1893, 93/93513/Misc., P.R.O.

76  *Committee on Living-in* (Mins. of Evidence), 1921, qq. 1556–7, 1047–8.

77  Smith, *Our Canal Population* (1875 ed.), p. 76.

78  *17th L. G. B. Report for 1887* (1888), pp. 120–1.

79  *Factory and Workshops Commission*, 1876, vol. I, appendix C, p. 129.

80  Letter to George Smith, reprinted in Smith, *Our Canal Population* (1879 ed.), p. 54.

81  *Ibid.*, p. 56.

82  See the numbers involved in the 'Report of the Canal Boat Inspector' in the *Annual Reports of the L. G. B.* (1889 to 1913).

83  *15th L. G. B. Report for 1885* (1886), p. cvi.

84  *16th L. G. B. Report for 1886* (1887), p. cxxv.

85  PIC 4/1, *The Morning Chronicle*, 30 July 1822, in Pickfords: Old Newspaper Cuttings and other Historical Documents, p. 10.

86  *17th L. G. B. Report for 1887* (1888), p. 122.

87  *22nd L. G. B. Report for 1892* (1893), pp. 131–2.

88  Roy M. Macleod, 'Social policy and the "Floating Population". The administration of the Canal Boats Acts, 1877–99', *Past and Present*, (1966), p. 108.

89  *34th L. G. B. Report for 1904* (1905), p. 301.

90  See appendix V*c*.

91  Canal Boat Registers, 1879–84, Burnley and Wigan Public Health Departments.

92  Canal Boat Registers, 1879–90, Reading Public Library (Tilehurst).

93  MH 32/94, John Brydone's Correspondence, 1883–99, 92359½/84, p. 14, P.R.O.

94  *Factory and Workshops Commission*, 1876, vol. I, appendix C, p. 118 (Inspector Redgrave).

95  *Ibid.*, p. 119.

96  Smith, *Our Canal Population* (1875 ed.), p. 76.

97  MH 32/94, 51409/85, pp. 38–9, P.R.O.

# X

# Improvement in the condition of the boat population 1879–1914

## ENFORCEMENT OF THE CANAL BOATS ACTS OF 1877 AND 1884

BROADBRIDGE, IN HIS STUDY of conditions upon midland canal boats, concluded that, in several respects, the Acts which had resulted from Smith's vigorous campaign had brought little improvement by the beginning of the twentieth century. He wrote:

> while cleanliness improved, overcrowding did not. The standards enforced were clearly low, yet they were constantly being infringed, each year showing twenty or thirty cases of overcrowding or inadequate separation of the sexes. As this represents up to ten per cent of the boats it probably means that most boats were overcrowded at some period of the growth of the family.[1]

Although a more critical appraisal of canal-boat life was timely, Broadbridge's conclusions are unnecessarily pessimistic. His assessment of 10 per cent of the boats being overcrowded and having the sexes inadequately separated is incorrect. The statistics presented below (see table 10) show that boats found to be infringing the Acts never rose to 10 per cent of those inspected from 1890 to 1913.

This percentage included boats involved with all types of infringement, many of which were relatively trivial. Registration offences, which might include a misplaced certificate or faded numbering on the boat, accounted for almost half of the total infringements in nearly every year. The more serious contraventions were very few. The details of infringements listed in Appendix VI show that not 10 per cent, but *less than 1·0 per cent* of all boats inspected were found to infringe the 'decency' regulations. And as Brydone had always been quick to point out, many of the cases of overcrowding were caused by a newly-arrived infant, and the female over age was often a daughter who had only recently entered the thirteenth year of age. In an exclusively narrow-boat area—Birmingham—where inspections were diligent and frequent, after the initial onslaught of the enforcement of the Acts, infringements also fell to 10 per cent and below (see table 11).

TABLE 10   *Number of boats infringing regulations of Canal Boats Acts in England and Wales, 1890–1913*

| Year | Number of boats inspected | Boats infringing regulations | |
|---|---|---|---|
| | | Number | % |
| 1890 | 29,575 | 2,331 | 7·8 |
| 1891 | 28,704 | 2,443 | 8·5 |
| 1892 | 31,280 | 2,450 | 7·8 |
| 1893 | 30,630 | 2,287 | 7·4 |
| 1894 | 33,944 | 2,621 | 7·7 |
| 1895 | 32,618 | 2,118 | 6·4 |
| 1896 | 35,443 | 2,385 | 7·1 |
| 1897 | 33,431 | 2,287 | 6·8 |
| 1898 | 35,240 | 2,201 | 6·2 |
| 1899 | 32,165 | 2,303 | 7·1 |
| 1900 | 33,620 | 2,119 | 6·3 |
| 1901 | 32,541 | 2,115 | 6.4 |
| 1902 | 33,158 | 2,655 | 8·0 |
| 1903 | 31,599 | 2,781 | 8·7 |
| 1904 | 33,335 | 2,779 | 8·3 |
| 1905 | 34,375 | 3,017 | 8·5 |
| 1906 | 35,534 | 2,489 | 7·1 |
| 1907 | 35,382 | 2,925 | 8·2 |
| 1908 | 34,617 | 2,656 | 7·6 |
| 1909 | 33,788 | 2,127 | 6·2 |
| 1910 | 34,694 | 2,742 | 7·9 |
| 1911 | 34,746 | 2,998 | 8·7 |
| 1912 | 33,767 | 3,189 | 9·4 |
| 1913 | 32,569 | 2,325 | 7·1 |

*Source*   Compiled from the 'Annual Reports of the Inspector of Canal Boats', found in the *Annual Reports of the Local Government Board* (1890–1913). Full details of these reports are given in the Bibliography.

TABLE 11   *Percentage number of boats infringing the Acts in Birmingham, 1886–1914*

| Year | % of boats infringing the Acts | Year | % of boats infringing the Acts |
|---|---|---|---|
| 1886 | 18·8 | 1903 | 9·7 |
| 1887 | 19·0 | 1904 | 7·1 |
| | | 1905 | 6·3 |
| 1894 | 10·6 | 1906 | 6·0 |
| 1895 | 11·7 | 1907 | 6·2 |
| 1896 | 8·3 | 1908 | 5.1 |
| 1897 | 10·5 | 1909 | 8·8 |
| | | 1910 | 8·4 |
| 1899 | 10·3 | 1911 | 8·4 |
| 1900 | 9·2 | 1912 | 9·0 |
| | | 1913 | 7·3 |
| 1902 | 8·9 | 1914 | 6·4 |

*Source*   Compiled from the *Annual Reports of the Medical Officer of Health . . . of Birmingham* (1886–1914).

These Birmingham boats were guilty of all kinds of offences under the Acts, many of them trivial, serious contraventions being relatively rare.

It is true that there were imperfections in the enforcement of the Acts. Both chief inspectors expressed their concern that sometimes as many as 6,000 inspections, supposedly carried out in certain districts, invariably found boats to be perfect year after year. One Thames-side inspector admitted that, although his records showed over a hundred inspections a year, he had never actually been on board a canal boat.[2] Obviously, this meant that boats used as dwellings remaining in such a district, and boats passing through such a district, would be untroubled by inspectors, save very occasionally by the chief inspector. However, most boats used as dwellings passed through several sanitary districts, and other inspectors more than made up for the laxity of a few of their colleagues. Inspections tended to be more perfunctory where the canal-boat inspector was the sanitary inspector of a small sanitary district, being paid little or nothing for the extra duties involved. The fact that there were such perfunctory inspections, becoming fewer after 1900,[3] is more than offset by the fact that the nationwide total of infringements included the same contraventions, on the same boats, being recorded over and over again, as they passed from one district to another, until the faults could be rectified.

It was, perhaps, as well that there were these dormant areas, or the life of the boat people must have become intolerable, as at times it came close to being. Llewellyn, the newly-appointed Chief Inspector of Canal Boats, revealed that

> Round Birmingham, as round many other big towns, the boat people often raise the cry of over-inspection. The master of a pair of boats complained to me one evening at Salford that the inspector there was the sixth who wanted to see his papers that day.[4]

When it is considered that the number of canal boats used as dwellings declined in the quarter of a century before 1914 whilst the number of boats inspected remained constant, the conclusion of the Birmingham Medical Officer of Health in 1906 seems particularly apt.

> The vigour with which the Canal Boats Acts and the Regulations made thereunder are carried out all over this country is quite exemplary; indeed, it may be a question as to whether in many districts the boats are not over-inspected.[5]

The actual number of boats used as dwellings at any one time is difficult to arrive at since, once on the register, abandoned and destroyed boats were slow to get off it. In 1891, Brydone estimated that of the 11,827 boats on the register, 10,000 would more than represent those used as dwellings.[6] This was almost certainly an overestimate since, by the end of 1896, only 7,820 dwelling boats were known to be working.[7] Another serious effort to establish the true number in 1908 produced 6,354 boats which had actually been seen and inspected.[8] In practice, more inspectors were searching fewer boats, and they were thus inspecting the same boats repeatedly. That obstructions to the local inspectors by the boatmen were so few was, in the circumstances, quite remarkable. Already, by 1885, it could be noted that 'although the class have a reputation for bad language and rough manners, scarcely a single instance has been reported in which an inspector's interference has been resented'.[9]

As for the standards enforced being 'clearly low', it could be argued that the exact opposite was the case. Obviously the framers of the regulations under the Acts recognised the limitations of canal boats as compared with houses when it came to the numbers allowed to occupy their cabins. On the other hand, even if the sanitary inspector had similar powers to those granted by the Canal Boats Acts, in relation to the land population in his area, it seems unlikely that he would have had the time, inclination or courage to attempt to enforce them with the vigour with which the Canal Boats Acts were implemented, with the exception perhaps of common lodging houses. One can hardly envisage sanitary inspectors calling upon and entering a house six times a day, or even thirteen times a year,[10] to ensure that the householder had a valid certificate; that the dwelling was in a 'cleanly and habitable condition'; that it had been painted within the last three years; that females over 12 years were not sleeping in the same room as a man and his wife, nor males over the age of 14 years in like circumstances; that rooms occupied as a sleeping place by a person of the male sex above the age of 14 years was not occupied by a female over 12 years, unless she were the wife of the male; and much besides.[11] This last edict made the living together of a man and woman, as man and wife in an unmarried state, illegal, and this provision was actually enforced in at least two instances; one of them resulting in a prosecution, which in fact failed.[12]

### BENEFICIAL RESULTS OF THE ACTS

The vast improvement which had taken place in all aspects of canal-boat life by the early twentieth century is indisputable. Not only did the Chief Inspector of Canal Boats, and all the local inspectors, claim that it was so, but their claims are verified by others equally knowledgeable of canal life. The Reverend S. Ventham was certainly reflecting the opinions of many when he said, in 1912, 'There is a general consension [*sic*] of opinion that the moral intellectual and spiritual condition of . . . canal boatmen has vastly improved of late years'.[13] The organisation which he represented—The Seamen and Boatmen's Friend Society—freely admitted that 'Legislation has played an important part in improving the lot and conditions of life of our boatpeople', although it was probably justified in some measure in claiming that

> through the efforts put forth by the Society, much has been done to elevate the social, moral and spiritual life of our boat people and their children. Today nearly all have homes ashore and have elevated ideas of home life. Immorality once the rule is now the exception and it is regarded as a disgrace by nearly everyone.[14]

John Brydone confirmed that the society had done much good work.[15]

Improvement resulted from the first Canal Boats Act of 1877, but only on a limited scale, since many local authorities did little beyond registering the boats to be used as dwellings, the Act being otherwise largely permissive. Also, by a quirk of law, those authorities attempting to enforce the Act were inhibited by a decision in 1881, in Manchester, which ruled that proceedings could be taken against owners and boatmen for evading the Act, but not for evading the subsequent Local Government Board regulations.[16] None the less, the mere existence of the Act, the process of registration, and the efforts of some local authorities (Runcorn for example was a particularly active area)[17] did have some effect in reducing overcrowding, not least through teenage girls leaving the boats for domestic service. Smith admitted, 'To a certain extent it has been [beneficial] but not altogether so'.[18]

Even this limited impact of the Act was soon to fade as enforcement remained sketchy. In 1884, after the amended Act had brought compulsion and a central inspector, the newly required annual reports from local authorities to the Local Government Board were 'alike in declaring that hitherto so little has been done beyond registration that they are not prepared with any lengthy report for 1884'.[19]

The 1884 Act did result in rapid and dramatic improvement. Already, by 1885, John Brydone could report,

> The progress made in restriction of the number of people occupying the cabins has become very noticeable, it being seldom now that one meets with more than the number for which the boat is actually registered . . . [and] the diminution in the number of girls on board is very observable.

Girls over 12 continued to find their way into domestic service. The cleanliness and habitable condition of the canal-boat cabins had also markedly improved. The whole tone of waterway life was elevated.[20] Boatmen increasingly took homes on shore, and more left their wives and children there while they continued to work the boat with their sons or a hired hand.

Most boatmen soon came to welcome the Act. It resulted in an improvement in living conditions by pressure being exerted upon the owners of boats, a pressure which the boatmen had, perhaps, been afraid to put upon their employers. Most canal-boat inspectors came to be recognised as friends of the boating class, to whom the boatmen were able to point out faults in the boats, secure in the knowledge that the employers would be forced to rectify them.[21]

In this respect it suited the boatmen to co-operate, but it must be admitted that there were those who adopted devious means to evade those regulations which suited them less. Surplus children might be unloaded at the beginning of a zealous inspector's territory, to rejoin the boat on the other side. If the inspector discovered irregularities in the shape of too many children or the wrong mixture of teenage sexes, the boat people were ever ready with the answer that such children were merely visiting for the day and not sleeping on the boat, were helping with the locks, or some other cock-and-bull story.[22] Equally, some boat owners—not the large carrying companies—were found to adopt devious means to evade the Acts.[23] Such practices were more frequent in the early days, but some boatmen, of course, were always to be found 'trying it on', as one exasperated carrier discovered in 1910. He had to explain to the Nantwich inspector that,

> When the steerer told you that I had a 'letter etc.', he told a lie. He informed me he had 2 children only and it would appear he has been keeping the 3rd in the background. These boatmen are a troublesome lot. It would make life much more pleasant if they would speak the truth and keep off the beer.[24]

Telling lies seems to have been one of the boatmen's special fortes, which proved resistant to improving influences. 'There is a good deal of trickery—on the canal side—trickery in little things' wrote E. Clarke.

> I have seen it frequently. Men trick each other up and down the locks, they trick each other about cargoes, and many other things. They don't 'play the game' always. They try to 'do' one another. If they think they can gain some small advantage they are quite ready with a 'fib'—a dozen of them if need be.[25]

However, those who persistently evaded the Acts were usually found out in the end, and the beneficial impact of legislation on the boating class, as a whole, cannot be denied.

### THE DRIFT FROM THE WATERWAYS

The boatmen adapted themselves to the 'overcrowding' and 'indecent occupation' regulations in several ways. As we have seen, many girls over 12 were pushed out into domestic service. Some boatmen began to work two boats in order to distribute their family between two cabins.[26] Others made use of a small cabin erected in the bows of the boat. This was never a very satisfactory arrangement, since, owing to the position, passage through locks left it invariably damp, as well as being cramped.[27] Finally, the boatmen's wives and children took land homes and deserted the waterways. In the long term it is clear that the first and last expedients were the ones generally adopted, not only from the rather suspect census data, but also from the observations of the inspectors. This, as we have seen, was apparently a trend already in evidence before legislation was passed, and, in the long run, one speeded up by it.[28]

The 1891 Census figures reveal a significant reversal in the trend. There are two possible, and probably complementary, explanations for this. Firstly, they almost certainly confirm other evidence that the decline in living-in was a disjointed process, a fact which census evidence, collected at ten-year intervals, is not generally sufficiently sophisticated to capture. The mid-1880s (c. 1884–7) were particularly unfavourable to the boating population. Mr George, in 1884, observed the beginnings of a short-term reversal of the trend towards living on shore.

> There has been a decrease in the number of children in the boats up to within a very recent period; there has been a little check in that lately in consequence of the great depression of trade; the people have not earned so much, and have not been able in two or three instances that I know of to keep up their homes on shore.[29]

Unusually severe weather conditions added to the difficulties created by the years of economic slump, which continued through the mid-1880s, when the freight rates paid to boatmen were reduced, if indeed work could be found at all in some areas. Inspectors remarked upon the increasing number of women and children to be found on board, as boatmen were compelled to break up their land home as their savings became exhausted, for not only did the boatman have to keep himself and his family, but he had often also to purchase feed for the horse as well as pay stable rent.[30] Boatmen employed by large companies built up substantial debts by way of advances. Even when commercial prosperity returned to the waterways, in 1888, although work increased and freight rates rose, another severe bout of frost in February and March of that year, and again in the winter of 1890,[31] delayed recovery of the boatmen's finances sufficient for them once again to be able to contemplate taking homes on shore in significant numbers.

The second explanation of the increase in the numbers sleeping on board in 1891, and particularly males, is that, in spite of the difficulties in the 1880s, the general prosperity of canal trading around the turn of the decade had attracted more men into it and, especially, a growth in the number of fly-boats had resulted in more men sleeping on board.

The 1890s saw a return to the practice of taking shore homes, apart from a significant set-back resulting again from a severe frost in the winter of 1895, when many of the canals were closed for from seven to eight weeks.[32] The data of the Census of 1901 are no doubt a true reflection of the permanent decline in the practice of living upon canal boats and the increasing drift from canal employment generally.[33] In 1900 the different local authorities were of the 'opinion that a continuous decrease has taken place in the number of women and children found on board'.[34] The number of females on the Shropshire Union Company's boats had fallen significantly:[35]

| Year | Number of boats | Number of females |
|------|-----------------|-------------------|
| 1884 | 363 | 189 |
| 1902 | 450 | 151 |

The fact that the decline was an uneven process, with women and children returning to the boats in hard times, is an interesting phenomenon. Llewellyn remarked on the fact that 'the better trade is on the canals, the fewer are the women and children found on the boats'.[36] Similar observations had been made frequently before. It would seem to prove John Hemelryk's theory that the permanent boating population had always been a very elastic one, waxing and waning with bad or good times. However, whereas in the earlier years of the nineteenth century each period of depression had brought more on to the boats, resulting in more living aboard, it is now clear that the opposite was taking place in the half century or so before 1914. Bad times attracted fewer and fewer boaters back to living on their boats.

From around 1900, however, the number of women and children on board seems to have remained fairly constant, at a very low figure. Llewellyn remarked, virtually every year, that the numbers of women and children showed little tendency to fall in those years, except where steam traction was rendering family boats redundant. The missionaries at Leeds, for example, were gratified

> to note that the number of women and children on the boats seems to diminish year by year. This is chiefly due to the increase of steam towage, which enables the men to make quicker passage and to get home more frequently.[37]

But where the narrow boat predominated, where steam haulage was uneconomic, a sticking point seems to have been reached. Unfortunately the number of women and children sleeping on board boats appears not to have been recorded in the Census of 1911, but the post-war statistics (listed in Appendix IV*d*) go some way to confirming Llewellyn's view that women and children had perhaps ceased to leave narrow boats in significant numbers from around 1900.

Indeed, there was no marked decline in the number of women and children on board the boats passing through Birmingham from as early as 1894 (see table 12).

TABLE 12  *Women and children as percentages of occupants on board boats passing through Birmingham, 1894–1914*

| Year | Women | Children | Year | Women | Children |
|------|-------|----------|------|-------|----------|
| 1894 | 20·4 | 24·4 | 1908 | 22·0 | 20·9 |
| 1895 | 19·1 | 22·5 | 1909 | 20·2 | 24·0 |
| 1896 | 18·7 | 22·2 | 1910 | 21·3 | 26·2 |
|      |      |      | 1911 | 23·9 | 25·9 |
| 1902 | 20·2 | 21·0 | 1912 | 23·4 | 26·1 |
|      |      |      | 1913 | 22·3 | 24·7 |
| 1907 | 20·7 | 20·8 | 1914 | 22·3 | 22·6 |

*Source*  Compiled from the *Annual Reports of the Medical Officer of Health on the Health of the City of Birmingham* (1895–1915).

However, such statistics thrown up by the inspection of boats mask many possible distortions of the existing state of affairs, and although these Birmingham figures are more stable than some others produced by inspectors, it would be foolish to put too much faith in them. The census material has of course equally grave disadvantages, but, in conjunction with Llewellyn's opinion, it seems probable that the exodus of women and children from the boats was slowing down from near the end of the nineteenth century.

Economic and other influences had probably led many of those women, who had always retained connections with the land, to remain there permanently and even to persuade their husbands to cut their ties with a boating life if need be, rather than return to the canal in bad times. Most of those families remaining on the boats were probably that hard core of boat dwellers who had always lived permanently on board. Such people were least susceptible to outside influences. They loved their way of life too much, they were fearful of the unknown world on land, or inadequacy and inertia continued to keep them in the paths of their forefathers. This permanent population was few in number. As early as 1892 John

Brydone had estimated that 1,000 would be the total number of boats acting as permanent homes.[38]

THE SEAMEN AND BOATMEN'S FRIEND SOCIETY

In some spheres the Boatmen's Friend Society could probably claim more credit for improvement than the legislators. The society had commenced operations in London in 1846, as the Seamen's Society. After the amalgamation with the Inland Navigation Society in 1851, as the Seamen and Boatmen's Friend Society, it extended its work to canal people, although it was not until the 1870s that it began to expand significantly. By 1910 it was organised into seven large districts, each having sub-districts attached to them, 'thus practically covering most of the available space where men . . . may be met on the canals of England'.[39]

This society got through to the boat people where others had failed. One old boatman told one of the Society's missionaries:

> Well, governor, I must say that the likes of you have helped us chaps a good deal. I have been a boatman over fifty years, so I can speak like what I know, and that is, that the boat people are a better lot of people than they were, and the likes of you men have done it.[40]

The provision of alternative diversions, other than the public house, by this society, did much to combat the evil of drunkenness. The Registrar General commented on the lower mortality from alcoholism among bargemen in the period 1900–2, as compared with 1890–2.[41] Already by 1888 Brydone could remark that,

> one circumstance has impressed itself upon me very much, and that is, that I have not met with this year a single case of drunkenness and the opinion among the local inspectors is that in this respect, as in many others, the greatest improvement is visible.[42]

Beginning with primitive mission rooms, the society increasingly began to provide rest rooms with recreational facilities and non-alcoholic refreshment, as well as periodic functions in them. At Leeds, the report for 1911 makes clear that a long-established aim of the society was to cater for other than the spiritual needs of the boatmen in declaring:

> your Committee realize that there is also a social side to the Boatman's life, to which the low-class Music Hall and Public House appeals, and they have striven to counteract the influence of such places by making the Institute as bright and attractive as their means permit.

Reference to a kitchen and washhouse also bears testimony to the practical needs of the boatmen being catered for.[43] The Birmingham society had written fifty-four letters for the boatmen in 1908, no doubt reflecting long-established practice.[44]

Such practical help, with regard to the problems peculiar to the boatmen, inspired their confidence, as also did the character of the men employed as full-time missionaries. There was 'nothing of the stiff clerical element about them'.

They were

> Bluff, hearty and even jovial in their intercourse with the men and women in the floating homes, and I could see with great pleasure how it was they were looked upon as such good friends of the boatmen and his little ones,

wrote the 'special commissioner'.[45] They were as likely to pass the time of day with the boatmen as to exhort them to leave their path of wickedness and sin, a more common approach by others not of the society. The missionaries visited them in their homes and boats, invariably bringing with them a keen understanding of waterway life, practical help and advice and, above all, friendliness.

And it was this last, brought by missionaries and many canal-boat inspectors, which probably played the most important part in causing such dramatic changes in the boaters' outlook. For long they had felt cut off and rejected by society. Now they felt that there was a genuine concern being expressed for their peculiar needs and problems, to which they responded in kind. As Brydone put it, in 1892:

> The boatman has realised that his position is not that of the despised member of society he was once considered. Under the good influences of so many agencies he has become another proof of what can be accomplished by persuasive efforts, . . . [and] it is a most remarkable fact that there is not one of the local inspectors against whom I ever now hear the slightest word of complaint from any of the boat people, but on the contrary, in many instances, I have been told of many acts of friendship experienced from them.[46]

### IMPROVEMENTS IN THE HEALTH OF THE BOATING CLASS

Apart from the decline in drinking, other factors where combining to improve the health of boatmen, especially that of younger boatmen. The gap between the death rates of boatmen and others narrowed (see table 13).

TABLE 13    *Death rates of males in the age group 24–45, during the periods 1900–2, 1890–2, 1880–2 and the years 1860, 1861 and 1871* (%)

|  | 1860, 1861, 1871 | 1880–2 | 1890–2 | 1900–2 |
|---|---|---|---|---|
| Occupied males | – | 9·71 | 9·52 | 7·84 |
| All males | 11·27 | 10·16 | 9·99 | 8·38 |
| Bargemen, watermen and lightermen | 14·99 | 14·25 | 13·04 | 10·98 |

*Source   65th Report of Registrar General (Supplement)*, 1908, table vii, p. cci.

In comparing the period 1900–2 with 1890–2, the Registrar General remarked upon the lower mortality from alcoholism and liver disease, as well as from tuberculous phthisis and from diseases of the nervous, circulatory and respiratory systems, and from accident. Deaths from rheumatic fever, diabetes mellitus, Bright's disease and suicide had increased.[47] Unfortunately the data for the two periods seem not to be strictly comparable, and it is difficult to assess the proportional decline in the various diseases; nor is light thrown upon the reasons for the declines.

However, it would seem not unlikely that the health of young boatmen benefited for the same reasons that the health of other young people improved. McKeon and Record, in an interesting and convincing piece of medical detection, came to the conclusion that the reasons for the falling death rate in the second half of the nineteenth century were as follows, and in the following order of importance: (*a*) a rising standard of living, of which the most significant result was an improved diet; (*b*) the hygienic changes introduced by the sanitary reformers; (*c*) a favourable trend in the relationship between the infectious agent and the human host; (*d*) the effect of therapy, which was restricted to smallpox and hence had only a trivial effect on the total reduction of the death rate.[48]

There is no reason to assume that the boatmen did not, like the rest of the population, benefit from falling prices during the 'Great Depression', and in particular from falling food prices,[49] which gave the working classes a wider and better diet, also in part facilitated by the consumption revolution which these falling prices produced.[50]

It would also be reasonable to assume that the Public Health Acts, especially the one of 1875, benefited the health of boatmen, by ensuring better urban conditions, since many of the canal boatmen and almost all the river boatmen (who continue, by their intrusion, to cloud the issue) lived on land, wholly or partially.

However, this does not explain why the gap between boatmen and others narrowed. Three additional factors suggest themselves. The Canal Boats Acts contributed, by reducing the death rate of those who lived wholly on board, and proved a double bonus to those who lived partly on board and partly on land. These Acts also contributed by playing a part in the reduction of drinking on the canals; by alleviating some of the causes of such drinking and by their psychological effects upon the boating population. Deaths from alcoholism were significantly reduced.

McKeon and Record insisted that the advances in medical knowledge and practice played little part in the reduction in the death rate before 1900, despite the discovery of anaesthesia which greatly increased the possibilities of surgery, and the knowledge of antisepsis which added to its safety. This may have been true for the population as a whole, but, obviously, men who worked in an accident-prone industry would benefit much more from advances in surgical knowledge and safety, and from improved nursing, especially towards the end of the century. Accidents which had previously proved fatal did not now necessarily end in tragedy, and this may be a third reason for the narrowing of the gap. It must be made clear however that fatal accidents remained high; bargemen (etc.) having fallen only to second place, below seamen, in the league table of deaths from accident by occupation.[51]

These conclusions are mainly conjecture. Suffice it to say that the health of boatmen improved rapidly towards the end of the century, and more rapidly than the rest of the population, though the death rate among boatmen remained above average.

It might be reasonable to assume that the health of canal-boat women also improved, although there are no statistics at all on this matter. There were those who assumed that the practice of giving birth to children in canal boats would not only be detrimental to the health of the mother, but would also result in a high infant mortality rate. J. Doig McCrindle, the Assistant Medical Officer of Health for Birmingham, calculated, from a survey of boats, that infant mortality stood at around 30 per cent, or twice as high as the rate for Birmingham.[52] The method by which he arrived at these figures (by asking the boatmen and women) renders them virtually useless. Later evidence suggests that infant mortality was surprisingly low. The nurse at Brentford had, by 1920, known only one infant death and no deaths of women in childbirth.[53] Whittam, the manager of the Shropshire Union Company, remarked, in 1920:

> it is a remarkable fact that on the Company's boats rarely, if ever, has mother or child been lost, whilst the infant mortality on the boats is exceptionally low, the children being invariably born healthy and strong. Deformed births are practically unknown and imbecility a rarity.[54]

Unfortunately, the veracity of any assertion in this direction hangs upon the opinions of two people, at a date when revolutionary changes had taken place in childbirth throughout the country. However, such opinions are verified in part by Llewellyn, who had observed twenty years before that 'Those who have been inside the cabin of a narrow boat will be surprised that the number of deaths during and after confinement are so exceedingly few'.[55]

### CONCLUSION

In spite of the imperfections of the enforcement of the Canal Boats Acts it would be fair to conclude that, along with other influences, they had been successful in causing a vast improvement in the whole tone of waterway life. Not least had the Acts succeeded (in conjunction no doubt with other economic and social factors) in significantly reducing the size of the population which was exposed to the disadvantages of canal life. By 1911 the waterway population, exclusive of river boatmen, day-boatmen and maintenance men must have been below 20,000 and, of these, probably fewer than 7,000 lived permanently on board.[56] How many women and children continued to live on board, permanently or temporarily, is difficult to assess, but by general testimony they had been greatly reduced in number, and there were probably not more than a few thousand. Those who were in a position to know compared the boating class very favourably with workers of a similar class on land.

At the same time it would be wrong to paint an unrealistic picture of the virtues of boatmen and boating. Although matters had in no way been as bad as Smith had painted them, there had been real evils and real slum boats. The evils had been much reduced and slum boats improved, but even if slum boats were fewer they were still to be found. As the inspector for Heston and Isleworth had remarked, back in 1891,

> The Acts are in my opinion certainly working well for the lifting up of the people occupying canal boats, and cleanliness and the preventing of overcrowding are the great means; there are exceptions, and I fear for years always will be.[57]

In 1904 the Medical Officer of Health for the Port of Manchester confirmed that there were still potential exceptions. He warned that 'If the inspection be in any way lax or inefficient, these boats will be found to fall far short of the attainment of sanitary efficiency'.[58] That there continued to be slum boats down to recent times is clear from Rolt's admission, in 1944, that 'the canal folk are either scrupulously clean or unbelievably squalid'. His explanation that 'on investigation the latter class usually turn out to be a family "off the land", the new poor without pride who are the product of industrial cities',[59] is hardly a satisfactory one.

Boatmen still drank more than missionaries thought was good for them, as no doubt did the rest of the population. 'Some of our Boatmen are still too fond of the public house; they like the drink and will have it; and there are such facilities for getting it; so many pubs on and near the canal side', wrote Mr Clarke in 1914.[60] Drunken excesses could still be found.[61] And boatmen were still ready to settle their differences by violence.

> Boatmen, and boatwomen, too, quarrel. They quarrel over little things as many other people do and quarrelling sometimes leads to fighting. I have seen in my time, a good deal of quarrelling and not a little fighting, on the canal side,[62]

Clarke wrote.

None the less there is no reason to deny the opinion expressed by William Bagnall, a 60-year-old boatman, that life on the canals had 'improved in everything to what it was when I was a boy . . . [the boats] more clean and decent . . . Everything has improved'.[63] Nor can we disagree with the conclusion of the 1921 Departmental Committee that, 'so far as health, cleanliness, morality, feeding and clothing are concerned, they are fully equal, if not superior, to town dwellers of a similar class'.[64]

## NOTES TO CHAPTER TEN

[1] S. R. Broadbridge, 'Living conditions on midland canal boats', *Transport History*, vol. III (1970), p. 44.

[2] *31st Annual Report of the Local Government Board for 1901* (1902), p. 166 (henceforward abbreviated to *L. G. B. Report*).

[3] *37th L. G. B. Report for 1907* (1908), p. 94.

[4] *29th L. G. B. Report for 1899* (1900), p. 194.

[5] 'Report on the conditions of life under which canal boat children are reared', *Annual Report of Medical Officer of Health . . . of Birmingham for 1905, Supplement* (1906), p. 1.

[6] *21st L. G. B. Report for 1891* (1892), p. 208.

[7] *26th L. G. B. Report for 1896* (1897), p. 149.

[8] *39th L. G. B. Report for 1909* (1910), p. 83.

[9]  *15th L. G. B. Report for 1885* (1886), p. cvi.

[10]  *29th L. G. B. Report for 1899* (1900), p. 185.

[11]  *Regulations by the Local Government Board under the Canal Boats Act of 1877*, 1878 (103), LXIV. See also the list of possible contraventions in Appendix VI.

[12]  *18th L. G. B. Report for 1888* (1889), p. 207, and *26th L. G. B. Report for 1896* (1897), p. 154. In the first case the inspector persuaded the boatman to marry the woman he was living with, in the second the magistrate felt that the Act did not cover such cases.

[13]  *The Waterman*, January 1912, p. 3.

[14]  *Ibid.*, November 1911, p. 122.

[15]  *20th L. G. B. Report for 1890* (1891), p. 323.

[16]  *S. C. on Canals*, 1883, qq. 3377, 3384–5, 3389.

[17]  Smith, *Canal Adventures by Moonlight* (1881), p. 149.

[18]  *S. C. on Canals*, 1883, q. 3088.

[19]  *14th L. G. B. Report for 1884* (1885), p. 74.

[20]  *15th L. G. B. Report for 1885* (1886), pp. civ, 70, 72.

[21]  *19th L. G. B. Report for 1889* (1890), p. 219.

[22]  *Ibid.*, p. 218.

[23]  *Ibid.*, p. 216.

[24]  Letter, T. and C. Southall to Canal Boats Inspector, August 1910, Canal Boat File, Nantwich Public Health Department.

[25]  *The Waterman*, November 1914, p. 126.

[26]  *17th L. G. B. Report for 1887* (1888), p. 116.

[27]  *18th L. G. B. Report for 1888* (1889), p. 206.

[28]  See Appendix IVd.

[29]  *S. C. on Canal Boats*, 1884, q. 305.

[30]  *16th L. G. B. Report for 1886* (1887), p. 173; *17th L. G. B. Report for 1887* (1888), pp. 115–26, and p. cxxxv.

[31]  *18th L. G. B. Report for 1888* (1889), pp. 203–4; *20th L. G. B. Report for 1890* (1891), p. 223.

[32]  *25th L. G. B. Report for 1895* (1896), pp. 240, 250.

[33]  See Appendices IVc and IVd.

[34]  *30th L. G. B. Report for 1900* (1901), p. 216.

[35]  SURC 1/25, 19 March 1902, minute 21741.

[36]  *35th L. G. B. Report for 1905* (1906), p. 83.

[37]  *13th Annual Report of the Incorporated Seamen and Boatmen's Friend Society (North Eastern District) for 1912* (1913), p. 11, Leeds Reference Library, 266 IN 2L.

[38]  *R. C. on Labour (group B)*, 1893–4, q. 17196.

[39]  *The Waterman*, October 1910, p. 209.

[40]  *Ibid.*, November 1910, p. 233.

[41]  *65th Report of Registrar General (Supplement)*, 1908 [Cd. 2619], XVIII, p. xli.

[42]  *18th L. G. B. Report for 1888* (1889), p. 215.

[43]  *12th Annual Report of the Incorporated Seamen and Boatmen's Friend Society (North Eastern District) for 1911* (1912), p. 13, Leeds Reference Library, 266 IN 2L.

[44]  *46th Annual Report of the Incorporated Seamen and Boatmen's Friend Society (Birmingham District) for 1908* (1909), p. 9, Birm. R.L., 21947 (in. 239999). .

[45]  Extract from the *Birmingham Daily Mail*, 5 March 1875, in Smith, *Our Canal Population* (1879 ed.), p. 70.

[46]  *22nd L. G. B. Report for 1892* (1893), p. 135.

[47]  *Ibid.*, p. xli.

[48]  T. McKeon and R. C. Record, 'Reasons for the decline of mortality in England and Wales during the nineteenth century', *Population Studies*, vol. 16 (1962–3), p. 120.

[49]  See above, pp. 91–6.

[50]  Charles Wilson, 'Economy and society in late Victorian Britain', *Economic History Review*, 2nd Series, vol. 18, No. 1 (August 1965), pp. 183–98.

[51] *65th Report of Registrar General (Supplement)*, 1908, p. xxxvii and table v, p. cxci.

[52] 'Report on the conditions of life under which canal boat children are reared', *Annual Report of Medical Officer of Health . . . of Birmingham for 1905, Supplement*, 1906, p. 8, Birm. R.L. 194999.

[53] *Committee on Living-in*, 1921 (Mins. of Evid.), qq. 1942–6.

[54] *Ibid.*, appendix L, p. 85.

[55] *30th L. G. B. Report for 1900* (1901), p. 218.

[56] See Appendix ivd for the total number of people sleeping on board in 1901.

[57] *21st L. G. B. Report for 1891* (1892), p. 217.

[58] *34th L. G. B. Report for 1904* (1905), p. 301.

[59] L. T. C. Rolt, *Narrow Boat* (1944; 1965 ed.), p. 36.

[60] *The Waterman*, April 1914, p. 39.

[61] *Ibid.*, February 1910, p. 113.

[62] *Ibid.*, June 1914, p. 68.

[63] *Committee on Living-in*, 1921 (Mins. of Evid.), qq. 2229–31.

[64] *Ibid.*, (Report), p. 4, paragraph 7.

# XI

# Canal-boat children
## Their condition
## in the half-century
## before 1914

### THE MISERY OF CANAL-BOAT CHILDREN

GEORGE SMITH had always insisted that the children upon the canals were his prime concern. They were

> growing up in the cabins in the most heathenish ignorance and squalor, receiving the most cruel treatment from the boaters—knocked 'from pillar to post'—thrashed, kicked and beaten with ropes, sticks and heavy-ironed boots, until many of the boys and girls become as stupid as the asses they drive.[1]

He spoke of the 'child slavery which the canal children have to endure in toiling and trudging on and after the canal boats from fourteen to sixteen hours daily, winter and summer'.[2]

He invariably spoke or wrote upon these matters in general terms, but he did, on occasion, give details of particular overworked and ill-treated children.[3] Many of these instances were convincingly denied, or clearly proved to be wild exaggerations.[4] On the other hand there was much about canal-boat life which would seem detrimental to the well-being of children. Hollingshead, in 1858, pointed to a few of the drawbacks, for some children at least, in this way of life.

> The youngest of these helpless little ones, dirty, ragged, and stunted in growth, are confined in the close recesses of the cabin . . . stuck round the bed, like images upon a shelf; sitting upon the cabin-seat; standing in pans and tubs; rolling helplessly upon the floor, within a few inches of a fierce fire, and a steaming kettle; leaning over the edge of the boat in the little passage between the cabin doorway and the tiller-platform, with their bodies nearly in the water; lying upon the poop with no barrier to protect them from being shaken into the canal; fretful for want of room, air and amusement; always beneath the feet of the mother, and being cuffed and scolded for that which they cannot avoid; sickly, even under their sunburnt skins; waiting wearily for the time when their little limbs will be strong enough to trot along the towing-path; or dropping suddenly over the gaudy sides of the boat, quietly into the open, hungry arms of death . . . Not a week passes, but one of these canal-children is

drowned in the silent by-way upon which they were born; and, painful as the incident is, it is too common to excite much observation.[5]

There is no doubt, too, that young children did help in driving the horse, in steering and unloading the boats, and in opening the locks. Their mere presence in proximity to these activities exposed them to dangers. Also, since boats were often hidden from the public gaze and from outside supervision, there was little, on many canals, to prevent unscrupulous parents from demanding more from their children than was really good for them. Living conditions were, on the face of it, not conducive to the moral and physical well-being of such children. They were denied advantages which other children had. Such children were often not vaccinated against smallpox, for instance.[6] Limited contact with the outside world and restricted educational opportunities condemned most children to follow their parents along the same ignorant paths.

A feature of canal life which particularly put young children at risk was the practice of loaning, giving away and even selling children to other boatmen and women, sometimes to complete strangers. The story of Elizabeth Lowkes was a sad demonstration of the evils which could result. She had been given by her father to a 23-year-old boatman, Frederick Musson, and Ann Maria Hillman, 21, presumably to help them with their boat. She received such cruel treatment from them that before she was 8 years old she was dead. A particularly severe beating at Aldersley Junction on the night of 31 July 1875 had proved too much.[7] In January 1877 a similar case at Runcorn fanned the sense of public outrage, which George Smith was careful to keep on the boil.[8]

Another instance of the practice was brought to light, again at Runcorn, when a reporter of the *Warrington Guardian* jumped upon a boat at the wharf there, and on being asked how many children she had the boatwoman said that she had:

> 'One of her own and one given to her.' 'Given to you.' I said, 'What do you mean?' 'Well this 'ere lad,' said the woman of a lad of about twelve years of age, 'he was gin to me.'[9]

The practice did not end with the Acts of 1877 and 1884. Legislation may even have increased the problem, since more, and younger, children had to be 'pushed out of the nest'. In 1903 the N.S.P.C.C. had come to hear of two boys on a canal boat who were being ill-treated and made to work all through the night. They were not the sons of the boatman employing them. Their father was found to be a man who had previously been warned in 1897 for ill-treating his sons, but he now claimed to have no responsibility for them since, four years before, he had legally transferred them to the other boatman. This 'legal transfer' was embodied in a document in the form of a will. It read; 'I William so-and-so give and bequeath my son Fred so-and-so and in order to make the transaction fully legal money to the value of 2/6d [12½p] changed hands'.[10] Even in 1929 the practice was said by some to be still in existence. Harry Gosling, M.P., the veteran transport worker, in introducing a Bill into the House of Commons to remove the children from boats, stated that 'it was not unknown for barge workers to give their children away to other boatmen, who compelled them to do heavy work in the vessels'.[11]

## A BALANCED VIEW

However, judging by the occupants of the boats that we have found in the census returns for 1861 and 1871, the abandonment of children of tender years to complete strangers was, in fact, rare.[12] Usually, young boys, and sometimes, regrettably, young girls, were at least 12 or 13 before they became a 'chap', working with another boatman and his wife, who had no children or only young children. More often than not they were sent to help relatives who were in such a position, and, in the case of younger children, invariably so. An older boatman and his wife might take their grandchild with them, either to give them assistance with their boat, or, in some instances, to alleviate the overcrowded family cabin. Sub-Inspector Blenkinsopp found one such boat in the Black Country, owned and crewed by a man and his wife, accompanied by their granddaughter, a little girl of 10.[13] Sometimes a young boatman would get married and his younger brother would help him and his wife until their children had grown older. In other instances a young boy might go off to help an older unmarried brother or uncle in the running of his boat.[14] Mr George, who had particular knowledge of the line from Birmingham to Gloucester, denied that many children were handed over to other masters. 'That', he said, 'is very rarely the case. Sometimes a handy boy may be lent to another captain they know and they can depend on, to go with him under circumstances. Perhaps a hired hand has run away, as I have known men run away from the boats sometimes and a boy has been lent from another boat.'[15] A Gloucester schoolteacher confirmed, in 1920, that young boys were only loaned (not given) to relatives.[16] Admittedly, Saunders, the Anderton agent to the Bridgewater Navigation Company, remarked, 'The moment a boy gets to the age of eight or nine years he leaves his father, and goes to other boatmen';[17] an opinion not borne out by the data, admittedly imperfect, thrown up by the census. However, if true, it would confirm our view that the canals of the north-west midlands witnessed more of the worst aspects of canal-boat life than did other canals. The inference that boatmen and women abandoned their children in large numbers, irrespective of the consequences, is not proved.

Nor, for that matter, is the suggestion that most fathers and mothers of canal-boat children were any less attached to their children than anybody else. Smith had many unkind things to say about waterway parents. Others who had had a long and sympathetic knowledge of these people were less critical. Mr George asserted, in answer to Smith's allegations:

> I have never seen an instance of unparental conduct on the part of the boatmen or the boatwomen. My experience of boat people is that they have a very tender solicitude for their children, and I am surprised to see the statements put forward. They are very cruel statements in many instances.[18]

The activities of Musson and Hillman had been roundly condemned by other boatmen and women. Brydone, who by 1889 had visited thousands of canal boats, must be given some credence when he observed, 'they evince as tender a regard in their own way [for their young ones] as do parents of other classes', and he described a moving incident at a lock, in Wolverhampton,

> to illustrate that the parental feelings of Boat people are not of that indifferent adamantine [kind] many have been led to suppose. They have affections as great and as tender as other people.[19]

It seems more likely that canal-boat parents were, with some exceptions, quite as good parents as any of the working class. While there is no denying that children did help in the running of the boat, parents were aware of the capabilities of their children and did not as a rule overtax their energies. Hales, a man of the highest integrity, and recognised as such by Brydone, denied that children were expected to drive the horse for cruelly long distances, and explained how members of the boat crew or family changed around every four-and-a-half miles or so.[20]

Allegations of cruelty continued to be aired in the press, but Hackett, the canal-boat officer of the N.S.P.C.C., had to admit that there was less cruelty upon canal boats than ashore. The majority of mothers and fathers looked after their children well.[21] His survey of canal-boat children reveals that most of those assisting in the working of the boats were 10 years of age and over.[22] It was the general conclusion of the 1921 Committee, about child labour, 'that it is little practised except among the older and stronger boys and girls', and, 'taking the evidence as a whole, we cannot assert that the health of canal boat children is worse than that of those who live in the crowded dwellings of our large cities'.[23]

As to the question of the exposure of children to accident, there were those who denied that accidents were frequent. They pointed out that, although boating could be a dangerous occupation, boat children soon became aware of the dangers and took greater care than other children. Further, they were isolated from many of those accidents to which other children were exposed, not least from the busy traffic in towns. Again, as others pointed out, they were forever under the eye of their parents, unlike many others. None the less, the fact remains that a study of the minutes of the Shropshire Union Canal Company, for the latter part of the nineteenth and the first part of this century, reveals that accidents to children (and adults) were far from infrequent, many of them fatal. Here a child was kicked by a horse; another one was drowned; a hand was crushed in a crane; a child killed by falling wood at the wharf, and so on.[24] On balance, canal-boat children were probably more subject to accident than were other children, although there are no statistics to back up such an assertion.

### ATTEMPTS TO EDUCATE THE BOAT CHILDREN

It has been widely accepted, both at the time and since, that all efforts to educate the boat children had failed, not only before the compulsive Acts following the

1870 Education Act, but also in the years down to 1914. This view must to some extent be modified.

Although there had been schools, such as mission schools and Sunday schools, which canal-boat children could, and did, attend long before 1870, Smith was probably correct in insisting that few could read and write, although, taking into account his penchant for exaggeration, 'the few' was probably larger than his arbitrary 5 per cent. He hoped that legislation would rectify this state of affairs, but the two resulting Acts of 1877 and 1884 had had their sharpest teeth drawn by the canal lobby, and by 'Clever drawing-room theorists with white kid gloves attempting to decry a subject past their comprehension'.[25] None the less, by section six of the Act of 1877, a child on a canal boat was theoretically drawn into the educational net, by being deemed registered (for educational purposes) at the place in which the boat was registered, and subject to the educational by-laws of that place. Secondly, a local education authority, on being satisfied that a child was attending school, or otherwise being efficiently educated, in the area of some other authority, might issue a certificate to this effect, whereupon the child was deemed to be resident with the second authority. By section six of the Act of 1884, the Education Department (later the Board of Education) had to report annually to Parliament as to the manner in which the Education Acts were being enforced, with respect to children in canal boats.

Some authorities, after 1884, began to implement the law with vigour. By 1890, Brydone could record that

> The Birmingham School Board, and their officials too, take exceptional interest in the matter, and the result is that Birmingham is one of the best worked centres in relation to the education question so far as boatmen's children are concerned.[26]

Many of the boat people had not taken kindly to this eagerness to have them become 'scholars'. 'One boatman with whom I expostulated for not sending his son to school', Brydone wrote, 'retorted thus, "If the lad grows up as good as his father he will do", adding, "I never had any schooling nor do I see what good it does them, it only makes them above their work." Such is some of the raw material one has to work upon.'[27] The Birmingham officer found that sometimes, if too much pressure was exerted, a master arranged to work two boats, one registered in Birmingham and the other elsewhere and, by transferring the children to the other boat, was able to put them beyond the jurisdiction of the Birmingham officer; and boatmen worked out other escape routes.[28]

Not all boatmen were opposed to the idea of education, but they justifiably complained that they were unfairly penalised in the matter of school fees since, for each school attended, which might be two or three in a week, they were compelled to pay a week's fees each time. Another complaint came from the size of the pass books, which were so large that the children were singled out for abuse.

> The mothers allege that they cannot get their children after they came to eight or ten years of age to carry the books, as the other children call names after them such as 'boatie', etc., etc.[29]

Both these complaints were soon to be rectified, the first by the coming of free education, and the second by the simple expedient of issuing small books, although discrimination by other children, and sometimes by teachers, continued to discourage boat children from attendance at school down to recent times.

None the less, in spite of these difficulties, it seems clear that many parents did wish to see their children educated, or at any rate fell in with the wishes of the authorities, for by 1892, Osmund Airy, a schools' inspector, was able to make an optimistic report to the Board of Education upon the working of the educational clauses of the 1877 Act, in Birmingham. Special officers were appointed and as a result,

> The parents of at least two thirds of the children have been induced to provide houses on land for their wives and families so that the children may regularly attend school. The children living in Birmingham Boats are supplied with School Books in which their attendances [at different schools] are registered; the parents whose children do not make a reasonable number of attendances receive notices to attend before an Appeals Committee; and obstinate neglect leads to prosecution . . .

> During 1891, 778 Boats were inspected in Birmingham: on these boats there were 308 children of School Age. But 136 of these were on boats not registered in Birmingham and notices respecting all of these were sent to Local Authorities of the districts in which the boats were registered. This leaves 172 children belonging to the Birmingham Boats: and in no instance was it necessary to serve a parent of a Birmingham child with a notice. Their school books gave evidence of a very fair amount of school attendance . . .

> The Elementary Education Acts are carried out in Birmingham in the case of Canal Boat Children in a decidedly satisfactory manner.[30]

Other school boards and their officers were equally active, for example Coventry and Runcorn, where, as in Birmingham, large numbers of boats had been registered by 1892.[31] At Runcorn, between 1877 and June 1910, 766 convictions were obtained in respect of canal-boat children.[32]

The Shropshire Union Company also encouraged the children on its boats to attend school. By 1900, of the ninety-seven children of school age, thirty-two could read and write, and, following the summonsing of several steerers before the Chester magistrates, the company took an even keener interest in the education and general welfare of the children.[33] It issued special cards for school attendances, to be filled in at the various termini, principally Ellesmere Port, Chester, Stoke, Birmingham and Wolverhampton, and the company's agents ensured that the children attended as often as possible. The directors were informed, at each meeting, of the numbers attending and of any defaulters, who were subsequently dealt with. In 1903 a woman, a 'Lady Inspector', was appointed at Ellesmere Port, to ensure that the boat children attended school, and generally to keep an eye upon them.[34]

The number of children registered with such large active authorities as Birmingham, together with those living on the canal boats of the largest employer, the Shropshire Union Company, must have accounted for a substantial percentage of the canal-boat children of school age attending school for some education.

## EDUCATIONAL RESULTS GENERALLY UNSATISFACTORY

However, it cannot be denied that the activity of some authorities was matched by the sloth of others. There were many who took little interest in the children registered with them. This was often understandable, since some registration authorities (those near a boat builder for example), never saw many of the boats, or children, registered with them. This meant that children in such boats could continue to evade the education authorities, since towns through which they passed were able to do little more than notify the registration authority of the boats, which in turn knew little of them. Others made a serious effort at first, but soon wilted under the difficulties. The Wolverhampton authority, for example, soon decided that the education of boat children was impossible unless they were banned from the boats.[35] In fact, a boatman determined to evade the embarrassment of educating his children could, with a little dedication, succeed, more or less, with impunity.

It cannot be denied, also, that even where canal-boat children attended school as often as possible, and many did, the total number of attendances was abysmally low, in consequence of their migratory life. In 1902, for example, in Runcorn, whereas the average percentage of attendances of ordinary children was 86·7 per cent, for canal-boat children it was 33·3 per cent.[36] This was not quite as bad as it might appear, since many would attend schools elsewhere, admittedly for a limited number of attendances, but it was clearly not good. At one of the two schools in Birmingham where canal-boat children attended, the average number of attendances was twenty-one out of a possible 242 per annum.[37] Even if they did attend other schools on their travels, the educational benefits must have been slim. A day, or even two or three, in some wayside school was of little good, since there was no opportunity to follow up the learning. Many schoolteachers did not welcome them, since they affected the percentage attendance; they were backward, undisciplined and different; and such teachers often attempted little with them. Some head teachers refused these children admission on the grounds that their school was full.

On the other hand there were schools and schoolteachers who took a real interest in them, and where such children reappeared at not infrequent intervals some good was done. The children on the Shropshire Union Company's boats moved between the same termini, and the teachers at Ellesmere Port were particularly helpful, for 'they were more "struck" on the children,' William Bagnall informed the Chamberlain committee, 'they used to make them do things, if a child went there they would make it understand what it was doing; they would not turn it out half learned; they would make it take notice of what it had to do. That is how our children learned to do as they did [read and write].'[38] At Brentford, also, the school opened by the London City Mission in the 1890s, exclusively for boat children, proved popular and was useful, since, being an important terminus, boats remained there for longer periods.[39]

None the less, for all these reasons, the results were generally unsatisfactory. In the survey carried out in 1904–5 of one hundred children in Birmingham, only 3 per cent could read fairly well and 54 per cent were completely unlettered.[40] By 1907 the Birmingham Education authority, once so optimistic, admitted that 'Great difficulty is experienced in enforcing attendances owing to boats moving from wharf to wharf; and as a rule they are not in Birmingham more than twenty-four hours'. The report confirmed the abysmally low standards achieved and concluded: 'The only hope for them is by legislation in the direction of making them live on shore'.[41]

Others had come to the same conclusion, including the officials at the Board of Education, who, none the less, remained content to continue to summarise the information sent to them every year. A motion from the Northwich Rural District Council on these lines submitted to the Board of Education in 1905 was one of many similar resolutions passed in those years. One schoolteacher in Cheshire considered 'The whole matter . . . a farce'.[42] In 1914 the Association of Education Committees passed a resolution, 'That it is desirable that the Canal Boat Act, 1877 should be amended as to provide adequate facilities with regard to the education of Canal Boat Children'.[43] The N.S.P.C.C. also pressed for legislation.[44] However, nothing emerged from such pressure then, or following the recommendations of the 1921 Committee, or indeed, ever. The problem was left to solve itself.

### EDUCATION—A QUALIFIED SUCCESS

There would seem, then, to be evidence enough to justify the assumption that the optimism of Brydone and others had not been rewarded, and to demonstrate that the attempts to educate this migratory population, with any measure of success, had failed. Such a conclusion would ignore the impact of the Canal Boats Acts, and other influences, in bringing changes to the canal scene. The problem children were those who lived and travelled permanently on the boats, and those whose parents had shore homes, but who spent little time there. There is no doubt that the numbers of such children had been dramatically reduced by 1914, as compared with 1884.

In other words, the various agencies had succeeded in persuading many parents to leave their children on land, with their mother, or with relatives. In 1891, Brydone recorded happily that 'everywhere it is apparent that the number of children of school age on board the boats is rapidly decreasing',[45] an opinion substantiated by those of many others.[46] The 1901 Census confirms that there had been a marked exodus.[47] Many mothers came to live more or less permanently on shore. Their children then, of course, ceased to be 'canal-boat children' as far as the education authorities were concerned. Indeed, we have seen already that it was not unusual for a mother, as the family grew up, to leave the boat, even before the Acts were passed. Equally children had stayed with relatives. In 1884 Hales had agreed that there were cases in which a man, accompanied by his wife and children, made some arrangement for the children to live with a relation during a part of the year, in order to get schooling.[48]

It would be wrong to pretend that these cases were frequent, but from 1884 there is no doubt that such arrangements became much more common. Not all boat people were as sceptical of the benefits of education as the boatman referred to by Brydone. Many increasingly felt their lack of scholarship in a literate society. 'It is not very nice to let everybody know yer business, as them is obliged to do who canner read and write', one boatman told Smith. 'They are always bothering the lock tenters to read and write their letters for 'em.'[49] 'The canal boatmen and more especially their wives are becoming more interested in seeing that the children are sent to school', Brydone reported in 1889.[50] The Nantwich inspector, among others, agreed with him.[51]

The exact degree of decline in the numbers of canal-boat children is difficult to assess. What is certain is that the number of children of school age had never remotely approached the 30,000 and even 40,000 quoted by Smith.[52] According to him there were as many as 60,000 boat children altogether.[53] Powell, in making allowance for the canals not covered by the Canal Associations survey of 1884, reckoned that there would be about 6,000 children in all, half of them of school age, and many of these already had shore homes.[54]

In 1894 Brydone made an estimate based upon the returns from the local inspectors, and reckoned that there would be 1,033 children of school age, although by the following year, as a result of the bad winter, 1,334 school-age children were found. It is interesting that the increase in the number of these children was markedly less than the increase in the numbers of other children.

*Children travelling on board canal boats*[55]

|  | 1894 | 1895 |
|---|---|---|
| Of school age | 1,033 | 1,334 |
| Under school age | 883 | 2,062 |
| Of ages not given (mostly infant) | 604 | 422 |
| *Total* | 2,520 | 3,818 |

Boat people were obviously trying to see that their children were educated. Even Smith in 1892 admitted that 'There are not nearly so many children on the boats as there were ten years ago. Many boatmen have found homes on shore.'[56] The statistics gathered by the Shropshire Union Company, the largest employer of canal-boat labour, perhaps give a rough indication of the order of decline.

*Number of school children travelling on Shropshire Union boats*[57]

|  | Boats | School children |
|---|---|---|
| 1884 | 363 | 151 |
| 1898 | 419 | 99 |
| 1902 | 450 | 97 |

The decline in the number of such children continued more slowly after 1900, but it was Llewellyn's opinion in 1903 that there were 'Not more than 400 children of school age . . . who have no other homes than the boats they live in'.[58] Not everyone agreed with this interpretation. Mr Johnson could not

> accept Mr Llewellyn's statement when he infers that there are only 400 boat children . . . who have no other homes than their boats, and that therefore it is only those children who do not go to school. I think it would be more correct to say that most of the 7,000 boats used as dwellings take their children with them; if not always, very often.[59]

Llewellyn remained convinced.

> My experience agrees with that of many inspectors and is that like a stage army the same children appear over and over again and the real number is much less than that popularly imagined.[60]

And he could not have been very far out in his estimate of those who were at the greatest educational disadvantage, by living permanently on board; nor were the numbers having homes on shore, but travelling with the boats, very high; for the first systematic survey of canal-boat children, carried out in 1920, found only 726 children of school age. There were 1,202 children under 14 in all travelling on boats.[61] At least some of these would be occasional trippers, for more children were found in the holiday time.[62]

### CONCLUSION

By 1914 the number of children on board boats was small, and the number of children excluded from the benefits of education, equally, was not large. They were very much fewer than had been the case in 1884. Sweeping statements of failure are not justified, for the Acts, and other agencies, had been instrumental in the reduction. Those boatpeople who had attended to the education of their children had seen them leave the canals. The missionary at Brentford remarked, 'they have some ambition when they have some education'.[63] Increasingly, there remained only those who saw little value in education and evaded it. There were those owner-boatmen who might wish to see their children educated, but for whom the choice lay between that and giving up their way of life. Being the most mobile, this class were the most difficult to attempt to educate. As the number of children fell, moreover, it became increasingly uneconomic to make special provision for them, since there was never a sufficient number in any one place for any length of time. Birmingham was but one of the mission schools which had to close down.[64] Only at Brentford were there enough children accumulated, at any one time, to justify a special school for them. Elsewhere they remained generally unpopular.

In the years immediately before 1914, then, there remained these few children largely excluded from the educational opportunities open to others, and in consequence they were condemned to follow their forefathers upon the water, for the gravest disadvantages was the restriction put in the way of their ever leaving such a life. On the other hand, they had advantages over other children. 'In my view', Llewellyn wrote,

> I do not exaggerate at all when I say that morally and physically the boat child is, for the most part, superior to the land child in a similar station of life. Its open air life inures it to all weathers, and its familiarity with its work from a very early age makes it reliant and strong and brings out its best qualities. . . . On the boats boys and girls whose contemporaries ashore are . . . a source of worry and anxiety to their parents, can be found doing their duty in a quiet matter-of-fact way, and taking a pride in its successful accomplishment. Undoubtedly, those ashore are more fully equipped in the matter of learning, but in the application of it I do not think most of them have any advantage over the boat children.[65]

A return to the Education Department, from Oxford, also found that 'Physically the chrn are superior to the ordinary school chrn of same age, they are more capable with regard to manual work and seem to possess a greater amount of reliance and common sense.'[66] Llewellyn concluded, in 1907, that 'they are superior [to land children in honesty, manners and physique] and grow up to be better citizens by reason of their training to face hard work and to fight life's battles on their own account'.[67]

### NOTES TO CHAPTER ELEVEN

[1] Smith, *Our Canal Population* (1879 ed.), pp. 15–16.

[2] *S. C. on Canals*, 1883, q. 3104.

[3] *Ibid.*, appendix 25.

[4] See especially evidence of Joshua Fellows, *S. C. on Canal Boats*, 1884, qq. 1325–38.

[5] *Household Words*, 18 September 1858, p. 322.

[6] MH 12/11645, 82/57441/430, 29 May 1882, P.R.O.

[7] *Staffordshire Advertiser*, 18 December 1875, p. 6.

[8] *Lancet*, 1877 (i), p. 29; *The Times*, 10 April 1877, quoted by MaCleod, 'Social policy and the "Floating Population". The administration of the Canal Boats Acts, 1877–99', *Past and Present* (1966), p. 110.

[9] *Warrington Guardian*, 12 September 1877, quoted in Miss F. M. Martin's 'Elementary education in the Poor Law Union of Runcorn, 1870–1903', unpublished M.Ed. thesis (1970), Durham University, p. 134.

[10] Robert J. Parr, *Canal Boat Children* (1911), pp. 11–12, quoted by Martin, *op. cit.*, p. 134.

[11] Cutting from the *Daily Mail*, 22 March 1929, in the Canal Boats Box, Coventry City Record Office.

[12] See Appendix V.

[13] *Factory and Workshops Commission*, 1876, vol. I appendix C, p. 133, 3*d*.

[14] *Ibid.*, 3*e*.

[15] *S. C. on Canal Boats*, 1884, q. 452.

[16] *Committee on Living-in* (Mins. of Evid. and henceforward Mins. of Evid. unless otherwise indicated), 1921, qq. 1289, 1294.

[17] *Factory and Workshops Commission*, 1876, vol. II, q. 10834.

[18] *S. C. on Canal Boats*, 1884, q. 486.

[19] MH 32/94, 'Draft Report for 1889', 39000/90, P.R.O.

[20] *S. C. on Canal Boats*, 1884, q. 1148.

[21] *Committee on Living-in*, 1921, qq. 1607–10.

[22] *Ibid.*, appendix M, p. 87.

[23] *Ibid.*, (Report), pp. 7, 5.

[24] SURC 1/22–7.

[25] Smith, *Canal Adventures by Moonlight* (1881), p. 202.

[26] *20th L. G. B. Report for 1890* (1891), p. 320.

[27] *16th L. G. B. Report for 1886* (1887), p. 172.

[28] *18th L. G. B. Report for 1888* (1889), p. 212; *19th L. G. B. Report for 1889* (1890), p. 223.

[29] *18th L. G. B. Report for 1888* (1889), p. 213.

[30] *ED 11/40*, 'Replies to Or. 283', No. 5266, 25 April 1892, P.R.O.

[31] *18th L. G. B. Report for 1888* (1889), p. 214.

[32] *Committee on Living-in*, 1921, appendix H, p. 80.

[33] SURC 1/25, 14 November 1900, minute 21362.

[34] *Ibid.*, 14 October 1903, 22099.

[35] *18th L. G. B. Report for 1888* (1889), p. 215.

[36] *Runcorn Examiner*, 20 March 1903, quoted by Miss Martin, *op. cit.*, p. 143.

[37] 'Report on the conditions of life under which canal boat children are reared', *Supplement to Annual Report of Medical Officer of Health for Birmingham for 1905* (1906), pp. 13–14.

[38] *Committee on Living-in*, 1921, q. 2269.

[39] ED 11/40, 'Extract from the *Morning Leader*', 3 October 1900; *ibid.*, pamphlet, *Sixth Annual Report of Canal Boatmen's Mission and Day School, Brentford 1901–2*, P.R.O.

[40] 'Report on the Conditions of life under which canal boat children are reared', *Supplement to Annual Report of Medical Officer of Health for Birmingham for 1905* (1906), pp. 13–14.

[41] ED 11/41, 'Summary of returns for 1907', 1169E, 16 December 1908, P.R.O.

[42] ED 11/40, T. A. Johnson, 'Notes on canal boat children', 322G, 10 February 1905, P.R.O.

[43] ED 11/87, 'Secretary of A.E.C. to President of the Board of Education', 566E, 16 April 1915, P.R.O.

[44] *Ibid.*, F. Horner, 'Memorandum on canal boat children'.

[45] *21st L. G. B. Report for 1891* (1892), p. 216.

[46] ED 11/1, 'Replies to Circular 283', 5711, 7125, 6673, (1887), P.R.O.

[47] See Appendix IV*d*.

[48] *S. C. on Canal Boats*, 1884 q. 1144; see also *ibid.*, 357; *Factory and Workshops Commission*, 1876, vol. I, appendix C., p. 122; *ibid.*, vol. II, q. 10883.

[49] Smith, *Canal Adventures by Moonlight*, (1881), p. 63.

[50] *19th L. G. B. Report for 1889* (1890), p. 224. He had already reported on how some boatmen in 1886, had taken homes on land so that their children could be educated; *16th L. G. B. Report for 1886* (1887), p. 172.

[51] *22nd L. G. B. Report for 1892* (1893), p. 138.

[52] Smith, *Canal Adventures by Moonlight* (1881), p. 169.

[53] *Ibid.*, p. 170.

[54] *S. C. on Canal Boats*, 1884, q. 206.

[55] *25th L. G. B. Report for 1895* (1896), p. 248.

[56] *R. C. on Labour (Group B)*, 1893–4, q. 28390.

[57] SURC 1/25, 19 March 1902, minute 21741.

[58] *33rd L. G. B. Report for 1903* (1904), p. 279.

[59] ED 11/40, 322G, 10 February 1905, p. 5, P.R.O.

[60] *39th L. G. B. Report for 1909* (1910), p. 83.

[61] *Committee on Living-in*, 1921, appendix M, p. 87.

[62] *Ibid.*, q. 1615.

[63] *Ibid.*, 692–3.

[64] ED 11/1, 'Replies to Circular 283', 6 June 1893, 10470, P.R.O.

[65] *35th L. G. B. Report for 1905* (1906), pp. 82–3.

[66] ED 11/41, 'Summary for 1907', 1169E, p. 4, P.R.O.

[67] *36th L. G. B. Report for 1906* (1907), p. 66.

# XII

# 'Sui Generis'
## The way of life of the
## boating population in the nineteenth
## and early twentieth centuries

A DISTINCTIVE SOCIAL GROUP

THE EARLY YEARS of the nineteenth century saw the emergence of a distinctive race of people, with a special way of life, living and working upon the narrow canals, and, to a lesser extent, upon the broad canals of England. This way of life came to have much in common with that of the gypsies, not because these people were gypsies, but because the similar circumstances of their existence encouraged similar developments. As the boating population became increasingly cut off from the main stream of society, customs and traditions grew up, which were perpetuated by the isolated life. Already by 1829 people referred to 'that veil of darkness in which they are enveloped',[1] although this referred as much to their reputed lives of sin as to the separate nature of their calling. By 1841, there was no disputing that they were 'a Class, in short, apart from Society?—Quite distinct'.[2] The Reverend John Davies considered them to be

> a Class of Men quite *sui Generis*. Their Habits and their whole Lives are detached as it were from those around them. They associate altogether; and their Feelings and Views lead me to think them quite a Class of Men *sui Generis*.[3]

The process continued because 'they intermarry almost universally with each other, and hence from Generation to Generation their Manners and Habits are perpetuated'.[4] In 1911 Joseph Phipkin could still inform Temple Thurston: 'Yer see they never 'malgamate. They fructify amongst themselves.'[5]

One particular difference common to these wandering tribes, like gypsies, was the distinctive style of dress which emerged and persisted, in some respects, into the twentieth century. The earliest boatman had worn a smock frock or flannel overshirt, like the carters and waggoners, from whose ranks we have presumed he emerged.[6] Such garments still persisted in 1832, since it was recorded: 'The Boatmen are usually in smock frocks, neatly worked, which are to them what finely worked collars are to ladies'.[7] By 1840 the boatman was becoming to an increasing extent jacketed in the red or brown plush waistcoat with fustian sleeves, for the three boatmen standing trial for their lives at the Staffordshire Assizes 'had on the sleeve waistcoat usually worn by boatmen'.[8] By 1858 they were an essential part of the boatman's wardrobe. Sometimes they were decorated with pearl buttons.[9]

Equally distinctive were the 'mighty hobnailed lace-up boots',[10] on the subject of which Hollingshead could barely contain his excitement.

> A bargeman's boot looks more as if it had been turned out of a blacksmith's forge, than a shoe-maker's stall . . . It is an easy full-sized blucher: with upper leather as thick as a moderate slice of bread and butter . . . Rude, uncultivated strength is the main feature of it. The sole absolutely bristles with a plantation of gooseberry-headed hob-nails; the toe and heel heavily strengthened with massive bandages of iron. Twelve shillings [60p] a pair is paid to makers who reside upon the canal banks, for these boots.

He was similarly impressed by the bargeman's stocking, which was equally distinctive, not only in volume but in colour, and served 'perhaps as a shield to protect the foot from the attacks of the heavy boot'. His fustian trousers were 'loose, short and Dutch built',[11] and had curious pockets sewn into the thick cord material. By 1886 the most common style of headgear was said to be a fur cap with side flaps.[12] A gay silk handkerchief slung loosely around the neck completed the boatman's wardrobe.[13] Such articles came to be supplied by special artisans living in particular waterside settlements. Some of the tailors who supplied 'the sleeved plush-fronted waistcoats, the thick blanket-coats, and beloved fur caps' were women.[14] William Edwards was one of the tailors who catered exclusively for boatmen, at one such canal centre. He came to regret the exclusiveness of his clientele, as he was compelled to solicit the indulgence of the Grand Junction Canal Committee.

> I am by trade a Tailor and have a small Shop beside the Canal at Braunston where I make Garments for the Boatmen working on the Canal but latterly many of my customers work on the Grand Union Canal this being the case I have lost part of my trade.

He was given permission to set up a small shop at Buckby top lock.[15]

The dress of the boatwomen seems to have been equally distinctive, although nineteenth-century chroniclers were less fulsome about female fashion. Boots and bonnets were the most remarkable items of the boating ladies' attire; both were in evidence by 1858. Hollingshead described a young woman who was

> dressed in a short-waisted, short-skirted blue cotton frock, a pair of laced-up heavy boots . . . and her bonnet was a quilted cowl that hung in flaps upon her shoulders; and formed a tunnel in front, at the dark end of which was her half-hidden face.[16]

George Smith added a little to the picture, when he described a boatwoman wearing 'a light blue dress, red shawl, with a coal scuttle kind of green silk velvet bonnet on her head, and strong heavy nailed boots upon her feet'.[17] From which we can deduce that the boatwoman's love of colour was not restricted to the landscapes of her cabin home.

The copious gypsy-like decoration and ornamentation of many canal-boat cabins has tempted numerous writers to prove the gypsy origins of their inhabitants thereby, almost certainly incorrectly. The exact origins of the 'roses and castles' have provoked interminable debate. Some declare that the connection with the castles of Hungary is indisputable; others are equally firm on their being Spanish. For some, Windsor Castle was the obvious model. Little useful purpose would be served by continuing the discussion and the conclusion of Barbara Jones has much to commend it, writing as she did in 1946, 'No one really has the slightest idea where they come from'.[18] Suffice it to say that by 1858 the practice was well established, since Hollingshead was able to write:

> The boatman lavishes all his taste; all his rude, uncultivated love for the fine arts, upon the external and internal ornaments of his floating home. His chosen colours are red, yellow, and blue.

The cabin sides might 'present a couple of landscapes, in which there is a lake, a castle, a sailing-boat, and a range of mountains'. The gaudy water-can had also found its way on to many cabin tops.[19]

There is no reason to suppose that it was a recent development, but rather that, as men came to spend more of their time upon the canal boat, at the end of the eighteenth century, and particularly as women and whole families came to live upon the boats, in the early years of the nineteenth century, there was a natural inclination to brighten up their abode. Boat people came to resent those parts of their cabins which were not adorned with something, and they decorated the bare boards as soon as possible with paint, or crockery, or some other camouflaging object. The boat of a newly-married couple would have the added ornament of a bunch of white ribbons tied to the funnel.[20] Often, a splash of natural colour would be wedged into the artificial ornamentation, in the form of a bowl of wild flowers on the top of the flat cabin, and it would not be unusual for a wild bird to be imprisoned in a cage on the same roof.[21]

Birds were not the only livestock aboard. If every French *peniche* could boast its mongrel cur by way of a watch-dog, so too could the English narrow boat.[22] Mr le Bas, the toll clerk at Buckby, complained in 1825 that 'he was impeded frequently in the execution of his Duty by the fierceness of the *Dogs* which are kept on board boats'.[23] They were not solely for the purpose of guarding the boat. Pickford told the Police Commissioners that 'they keep a sort of greyhound, that is a decided poaching dog,—no doubt about it'.[24] It continued to be the practice to keep dogs on board for one reason or the other, or both.

The coloration of their cabins went well with their swarthy complexions, which again tempted the connection with gypsies. Captain Colville recognised them 'by their peculiar cast of countenance'.[25] However, the constant exposure to wind and sun, and, in some cases no doubt, the inadequacy of washing facilities, would appear to be the real causes. In the United States also, the boatmen were as 'Dusky as gypsies, and as picturesque in their costume'.[26] The red faces of the French boatmen earned them a dubious nickname.[27]

As with other closely-knit communities such as the gypsies and the railway nav-vies,[28] the practice of recognising people by their nicknames, rather than by their real names, became a marked feature of canal life. Pickfords' boatmen, standing before the magistrates at Hatton Gardens,

> were severally asked how they came to have nicknames in addition to their real names and they said that those employed on the canal had *two names* and were known by their *bye-names* rather than by their real names.

Before the bench were John Maxwell, 'Redman', Peter Hand, 'St Peter', Thomas Owens, 'Stour', and William Pickering, 'Shiner', this last young man being so dubbed from a suspicion of his having been previously 'engaged in shining "Tiz-zies, Bobs, Half Bulls, and Bulls", of the manufacture of his town [Birming-ham]'.[29] William Hatton's nickname, 'Moucher', is preserved for posterity, since the Manchester boatman featured briefly in the drama of the murder of Christina Collins, in 1839.[30] Mrs Phipps was a poor boatwoman known on the 'cut' as 'Ban-bury Bess',[31] and it was also to his place of origin that the now legendary 'Eyn-sham Harry' owed his 'bye-name'.[32]

There seems to have been nothing akin to the rhyming slang common to such people as railway navvies and Cockneys in the language of the boaters.[33] There was of course the technical language of the 'cut'. A 'monkey-boat' (narrow boat) might get 'stemmed up' (aground).[34] The steerer would be directed to 'hold out' or 'hold in'.[35] 'Butty boat' was an expression which came to describe the boat towed by a motor-boat, but its origins seem to have emerged from the practice of forbidding single narrow boats to travel, except under special circumstances, upon the broad Grand Junction canal, in order to save water. Hence each narrow boat must be accompanied by a mate or 'butty'. The word was used in the Grand Junction Company's minutes in 1850, when a Mr Broughton wrote 'as to the di-fficulty in providing a Butty for a Boat occasionally loaded with salt'.[36] There were also, of course, the 'Fly-Boats', 'Day-Boats', 'Long-Boats', 'Rodney-Boats', and innumerable other descriptions of the many different types of vessel trading upon inland waterways. Boats were 'legged' through tunnels on 'wings' attached to the front of the boat, on which lay hired 'leggers', or the boatmen themselves. The operation consisted of walking the boat through the tunnel, by side-stepping on its walls, 'like the operation known as "hands over" by young ladies who play upon the piano in a showy and gymnastic manner'.[37] Boats 'swam' rather than sailed.[38] In going around a sharp corner, such as the elbow-like bend at Brindley's Bank, the boat would tumble on to one side in what was technically known as a 'drop' or a 'lurch'.[39] People who came on to the canals after their youth was passed were said to 'go boating'. They usually stayed 'about a month or six weeks, while they knock the boat all to pieces!' Slum boaters were sometimes said to be 'back of the map'.[40]

Apart from such expressions, and many more,[41] the language of the boatman had the peculiarity of being sprinkled with numerous mispronunciations. Like other illiterate people, such as gypsies, having misheard names and words, the

PLATE 1  Michael Ward and his family. 'A fireless stove and an empty locker in a cabin on a wet, cold wintry day are not pleasant companions for a man, wife and three children'

PLATE 2  Michael Ward and his family iced up on the North Oxford canal in the 1920s

PLATE 3    Barges *Shamrock* and *Peter* frozen in on the Rochdale canal (Chadderton, Lancs.), 1895. The bridge is painted white for the guidance of night traffic

PLATE 4 (*left*)    A canal-boat horse. 'They are frequently of the very poorest description. . .'

PLATE 5 (*right*) George Smith of Coalville (1831–95). 'A remarkable man who did a remarkable work in a remarkable manner'

PLATE 6    A canal-boat inspection in recent times. Jack Lanigan checking registration particulars on the Bridgewater canal near Hulme locks, Manchester

PLATE 7    '... they keep a sort of greyhound, that is, a decided poaching dog – no doubt about it.' Dog and family pose for their photograph aboard the *Foxland* before loading flints for the pottery industry at the Longport (Burslem) wharf of the Mersey & Weaver company about 1910

subsequent mispronunciations became a part of their language.[42] When Christina Collins first came on board the fly-boat which was to carry her to her unhappy end, she was later reported, by the boatmen, as having said: 'if any one "mislested" her she would make herself away'.[43] Words similar in sound but dissimilar in meaning came to be used. The Shropshire Union canal was the 'Sloppy Cut', a corruption of Salop.[44] 'Harmonium' boats were unpopular, being little more than floating wooden tanks that carried ammonia and other noxious cargoes.[45]

Most canal-boat children (and no doubt many adults as well) had never seen the sea and had no idea what lay on the other side of the Channel, but they 'knew of all sorts of little out-of-the-way, almost unknown inland places in "the shires"', to which they often gave peculiar names for little apparent reason. 'Brumagem' was better known than Birmingham,[46] and to go through 'The Ganzees' was to pass through Walsall.[47] One might have expected also that, leading an isolated life, similar to that of the gypsies, the boatmen would retain archaic words and phrases in their language, but there is no evidence of this.

Even the boatmen's voices had a distinctive falsetto ring, as a necessary part of the art of their calling. In 1886 it was observed that, when their voices rose,

> they still speak in the curious tremolo in which the experience of the generations has taught them it is most effective to address their steeds. A bargee who did not encourage his horse with an expression sounding something like 'k—a—a—am a—ap' would be at once detected as an amateur.[48]

They also walked with a 'strange lateral swing of the hands . . . to every step with an automatic action which is inseparable from their stride'.[49]

One final aspect of the boating vernacular, usually a broad dialect, was the presence in it of a liberal dosage of profanities and swear words, fit only for the horse's ears, but invariably falling on others less immune. In 1832 Panther agreed that they 'swear inordinately'.[50] Chetwynd said 'Boatmen are in the habit of making use of the most obscene language',[51] a statement verified by the trial of the three Pickford boatmen.[52] Whitman noted in 1880 that the waterman 'is ever ready to chaff and scarcely any passer-by escapes his vulgar sarcasm. He will sustain sallies of repartee until his voice is no longer audible'.[53] 'Hercules' in 1885 admitted discreetly that their vocabulary was 'not strictly parliamentary'.[54] Course language was a failing not restricted to English watermen. On the canals of the U.S.A. it was said that,

> Profanity by-the-bye, is the commonest sin of the boatmen and they blaspheme in cold blood, without the enthusiasm of the sailor and without the idiomatic richness of the Californian.[55]

The love of the French boatmen for excruciatingly dirty jokes caused them to be dubbed 'Les Couillons Rouges', an expression as indelicate as any of their jokes, and one of which they were extremely proud.[56]

Apart from the lack of vocabulary as an obvious cause, at least one reason for the propensity to unsavoury speech—in so far as it fell upon the ears of outsiders—was that it was something in the nature of a defensive mechanism against the abuse and discrimination which was the lot of these 'water Ishmaels'. Taunting of boatmen had always been a popular pastime. Pepys noted in his diary for 14 May 1669: 'By water with my brother as high as Fulham, talking and singing and playing the rogue with the Western bargemen about the women of Woolwich, which mads them'.[57] The boys who infested the banks of canals in towns were adept at stirring up the boatmen. One bargeman, on the Regent's Canal, complained of

> blackguard boys wot calls yer names and spits on yer and throws stones at yer—nothin' else. Then, if yer complains they pelts yer with brickbats wuss 'n ever and the hull country and the magistrates sides with 'em![58]

The antics of Birmingham boys are well known. The Lord Mayor of Birmingham, Lieutenant-Colonel E. Martineau, admitted to having 'discharged various missiles at the passing boats in his youth'.[59] Such antics were not restricted to future leaders of men, for 'Even the children out of the gutters get upon the bridges to throw all manner of filth at them as they pass along'.[60] Boatmen, being in a disadvantageous position for the exacting of retribution, had to remain content with verbal attacks.

Such invective was also, no doubt, a direct result of the boating population's feelings of inferiority in the same way that gypsies, apparently, lacking other means of defence, must resort to the use of abusive language against officials who are trying to shift them.[61] Boat children had the same feeling of inferiority, being reluctant to attend school, for 'they say they would not like to be laughed at in consequence of being very backward in their learning'.[62] Such feelings persisted down to the present century, lessened somewhat by the efforts of canal-boat inspectors and sympathetic missionaries.

So long as they remained on the boats, illiteracy was not a grave disadvantage. Jones found them to be 'very adept at figuring; they know how to calculate their wages',[63] an observation confirmed by Whittam of the Shropshire Union Company.[64] Forrester Clayton related how boatmen might return to the head office, after having had money on account during three months, and having paid numerous small bills, yet they were still able to calculate, to a penny, without writing anything down, exactly how much was owing to them. The manager told the Committee 'It is all here [Pointing to his head]'.[65] They were a simple but shrewd people.[66] The examination of the 'Shiner', in 1822, had 'caused much merriment in the Court from the mixture of simplicity and archness of his manner'.[67] It was only when they left the canals that illiteracy became a real physical and psychological handicap.

### THE WATERWAY CODE OF CONDUCT

It is not difficult to understand how violence could enter into canal-boat life, and how circumstances might lead to the use of strong language. None the less, there is

PLATE 8   The boat people: a family gathering in two narrow boats at Runcorn on the Runcorn and Weston canal about 1900

PLATE 9   Narrow boats at Runcorn locks on the Bridgewater canal. '. . . .a coal scuttle kind of . . . silk velvet bonnet on her head' . . . 'a quilted cowl that hung in flaps upon her shoulders; and formed a tunnel in front, at the dark end of which was her half-hidden face . . .'

PLATE 10 Interior of a narrow-boat cabin. 'Boat people came to resent those parts of their cabins which were not adorned with something . . .'

PLATE 11 '. . . a couple of landscapes in which there is a lake, a castle, a sailing boat, and a range of mountains.' Only the modern clothes of Mrs Evans and her son on board *Snowflake* show that this photograph was taken in 1954 and not 1854

PLATE 12 *Java* and *Pekin* moored among Weaver flats at Runcorn on the Runcorn and Weston canal

PLATE 13   A canal burst: at Marbury on the Trent and Mersey canal, 21 July 1907

no doubt that, in these particulars as in many others, the boating population had come to suffer from a bad press. Mr Watts had to admit, in 1921, that boatmen, in fact, swore less than people on shore, in general, and he also agreed that, 'The bargee is a much maligned individual'.[68] Alfred Colwell, a Gloucester schoolteacher, also admitted that the language of boat children was no worse than other children, but different.[69]

It is true that boatmen did not always 'play the game' with each other. This was often a part of the competitive spirit of the canals. At the same time, boaters closed ranks against outsiders, particularly outsiders representing authority. The Yorkshire boatman, for example, was said to be 'a clannish fellow [who] found his companions among the men of his own class. He was reserved in manner and did not readily make friends with strangers.'[70] In times of real trouble and need, Nurse Jones found that 'they do help each other wonderfully', especially when children were born.[71] It was not so much a question of doing somebody else a 'good turn', in the sense that the donor could please himself whether he did it or not, but rather it was the normal procedure to help those in need. Thanks were neither expected nor given, for each would have done the same for another, in similar circumstances, without expecting any comment.[72]

There was also a code of conduct to which boat people generally conformed. Hales gave one example. He

knew [of when] steerers have been anxious to get employment and get into a better boat; they invariably make application in the case of another steerer giving it up. A boatman would not ask for a boat that another man is working in; we find that to be an invariable rule with the boating people.[73]

In recent times it was generally accepted that a boatman never left his employer if his boat was loaded, and there is no reason to presume that this was not a long-established practice.[74] It was also always the custom to set the locks ready for the next boat, if one was in sight. But there was no surplus politeness. It was strictly first come first served at locks and at other impediments, although this was a custom which had to be defended more often than other codes of conduct.[75]

Although they were a clannish race, many people were surprised to find that, considering all that they had read and heard about the boaters, they were not an unfriendly people, provided that they were treated with some measure of respect, which often they were not. Chetwynd remarked on how 'Boatmen are quite surprised if you talk to them in a friendly way'.[76] They were 'very civil to those who treat them properly'.[77] Brydone had often commented on the friendliness of these people once he had gained their confidence, and his successor came to be equally impressed.

The supposed dishonesty of boatmen in the first part of the nineteenth century had almost certainly been exaggerated, and complaints of dishonesty against the boatmen in the second half of the century were few. This may, of course, have been due to the fact that the carriage of valuable goods had been much reduced.

There were still dodges with cargoes. Mr Scantlebury complained that some boatmen were

> mixing the water with manure in order that the gauge of the Boat may shew a grea-
> ter freight on board than is actually there . . . and after . . . the Boatman pumps the
> water from his Boat into the Canal much to the annoyance of the Inhabitants living
> in the vicinity.[78]

Water was still finding its way in to coal boats in 1900.[79] It is true that Saunders informed the Commission of 1875 that 'there is an element of pilferage in the canal traffic'.[80] And at Burslem one Jones, the hand of the boat *Dog*, was discovered 'breaking open a case of Salmon and attempting to steal two tins'.[81] It was also re-ported that '14 sacks of flour etc. had been stolen by Boatmen from the Co's Warehouse at . . . Oswestry . . . Proceedings were taken against Steerer Wood, his 2 Hands, Wood and Robinson.'[82] Some boatmen continued to have few qualms about helping themselves to articles by the canal side. The Chief Consta-ble of Cheshire wrote to the Shropshire Union Company about 'the alleged fowl robbery by one of the company's boatmen at Nantwich'.[83]

However, apart from such petty pilfering and the occasional grand felony by an element of the boating class, it is clear that the majority of boating people had a high standard of honesty. The manager of the Birmingham Warwick and Napton canals gave them the 'highest character for honesty'.[84] Hales observed that

> We have advanced large sums of money to boat people at the time that their boats
> have been tied up, and they invariably pay the money before they leave the service
> should they intend leaving at all, they will not do so until the money has been paid,[85]

an opinion which was verified by his report to the Shropshire Union Committee that 'up to date upwards of £8,000 had been advanced and . . . only £10 17s 8d [£10·88½p] had been required to be written off'.[86] The managing director of Thomas Clayton (Oldbury) Ltd. found them to be 'sober, industrious and honest, in fact I recollect times when some boatmen have been in our debt to the extent of £70 or £80, all of which has been repaid'.[87] And Nurse Jones found them to be 'a clean, honest, hard-working race of people, and very good to pay up. When your work is finished there is your money for you'.[88]

We have already seen how in many other aspects of life, not least in cleanliness and morality, boat people were generally in advance of a similar class on land by the beginning of the twentieth century. The future Prime Minister, Neville Chamberlain, astutely put the question

> Do you consider that the fact that boatmen have lived with their wives and families
> on boats for generations has made it so much a matter of course to have the two sexes
> in close proximity that there is no longer the same novelty about it which might lead
> to immorality in the case of people who were not so accustomed?

The London City Missionary at Paddington and Brentford, R. A. Knight, agreed with him, and went on to add 'they are living the simpler life; their lives are much cleaner and purer'.[89] It may not always have been universally so, and there

PLATE 14    A loaded horse-drawn narrow boat passes timelessly through the deep Tyrley cutting on the Shropshire Union canal in the 1920s. The old way . . .

PLATE 15    . . . and the new. Runcorn-bound motorised coal boat and butty *Merver* at Fenton's lock, Stoke, on the Trent and Mersey canal, 1950. 'Only the introduction of motor boats, probably, enabled canal boating to survive until recent times.'

remained exceptions, but it is clear that by the end of the nineteenth century the majority of the boating class were decent people.

## WORKING LIFE

The occupation of boating was one full of difficulties conducive to the creating of short tempers. There were some outside observers who felt that there was nothing

> more charmingly picturesque, nothing more Arcadian than the bright coloured top of the bow and cabin of the canal boat, gliding easily and silently along after the apparently sauntering horse. Nobody seems to be doing anything like hard work. Life goes on with calm enjoyment at the rate of two miles an hour about.[90]

But nothing could have been further from the truth.

Boating involved long hours of hard work, the boat people being exposed, more often than not, to inclement weather. 'This be a hard life, Must'r Olly, in winter time', Captain Randle admitted.[91] But there was much besides to test a man's patience. There had always been delays for one reason or another. Owing to the pressure of traffic, long lines of boats had to wait their turn through certain locks. Similarly, at narrow tunnels, where entry was restricted to certain hours of the day, boats had to wait for hours before they could begin to be legged through the tunnel. Before the second Harecastle tunnel was built, Pommeuse reported in 1822 that 'A l'heure du passage, les bateaux sont quelquefois amoncelés à l'entrée du tunnel sur un mile de longueur'.[92] It was said in 1836 that the impediment at the tunnel between the Rochdale and the Bridgewater canals in Manchester was so great that a letter could be sent from Manchester to Liverpool and an answer received before a boat could get through the tunnel.[93] In Birmingham Samuel Parkes had seen over eighty boats waiting their turn at the Farmers Bridge Locks, in the years before they were opened night and day.[94] No doubt both had been exceptional occurrences, but regular delays were common. There were delays in loading and delays in unloading. And such delays were to continue down to recent times. The introduction of steam tugs, in the later part of the nineteenth century, did lessen the delays at some tunnels, but other difficulties presented themselves. For, as the money available to canal companies dwindled, in the second half of the nineteenth century, the fabric of canal works began to deteriorate. Mud deepened in the bottom of the canal, increasing the danger of running aground and restricting the loading of the boat. The bargeman upon the Regent's Canal complained:

> There! her starn's all afloat now; its 'er 'ead as 'as got it; yer never know 'ow to load your barge; they never tells you w'en they're goin' to lower the water, nor nothin'. It's a disgrace to the country, the hull thing; nothin' right. It's never clean, an' it's allers low water, and there's nothin' but naked men a-bathin', and thieves wot robs your barge and takes all they can git out of 'er.[95]

Inadequate maintenance reduced the efficiency of locks and increased the wastage of water, as well as causing dangerous collapses which increased the number of stoppages. Lock-keepers ceased to help boats through, in order to save money, which increased the labour of the boatmen and the time needed to pass. Long lines of boats still built up at certain locks. The reporter of the *Birmingham Daily Mail*, struggling along the muddy towpath in 1875, came upon

a great fleet of these boats waiting their turns at a tedious 'block' at one of the locks, some of the unfortunates have been there an hour, and have every prospect of waiting another hour; darkness is coming on and the night is intensely cold.[96]

The most depressing feature of canal life was no doubt the necessity of passing through long tunnels, of which there were many. According to Hadfield, forty-two miles of canal tunnel had been built in England and Wales.[97] To pass once through one of these interminable 'sunless seas' is an experience. To do so week in and week out must have been unpleasant to say the least of it. It was dangerous, hard work and awesome. Sutcliffe, in 1816, thought

the slavery of working vessels through the tunnel [Standedge or Stanedge] is much greater than working upon the hulks, as the men have generally to lie on their backs and paw with their feet, against the top, or sides of the tunnel for three hours, and upwards, till they have pushed the vessel through.[98]

Lying within a few inches of a black and watery death, soaked by the interminable drippings, lulled and mesmerised by the mechanical nature of the task, it was not uncommon for boatmen to fall asleep and slide into the water.[99] The lantern at the front of the boat created fantastic and eerie shadows out of the movement of the leggers.[100]

To keep up the spirits of all concerned, and in particular to encourage the toiling leggers, the boatmen sang. Hymns were popular. Boats passing through the Islington tunnel were 'surrounded by night and silence broken only by the blasphemous bargees singing snatches of Moody and Sankey hymns'.[101] George Smith described how, in following behind the steam tug through Blisworth tunnel,

In the midst of these thundering groaning and unearthly sounds, Mrs ———, of the Birmingham boat . . . would strike up with a good clear voice, but with a kind of 'tin-can' ring about it . . . [with a] strange mixture of songs and hymns.[102]

Hollingshead, however, had noted in 1858, as Captain Randle's boat was legged through the same tunnel, that the favourite then was the plaintive ballad which contained a story and was written in a measure that fitted easily into a slow, drawling, breath-taking tune, which had been handed down from generation to generation without ever having been written down. 'The plots of these ballad stories, are generally based upon the passion of love,' he wrote, 'love of the most hopeless and melancholy kind; and the suicide of the heroine, by drowning in a river is a poetical occurrence as common as jealousy.' He reckoned that 'There may have been a dozen of these ballads chanted in the Blisworth tunnel at the same time', and

They came upon our ears, mixed with the splashing of water, in drowsy cadences, and at long intervals, like the moaning of a maniac chained to a wall. The effect upon the mind was, in this dark passage, to create a wholesome belief in the existence of large masses of misery, and the utter nothingness of the things of the upper world.[103]

In addition to such frustrations, discomforts and even fearsome aspects of canal-boat life it should also be noted that, contrary to appearances, the nature of the work was highly competitive in character. The roots of this lay in the practice, from the earliest days, of paying the boatmen piece rates, and, since delays at locks and wharves cost money, there soon grew up a rivalry between boatmen and boating families, invariably for financial reasons, but one which came to involve the egos of the boatmen as well. Hence they were always reluctant to be over-taken by other boats, especially if approaching locks or wharves. Mr Ward, of Oxford, informed the 1841 Committee of how it happened that 'If a Man passes by them he goes and loads before they can—a Man who passes by them who is going to the same Colliery to load. They may lose a Day or two by it'.[104] 'Time [was] . . . the essence of life to the bargee',[105] and boatmen invariably asked pas-sers-by on the towpath 'Do you know about the time please?'[106]

The annual stoppage invariably produced chaos. According to Twemlow, 'the Moment that Stoppage is at an end great Confusion and Inconveniences arise; Quarrels between Boatmen, whose Boat shall start first, racing to arrive first at a Lock; sometimes injury to the Locks'.[107] When boats raced for the locks, if they arrived both at the same time, the lock invariably became 'jammed' (i.e. the two boats became stuck fast in the entrance to the lock), and often it was hours before they could be freed, thus causing a bottleneck.

Such incidents were often attended by violent scenes. One of Aaron Manby's boatmen, Joseph Walton, had

caused a stoppage or obstruction to the Trade upon the Canal by Jambing a Boat navigated by Jn[h.] Whitehouse in one of the Locks near your works the 29th ult. . . .; several of the Canal Cos. Labourers were at work near the spot, who attempted to separate the Boats and open the passage but were overpowered and prevented by a great no. of persons collected together on the spot by Walton or his men and . . . the passage of the Canal was thereby interrupted more than two Hours.[108]

It was obviously a practice which continued to trouble canal management, since it was still not uncommon for the locks to become 'jammed' in 1913.[109] It is not sur-prising that bad blood between boatmen and their families grew out of such clashes which long outlasted its initial cause.

There is no doubt, also, that financial considerations were largely responsible for creating the restless race of people that the boaters came to be. They were for ever on the *qui vive*. Nurse Jones remarked on how 'very often they are confined today, and when you go to look for them the next day they are gone'.[110] One reason for the boatmen being so reluctant to send their children to school was that, although they might have to wait for days for orders from their employers to pro-ceed, several hours might be lost in waiting for their children when the order did come.[111] Although many company boatmen travelled regularly over the same route (or routes), there was an element of the boating population that wandered all over the country, or over a particularly extensive region, at least. Many were of course owner-boatmen. Inspector Bowling had been informed that 'some of the men after leaving Birmingham are not seen again for a year, during which time they may have been all over North and South Wales, Cheshire or Lancashire'.[112] Some of the Yorkshire keelmen might be away from home for eight months and more, the Reverend Bell assured the 1876 Commission.[113]

In spite of the obvious disadvantages of canal-boat life, including the hard work for long hours, often in bad weather conditions, the boat people seem to have been generally contented with their lot in so far as anyone was, or is, contented. Much depended, of course, on when a boatman or woman was asked his or her opinion. The canal-boat inspector, at Birmingham, found them

> very 'moody' . . . sometimes they will abuse it [their job] and at other times they are the reverse. The opinion of the average canal boatman or woman in that connection is really worthless.[114]

However, the Rev. W. Ward thought they were 'quite as contented as any other class, if not more so'. In 1920 the boatmen were preparing to defend, by strike action, their traditional family life on board boats.[115] Of course, at that time, when more insight became available into the sociology of canal-boat life, the canals were in a relatively prosperous state, owing to the post-war boom in general and to a shortage of railway trucks in particular; and also by that time most of the malcontents had left. None the less, the statistical evidence of the Registrar General for the 1880s and 1890s shows that suicides among watermen were very few, being far below the national average.[116]

It is true that the contentment often stemmed from the fact that they knew little of any better way of life, and, when the First World War widened the horizons of many boatmen, some did not return to the boats.[117] However, when Mr Jones, manager of Fellows Morton and Clayton, was asked 'Are there any instances of people having left your employ and gone into munitions works and come back to the boats because they did not like shore work?' he replied, 'Dozens of them . . . The workers on canals are contented absolutely contented; and if they do leave that employment, they invariably want to come back again.'[118] And, of course, another reason for their reluctance to leave, and, often, their anxiety to return, was that they were not really suited, or skilled, for any work other than casual labour. 'They are really no good for anything else except going down the pit', said Mr Forrester Clayton. 'They have tried, but they always come back.'[119] It was said of the teenagers who left the boats in Gloucester that

> On account of their lack of education they are not able to take anything better— They know nothing; they hang about the docks, and sometimes they become corn porters and that kind of thing.[120]

Equally, boatmen could not live as well on shore as on the boats, certain obvious disadvantages apart. This was especially true of those who substituted their wives and families for hired labour. It is clear that boat people generally lived well, even if by 1921 the rewards were perhaps not as high as they had been before the railways came. Mr Childs, the Birmingham canal-boat inspector, was not alone when he begged 'to suggest that poverty among canal boat people today is practically unknown',[121] although a frost, a strike, or some other unprecedented event, could bring extensive, if temporary, privation.

The representative of a large employer of canal boatmen, Fellows Morton and Clayton, observed that 'they feed extraordinarily well'.[122] The manager of the Shropshire Union Company, possibly still the largest employer of canal boatmen in 1920, mentioned that

> They buy substantial, if plain joints of meat, their principal food being beef, bacon, cheese and butter; and in most instances they purchase at regular places sufficient to last them for the entire journey. Boat people are noted for living well.[123]

### CONCLUSION

We might conclude by quoting the assessment of Mr Clarke, who had been a missionary to boatmen since the 1870s. They were, he said, with some exceptions, 'good and God-fearing men and women . . . living honest, sober, industrious, clean upright lives'.[124]

There is no doubt that boatmen and women, while not without their faults, had habitually suffered from a bad press. This was principally because they were different, and a good deal of ignorance about their special way of life prevailed among the general public. It was not difficult for a person such as George Smith to play upon the prejudices and fears of the unknown and the unusual, which are invarably a part of the human condition. Also, like the early factory workers, since they were so distinct from the rest of the population, they invited criticism. Mr George summed up this phenomenon, when he remarked in 1884:

> I am quite of the opinion that they would compare favourably with any other portion of the labouring class, if fairly judged. I would just say that their occupation stands out so distinctly from that of any other class, that they are easily criticised; and that if the same criticism were applied to the other labouring classes, and to their domestic affairs, I am quite sure boat people would not come out less favourably than other people.[125]

Those who had approached the boat people with an open mind, even before the improvements resulting from the Canal Boats Acts, had found many of the accepted prejudices about them to be untrue. Temple Thurston and Aubertin held many of them to be 'Nature's gentlemen'.[126]

It might also be mentioned, in passing, that boatmen were more than equal to the call to defend the country in the First World War, in spite of their isolated life, for there were no restrictions on their recruitment until 1917. Their patriotism cannot be questioned since many fought and died in the trenches, on barges on the Belgian and French canals, and in the Navy, especially in the patrol service and in minesweepers.[127]

The patriarchal way of life, with the whole family living and working together, week in and week out, must have been almost unique in the England of the late nineteenth and early twentieth centuries. There was much that was 'pre-industrial' about it, with all the family working together, the boatman being his own master, within limits, and leading a leisured existence in so far as he could work or play when he felt like it (which was not, of course, really true in practice). Our assumption that they were generally contented might tempt some to denounce the industrial way of life, by comparing it unfavourably with this survival of a supposed 'pre-industrial' *modus vivendi*. Indeed, some have already done so, in much the same way that various writers have denounced the destruction of the blissful, contented, pastoral, domestic, and largely mythical eighteenth-century way of life in the flood of industrialisation. However, it would be a brave man who set out to prove such a thesis. The employment of boatmen in large numbers was, after all, largely a product of industrialisation. In spite of its isolation, the boating population was not so cut off from the march of progress as it would appear, or as it would be necessary to prove to sustain any such idea. To take but two examples: the boat population benefited as much as every one else from cheaper and better food, and from improved medical facilities. Again, while it is true that organised unions—a recognised feature of an industrial society—remained weak, the boatmen were always ready to combine together sporadically and take industrial action. It is impossible, despite the separateness of these people, to insist that they were isolated from the influences of industrialisation felt by the rest of the population. Further, while it seems probable that the family-boat man tended to be more tenacious in remaining on the 'cut', the desertion of the canals by boatmen at the end of the nineteenth and early twentieth centuries was not all made up of non-family boatmen; many were clearly discontented with their lot.

The way in which the boatmen created their own amusements has tempted some writers to look back with envy to the days of this simple rustic culture, where sturdy independent peasants enjoyed the pleasures and charms of their unspoiled traditional folklore. Rolt clearly felt this way about it. But an unbiased observer must place beside the alleged advantages of this 'pre-industrial' way of life all the numerous disadvantages, just as Dorothy Marshall's study of the eighteenth century has highlighted some of its unpleasant aspects. They would have to point to the massive ignorance of the boaters and some of its results; to the extremely narrow way of life; to the excessive drinking; to the lack of social facilities; and to the casual nature of employment, as being some of the disadvantages suffered by boat people, as compared with the 'industrial' population.

### NOTES ON CHAPTER TWELVE

[1] *Canal Boatmen's Magazine*, May 1829, p. 17, British Museum, PP. 1090 c.
[2] *S. C. on Sunday Trading*, 1841, q. 889. Evidence of William Ward, canal trader.
[3] *Ibid.*, 739.

⁴ *Ibid.*, 952.

⁵ Temple Thurston, *The Flower of Gloster* (1911; 1968 ed.), p. 30.

⁶ 'Maritime Birmingham', an extract from *The Mail* (probably *The Birmingham Daily Mail*), 8 February 1886, in Newspaper Cuttings relating to Canals, collected by G. H. Osborne, p. 3, Birm. R.L. 243972. (Referred to in this chapter as 'Maritime Birmingham'.)

⁷ *The Canal Boatmen's Magazine*, February 1832, p. 16.

⁸ *Staffordshire Advertiser*, 21 March 1840.

⁹ *Household Words*, 11 September 1858, p. 290.

¹⁰ *Birmingham Daily Mail*, 12 March 1875, reprinted in George Smith, *Our Canal Population* (1879 ed.), p. 77.

¹¹ *Household Words*, 18 September 1858, p. 318.

¹² 'Maritime Birmingham'.

¹³ *Household Words*, 11 September 1858, p. 290.

¹⁴ *Birmingham Daily Mail*, 12 March 1875, *op. cit.*, p. 76.

¹⁵ GJC 1/9, 2 August 1844, p. 125.

¹⁶ *Household Words*, 25 September 1858, p. 358.

¹⁷ Smith, *Canal Adventures by Moonlight* (1881), p. 3; Rolt gives a detailed description of the dress of boatmen and women as it was said to exist not so long before he made his voyage (recorded in *Narrow Boat*, pp. 36–7) in 1939–40.

¹⁸ Barbara Jones, 'The rose and the castle', *Architectural Review*, December 1946, p. 162.

¹⁹ *Household Words*, 18 September 1858, p. 322.

²⁰ *Ibid.*, 25 September 1858, p. 358.

²¹ Temple Thurston, *op. cit.*, p. 212.

²² R. L. Stevenson, *An Inland Voyage* (1888; 1919 ed.), p. 76.

²³ GJC 1/3, 28 June 1825, p. 376.

²⁴ *Constabulary Force Report*, 1839, p. 54.

²⁵ *Factory and Workshops Commission*, 1876, vol. II, q. 10440.

²⁶ William H. Rideing, 'The waterways of New York', in *Harper's New Monthly Magazine*, vol. 48, December 1873, p. 2.

²⁷ See below, p. 173, Jean Anglade, *Vie quotidienne dans le Massif Central au 19e siècle* (1971), p. 49.

²⁸ See Terry Coleman, *The Railway Navvies* (1965).

²⁹ PIC 4/1, Extract from the *Morning Chronicle*, 30 July 1822, in Pickfords' Old Newspaper Cuttings and other Historical Documents, p. 10.

³⁰ *Staffordshire Advertiser*, 29 June 1839.

³¹ Smith, *Canal Adventures by Moonlight* (1881), p. 44.

³² Temple Thurston, *op. cit.*

³³ See Coleman, *op. cit.*

³⁴ De Maré, *The Canals of England*, p. 109.

³⁵ Smith, *Canal Adventures by Moonlight* (1881), p. 95.

³⁶ GJC 1/11, 14 March 1850, p. 223.

³⁷ *Household Words*, 11 September 1858, p. 291.

³⁸ OXC 1/4, 13 November 1793.

³⁹ *Staffordshire Advertiser*, 21 March 1840. Evidence of James Willday.

⁴⁰ *Committee on Living-in*, 1921, evidence of William Bagnall, boatman, qq. 2290–3, 2289.

⁴¹ Rolt, in his *Narrow Boat*, provides a glossary of some of the technical waterway terms (pp. 201–8).

⁴² Ministry of Housing and Local Government and the Welsh Office, *Gypsies and other Travellers* (1967), p. 46.

⁴³ *Staffordshire Advertiser*, 22 June 1839.

⁴⁴ Mr D. Campbell supplied this information. It has also been suggested that 'Sloppy' is a mispronunciation of 'Shroppy', the still popular name for the Shropshire Union canal.

[45] Ellis-Martin, 'Through London by canal', *Harpers New Monthly Magazine*, vol. 70 (1885), p. 871.

[46] Article on the school at Brentford from the *Morning Leader*, 3 October 1900, reprinted as a pamphlet found in ED 11/40, P.R.O.

[47] 'The canal people' in the *Birmingham Sketch*, May 1967, preserved in Birmingham Newspaper Cuttings: Canals and Waterways, p. 79, Birm. R.L., 662820; other place names that were corruptions of the existing ones and some that were peculiar to the boat population are given in Rolt's *Inland Waterways of England*, p. 187.

[48] 'Maritime Birmingham'.

[49] Temple Thurston, *op. cit.*, p. 197.

[50] *S. C. on the Observance of the Sabbath*, 1832, q. 1806.

[51] *S. C. on Sunday Trading*, 1841, q. 71.

[52] *Staffordshire Advertiser*, 21 March 1840.

[53] James S. Whitman 'Down the Thames in a birch-bark canoe', in *Harpers Monthly Magazine*, vol. 62 (1880–1), p. 212.

[54] 'Hercules', *British Railways and Canals* (1886), p. 91.

[55] Rideing, *op. cit.*, p. 10.

[56] Anglade, *op. cit.*, p. 49.

[57] F. S. Thacker, *The Thames Highway*, vol. 1, *General History* (1914; 1968 ed.), p. 100, quoted in Willan, *River Navigation in England*, p. 109, as Pepys Diary, ii, p. 691.

[58] Ellis-Martin, *op. cit.*, p. 863.

[59] *The Waterman*, May 1913, p. 50.

[60] Smith, *Our Canal Population* (1875 ed.), p. 99.

[61] Ministry of Housing and Local Government and the Welsh Office, *Gypsies and Other Travellers* (1967), p. 46.

[62] *S. C. on Sunday Trading*, 1841, q. 966.

[63] *Committee on Living-in*, 1921, q. 307.

[64] *Ibid.*, appendix C, p. 85.

[65] *Ibid.*, qq. 571–4.

[66] *The Waterman*, September 1913, p. 105.

[67] PIC 4/1, extract from the *Morning Chronicle*, 30 July 1822, in Pickfords' Old Newspaper Cuttings and other Historical Documents, p. 10.

[68] *Committee on Living-in*, q. 176.

[69] *Ibid.*, 1327.

[70] *The Waterman*, April 1914, p. 42.

[71] *Committee on Living-in*, 1921, q. 1983.

[72] Aubertin, *op. cit.*, p. 98.

[73] *S. C. on Canal Boats*, 1884, q. 1214.

[74] Information from Mr D. Campbell.

[75] Aubertin, *op. cit.*, p. 98–9.

[76] *S. C. on Sunday Trading*, 1841, q. 87.

[77] 'Hercules', *op. cit.*, p. 92.

[78] GJC 1/16, 25 October 1861, p. 151.

[79] OXC 4/110, 26 June 1900, p. 65.

[80] *Factory and Workshops Commission*, 1876, vol. II, q. 10862.

[81] SURC 1/26, 12 August 1908, 23149 (21068).

[82] SURC 1/27, 15 October 1913, 24237 (21998).

[83] SURC 1/25, 14 May 1902, Min. 21782.

[84] *Factory and Workshops Commission*, 1876, vol. I, p. 119.

[85] *S. C. on Canal Boats*, 1884, q. 1214.

[86] SURC 1/25, 17 October 1900, 21323.

[87] *Committee on Living-in*, 1921, appendix C, p. 76.

[88] *Ibid.*, q. 1948.

[89] *Ibid.*, 735–6.

[90] 'Hercules', *op. cit.*, p. 93.

[91] *Household Words*, 18 September 1858, p. 321.

[92] Huerne de Pommeuse, *Des canaux navigable*, vol. 2. (1822), p. 19.

[93] H.L.R.O., MS., Mins. of Evid., H.C., vol. 24, Manchester and Salford Canal Bill, 19 May 1836, pp. 103–5.

[94] Birmingham Canal Bill, 25 April 1839, p. 165.

[95] Ellis-Martin, *op. cit.*, pp. 862–3.

[96] *Birmingham Daily Mail*, 12 March 1875, in Smith, *Our Canal Population* (1879), pp. 75–6.

[97] Hadfield, *The Canal Age*, p. 60.

[98] John Sutcliffe, *A Treatise on Canals and Reservoirs* (1816), p. 122.

[99] *Ibid.*, p. 237.

[100] *Household Words*, 25 September 1858, p. 358.

[101] Ellis-Martin, *op. cit.*, p. 870.

[102] Smith, *Canal Adventures by Moonlight* (1881), p. 91.

[103] *Household Words*, 25 September 1858, p. 357.

[104] *S. C. on Sunday Trading*, 1841, q. 857.

[105] Aubertin, *A Caravan Afloat* (c. 1918), p. 97.

[106] 'Hercules', *op. cit.*, p. 92.

[107] *S. C. on Sunday Trading*, 1841, q. 418.

[108] BCN 4/373, Houghton to Manby, 2 November 1817.

[109] *The Waterman*, September 1913, p. 98.

[110] *Committee on Living-in*, 1921, q. 1948.

[111] *Ibid.*, 1026; *19th L. G. B. Report for 1889* (1890), p. 224.

[112] *Factory and Workshops Commission*, 1876, vol. I, appendix C, p. 123.

[113] *Ibid.*, vol. II, q. 12898; see also *Committee on Living-in*, 1921, q. 1004.

[114] *Committee on Living-in*, 1921, q. 1010.

[115] *Ibid.*, 836–7, 1380.

[116] *55th Report of the Registrar General (Supplement)*, 1897, p. xxviii; *65th Report of the Registrar General (Supplement)*, 1908, p. xxvii; see above, table 9, p. 134.

[117] *Committee on Living-in*, 1921, q. 458.

[118] *Ibid.*, 494.

[119] *Ibid.*, 545.

[120] *Ibid.*, 1333.

[121] *Ibid.*, 1015; see also *ibid.*, 259, 857, 1907.

[122] *Ibid.*, 353.

[123] *Ibid.*, appendix L, p. 85.

[124] *The Waterman*, October 1914, p. 115.

[125] *S. C. on Canal Boats*, 1884, q. 342; see also MH 32/94, 'Draft Report for 1890', 38536/91, p. 39, P.R.O. (Lichfield Barge Missionary).

[126] Temple Thurston, *op. cit.*, p. 7; Aubertin, *op. cit.*, p. 96.

[127] *Committee on Living-in*, 1921, q. 458; *Annual Report of the Seamen and Boatmen's Friend Society* (Birmingham), 1917, Birm. R.L. 239999; *ibid.*, (Leeds), 1914, 1915, 1916, Leeds Reference Library, 266 IN 2L.

# APPENDIX I

## Notes on the registers of boats and barges, 1795 —gypsy names

(i) The figure of 898 masters of boats is an abstraction from the registers of the seven counties[1] made up of the masters of boats registered between 1795 and 1798, the bulk of them in 1795. Registrations later than 1798 have been ignored, as also have ferry-boat men on the Severn and members of the crews of boats, where they are named. Many names reappear several times, and in most cases it seems clear where they are the same person. For example, it is most unlikely that there were five men by the name of Nathaniel Lawrence all living in Brimscombe, and all navigating between Brimscombe and London (G.R.O. 18, 24, 26, 66, 81).[2] Again it would be surprising if the two Richard Corns were not one and the same:

| Name of master | No. on register | Record Office | No. or name of boat | Place of residence | Crew | Tons | Owner and residence | Date registered | Usual route and mileage |
|---|---|---|---|---|---|---|---|---|---|
| Richard Corns | 159 | S.R.O. | 20 | Stone | 1 | 21 | Hugh Henshall & Co. of Stone | 21.8.95 | Stourport to the Pottery 66 miles |
| Richard Corns | 475 | S.R.O. | – | Stone | 1 steering and driving the horse | 21 | Hugh Henshall & Co. of Stone | 5.9.95 | Shardlow to Manchester 117 miles |

The same applied to the Thomas Crossleys:

| Thomas Crossley | 358⎫ 365⎭ | S.R.O. | – | Ball Edge | 1 | ⎧20 ⎩18 | John Sparrow Esq. & Co. of Cockshead | 29.8.95 | Shardlow to Froghall 24 miles |

In such cases the likeliest source of error, where men of the same name lived in the same place, might come through the registration of father and son. Fortunately, a distinction was made between father and son, as in the case of William Hughes (the elder) and William Hughes (the younger) (S.R.O. 386–8 and 389–90), both living in Wombourn, and navigating the boats of Thomas Law of Bilston on the same routes. In other instances it is not so easy to be sure, and the decision to eliminate a possible duplication is a purely arbitrary one. It is inevitable that some inaccuracy must creep in here, especially with the Derbyshire and Leicestershire registers, where fewer details accompany each name. Also, in the case of the Warwickshire register, the absence of the place of residence of the boatmen creates difficulties. For example, there are two Thomas Hansons:

| Thomas Hanson | 136 147 | W.R.O. | – | – | 1 boy | 20 20 | Duncan Mac-korkell | 24.8.95 | Tipton to Birmingham 12 miles |

Were they the same man? It was decided that they were. More difficult is Thomas Fisher. It was decided that the two names also represented the same man. On the other hand, of the seven Abraham Fishers named, it was decided that they were in fact two men, although it may, indeed, have been a case of one man who had changed his employers or even taken on extra boats.

| Thomas Fisher | 138 | W.R.O. | – | – | 1 boy | 17 | Richard White-house | 24.8.95 | Tipton to Oxford 140 miles |
| Thomas Fisher | 291 | W.R.O. | – | – | 1 boy | 17 | William Davies | 1.9.95 | Tipton to Oxford 140 miles |
| Abraham Fisher | 422 | S.R.O. | – | Tipton | 1 boy | 22 | Richard Bissell & Co. of Tipton | 31.8.95 | Autherley to Birmingham 22 miles |
| Abraham Fisher | 425 | S.R.O. | – | Tipton | 1 boy | 22 | Richard Bissell & Co. of Tipton | 31.8.95 | Autherley to Birmingham 22 miles |
| Abraham Fisher | 344–8 | W.R.O. | – | – | 1 boy | 20 | Hockley Boat & Coal Co. | 1.8.96 | Birmingham to Hockley 12 miles |

The two John Brindleys lived in different places:

| John Brindley | 362 | S.R.O. | – | Baddeley Edge | 1 | 20 | John Sparrow & Co. of Cocks-head | 29.8.95 | Shardlow to Froghall 24 miles |

| John Brindley | 512 | S.R.O. | – | Cocks-head | 1 | 18 | John Sparrow & Co. of Cocks-head | 17.11.95 | Shardlow to Froghall 24 miles |

The two places (probably near Stoke-on-Trent) may be so near as to be virtually the same place, or he may have removed in the period between the two registrations. At any rate it was decided that the two Brindleys were one, whereas the Richard Brittains were thought to be two men:

| Richard Brittain | 332 | S.R.O. | – | Sand-bach (although regis-tered at Stafford) | 1 boy | 20 | George Cope of Milton | 29.8.95 | Runcorn to Shardlow |
| Richard Brittain | 141 | C.R.O. | – | – | 1 | 14¾ | Peter Lead-better of Preston o' the Hill | 5.9.95 | Stourport to Manchester 120 miles |

However, the potential source of inaccuracy is not as grave as it at first appears. There are 1,020 named masters in all, before possible duplicates have been discarded, but there can only be any really serious doubt in the case of about thirty masters. The amount of error cannot be too damaging.

Again, it might be argued that not all the boats were registered, and it is true that in Lancashire, for example, in spite of the Leeds and Liverpool canal being opened from Liverpool to Newburgh by 1775, no boats are registered for that canal, nor are any of the Duke of Bridgewater or Mersey and Irwell Company's 'flats' included. Many of the duke's boatmen are not named. But even if boats and names are missing from the registers, there is no reason to assume that any particular group would be omitted disproportionately, whether they were gypsies, owner-boatmen or whatever.

(ii)[3] It should be noted that, in drawing up the list of boatmen with gypsy names, the latitude has been towards dragging as many names as possible into the Romany net. Hence, while Leland quotes Bailey we have none the less found a place for Bayley; Clark has been extended to Clarke, Herne to Hearne, Davis has been given the benefit of the doubt for Davies, and so on. In Wales, according to Leland, the gypsies were Woods, Roberts, Williams and Jones and, despite the commonplace nature of such names in Wales (and England too), they have been religiously included. The 103 gypsy names collected must represent the most generous interpretation of Romany names.

(iii)[3] These statistics represent a blanket coverage of all kinds of boatmen (except ferrymen and crewmen), and include the flatmen of the Sankey Navigation, and Weaver and Mersey rivers, as well as Trent bargemen and Severn trowmen, which leads us to the difficult question of when a canal boatman is not a canal boatman, but a river boatman. For a low percentage of gypsy names among the longer-established river boatmen could disguise a much higher percentage of possible gypsies among canal boatmen proper. However, the elimination of all vessels trading exclusively on a river, but not those trading partly on canals as well (with the exception of vessels starting at Brimscombe and moving westward into the Severn and Severn estuary and, perhaps arbitrarily, those on the Sankey Navigation), reveals much the same picture. In other words, the exclusion of rivermen reveals 714 named masters, eighty-five of whom had gypsy names, i.e. about 12 per cent. And in Warwickshire, where only narrow boats are registered, only 10 per cent of masters might be said to have gypsy names. One wonders, in fact, if a study of almost any occupational group, both now and then, with the possible exception of fortune-tellers, clothes-peg sellers and scrap-metal dealers, might not produce similar results.

(iv)[3] The 1879–84 statistics have been worked out in the same way as those for 1795, with attempts to eliminate duplicates as before.

NOTES TO APPENDIX I

[1] See above, p. 2.
[2] Record Office and number of boat on register.
[3] See above, pp. 2–3.

# APPENDIX II

## *Notes on the registers of boats and barges, 1795 —details of ownership*

(i) The statistics of ownership quoted in Chapter II are again derived from the registers of boats and barges in the five counties where details of ownership are given. Only boats (and flats, barges, etc.) registered between 1795 and 1798 are included. Ferry boats have again been ignored. To arrive at an accurate list of boat owners is less difficult than the compiling of a list of boat masters, since the possibility of men with the same name (who are scattered throughout the registers) being different people is more remote. For example, there are three entries for a Richard Caulton of Wheelock.

| Name of owner and residence | Regis- tration number of boat | Record Office | Name or number of boat | Tons | Boatman and residence | Date regis- tered | Normal route | Mileage |
|---|---|---|---|---|---|---|---|---|
| Richard Caulton, Wheelock | 151 | C.R.O. | Swan | 14¾ | Joseph Bayley (the younger), Middlewich | 8.9.95 | Wheelock Wharf to Manchester | 46 |
| Richard Caulton, Wheelock | 152 | C.R.O. | Heart of Oak | 15 | Joseph Bayley (the elder), Middlewich | 8.9.95 | Wheelock Wharf to Manchester | 46 |
| Richard Caulton, Wheelock | 158 | C.R.O. | Trial | 15½ | Ralph Taylor, Middlewich | 22.9.95 | Wheelock Wharf to Manchester | 46 |

It would be difficult to credit that there could be two Richard Caultons of Wheelock, both trading between Wheelock Wharf and Manchester. It was the practice to distinguish between father and son as with Robert Deakin (C.R.O., 5–6). Most owners are, in fact, usually listed under consecutive entries. Those who are not are usually, like Richard Caulton, instantly recognisable. More difficult is Warwickshire, where the place of residence is not usually given, but, again, the chances of the five John Iddins, for example, being the same man are strong, particularly as the routes of the different boats are so similar.

| John Iddins | 328 | W.R.O. | – | 20 J. Lucas | 17.11.95 | Wednesbury to Birmingham | 10 |
| John Iddins and son | 351–4 | W.R.O. | – | 20 Gosling | 12.8.96 | Tipton to Birmingham | 12 |

Often the boatmen attached to the separate registrations are of the same name. The real difficulty arises where no forename is given, the same name appearing several times. This would be most problematical in Warwickshire, but, fortunately, this occurrence is restricted to one Fox, in partnership with Edward Wright for one boat, and with William Bayliss for a further six.

| —— Fox Edward Wright | 12 | W.R.O. | 12 | 20 John White | 20.8.98 | Birmingham to Tipton and Wednesbury | 12 |
| —— Fox William Bayliss | 13–18 | W.R.O. | 1–6 | 20 Isaac Pursal | 20.8.98 | Birmingham to Tipton and Wednesbury | 12 |

Since the routes were the same, and they also formed consecutive entries in the register, it was decided that Fox was the same man. There are many Gilberts, some with forenames and some not, but only one boat (owned by Gilbert and Burgess; L.R.O., no number) has no obvious place, and was left unattached to the other Gilberts. There are one or two other entries which are doubtful, but neither the number of 'displaced persons', nor the number of boats involved, is sufficient to cast doubt upon the statistics emerging from the piecing together of the registers.

(ii) Statistics relating to the ownership of boats in Lancashire, Cheshire, Staffordshire, Warwickshire and Gloucestershire, taken from the Registers of Boats and Barges, 1795 for those counties:

| Class | Boats owned | Number of boats involved | Percentage of total boats | Number of owners or part-owners[a] | Percentage of total owners and part-owners |
|---|---|---|---|---|---|
| I | Over 12 | 360 | 28·3 | 14 | 3·5 |
| II | Under 13 but over 5 | 411 | 32·3 | 76 | 18·7 |
| III | Under 6 | 501 | 39·4 | 316 | 77·8 |
| *Total* | | 1,272 | | 406 | |
| Boats owned by canal companies | | 242 | 20 | 10 | 2·5 |

| | | | | |
|---|---|---|---|---|
| Other classifications | Over 5 | 771 | 60·5 | 90 | 22·2 |
| | 1 only[b] | 129[c] | 10 | 165[d] | 40·5 |
| Owner-steerers | 1 only | 45 | 3·5 | 45 | 11 |

*Notes*
[a] Canal and other companies counted as one owner.
[b] Only 101 single owner/single boat combinations existed.
[c] Excluding those part-owned by people who had more than one boat.
[d] Excluding part-owners who had shares in other boats.

(iii) In establishing the identity of the various boat owners and boatmen listed in the registers (although not all the people mentioned in the text are to be found in the registers), the sources of reference providing proof of identity are given, without (for the sake of brevity) going into the details of that proof. In the case of Charles Moore (see Chapter II, note 8) the register gives his place of residence as Shirleywich, and lists boats travelling to Norton, Shardlow, Oxford and Bilston. The letter OXC 4/81/1, 2 April 1799, clearly shows that Charles Moore was the owner of a salt works at Shirleywich and that he traded to Oxford. Not all proprietors of boats are so easily recognisable, and it needs several points of reference to establish that a given owner is a coal-mine owner, ironmaster or whatever.

There are many examples of owners, other than those listed in the text, who are clearly identifiable, which shows that boat owners were generally men of some substance, and no doubt a close study of the directories and newspapers of the midland region would establish the identity of even more of the names listed in the 1795 registers. However, there are more than enough cases of established identity to show the types of people who owned boats, and, in conjunction with the statistics emerging from the registers, to suggest in what proportions they were to be found. Even without such examples, the number of owner-steerers found in these counties conclusively proves that, in 1795 at least, the idea of large numbers of 'number ones' moving the bulk of England's goods is a myth.

## Table showing the tonnages carried on the main canals 1828–98

| Name of canal | Mileage | Tonnage carried | | | | | | |
|---|---|---|---|---|---|---|---|---|
| | | 1828 | 1838 | 1848 | 1858 | 1868 | 1888 | 1898 |
| Birmingham | 169 | – | 3,332,709 | 4,696,192 | 6,162,981 | 6,982,773 | 7,713,047 | 8,627,074[a] |
| Coventry | 32½ | approx. 550,000 | 550,000 | 520,000 | 496,624 | 427,808 | 451,521 | 366,842 |
| Grand Junction | 140 | – | 948,481 | 1,031,284 | 1,142,450 | 1,404,012 | 1,172,463 | 1,620,552 |
| Kennet & Avon<br>Rivers Kennet & Avon | } 86 | – | 341,878 | 360,610 | 161,822 | 210,567 | 135,802 | 112,716 |
| Leeds & Liverpool | 142 | 1,436,160 | 2,220,468 | 2,601,577 | 2,160,256 | 2,141,151 | 2,016,976 | 2,323,968 |
| Trent & Mersey | 118 | – | – | 1,341,611 | 1,363,384 | 1,494,524 | 1,139,098 | 1,215,540 |
| Oxford | 91 | 450,000 | 520,000 | 420,000 | 400,000 | 482,000 | 450,000 | 421,507 |
| Staffordshire & Worcestershire | 50 | – | 680,479 | 843,540 | 895,054 | 798,780 | 646,038 | 767,577 |
| Warwick & Birmingham | 22½ | 216,563 | 319,926 | 226,084 | 208,071 | 243,373 | 353,118 | 354,022 |
| Warwick & Napton | 14⅜ | 203,286 | 308,045 | 219,643 | 201,789 | 212,789 | 236,353 | 196,842 |
| Aire & Calder | 85 | – | 1,383,971 | 1,335,783 | 1,098,149 | 1,747,251 | 2,210,692 | 2,412,062 |

*Note*
[a] 7,180,000 was local traffic.

*Source* Compiled from the returns presented to Parliament in 1870 and from the Board of Trade Canal Returns 1888 and 1898 (*Royal Commission on Canals and Inland Navigations in the United Kingdom*, vol. I, 1906 [Cd. 3183–4], xxxii, appendix I, statement I).

(iii) Magnitude of the changes in the numbers of bargemen, watermen and lightermen, in each age group, 1851–1911 (comparison for each year is made with the figures in the preceding census)

| Age Group | 1861 No. | 1861 % | 1871 No. | 1871 % | 1881 No. | 1881 % | 1891 No. | 1891 % | 1901 No. | 1901 % | 1911 No. | 1911 % |
|---|---|---|---|---|---|---|---|---|---|---|---|---|
| 10–15 | +449 | ? | −316 | −21·8 | −371 | −32·8 | +70 | +9·2 | −358 | −43·0 | −218 | −46·0 |
| 15–20 | −379 | −8·6 | −314 | −7·8 | +61 | +1·6 | +208 | +5·5 | −698 | −17·6 | −967 | −29·6 |
| 20–25 | −437 | −10·0 | +61 | +1·5 | +259 | +6·5 | −179 | −4·2 | −190 | −4·6 | −836 | −21·6 |
| 25–35 | −1,357 | −16·5 | −285 | −4·1 | — | — | — | — | −190 | −2·6 | −365 | −5·1 |
| 35–45 | +645 | +12·3 | −639 | −1·6 | — | — | — | — | −31 | −0·5 | +129 | +2·4 |
| 45–55 | −419 | −8·8 | −172 | −3·9 | — | — | — | — | +230 | +5·0 | +27 | +0·5 |
| 55–65 | −295 | −9·5 | −139 | −4·9 | — | — | — | — | +346 | +13·0 | +142 | +4·7 |
| 65 and over | +291 | +18·7 | +136 | +7·3 | −510 | −25·7 | −69 | −4·7 | −139 | −9·9 | +109 | +8·6 |

(iv) *Changes in the relative importance of each age group, as a percentage of the total labour force, 1851–1911*

| Age group | 1851 | 1861 | 1871 | 1881 | 1891 | 1901 | 1911 |
|---|---|---|---|---|---|---|---|
| 10–15 | 3·16 | 4·65 | 3·8 | 2·5 | 2·7 | 1·6 | 0·9 |
| 15–20 | 13·4 | 12·8 | 12·5 | 12·6 | 12·8 | 10·9 | 8·2 |
| 20–25 | 12·3 | 12·5 | 13·4 | 14·2 | 13·1 | 13·0 | 11·2 |
| 25–35 | 25·2 | 22·0 | 22·3 | – | 23·4 | 23·6 | 24·0 |
| 35–45 | 16·0 | 18·9 | 18·0 | – | 19·8 | 20·4 | 22·3 |
| 45–55 | 14·6 | 13·8 | 14·1 | – | 15·5 | 16·2 | 17·3 |
| 55–65 | 9·5 | 9·0 | 9·0 | – | 8·0 | 10·0 | 11·2 |
| 65 and over | 4·7 | 5·9 | 6·7 | 4·9 | 4·5 | 4·2 | 4·9 |
| 35 and over | 44·8 | 47 6 | 47·1 | – | 47·7 | 50·4 | 55·7 |

#### NOTES TO APPENDIX FOUR

[1] *Population Census of England and Wales, 1841: Occupation Abstract*, 1844, p. 32.

[2] *Ibid.*, p. 48.

[3] Written with a capital *W* here to make clear the difference between the word *watermen* used to describe all manner of boat people, and *Watermen* as a specific type of river boatmen.

[4] *R. C. on Labour (group B)*, 1893–4, q. 16897.

[5] *Population Census of England and Wales, 1841: Occupation Abstract*, 1844, pp. 32 and 48; for the sources for later years see the *second* volume in each census year listed under *The Census* in the Bibliography.

[6] In the interests of brevity, the sources for these statistics are given with the *second* volume listed for each census year, 1851–1911, in the Bibliography, under the heading *The Census*.

[7] The estimates for boys in the 10 to 15 age group, in 1851 and 1881, are arrived at by subtracting the numbers in other age groups from the total number of bargemen, watermen and lightermen. The seemingly untypical increase in the number of boys in this age group in 1861 is probably explained by the fact that for the first time apprentice lightermen seem to have been included.

IVd PEOPLE SLEEPING ON BOARD BOATS ON THE NIGHT OF THE CENSUS 1851–1931

| Year | Boats | | | People | | | | Males | | | Females | | |
|---|---|---|---|---|---|---|---|---|---|---|---|---|---|
| | Number | Increase/ decrease | % increase/ decrease | Number per boat | Total number | Increase/ decrease | % increase/ decrease | Number | Increase/ decrease | % increase/ decrease | Number | Increase/ decrease | % increase/ decrease |
| 1851 | – | – | – | – | 12,562 | – | – | 10,059 | – | – | 2,503 | – | – |
| 1861 | – | – | – | – | 11,915 | −647 | −5·1 | 8,494 | −1,563 | −15·5 | 3,421 | +918 | +36·6 |
| 1871 | – | – | – | – | 10,976 | −939 | −7·9 | 7,616 | −818 | −9·6 | 3,360 | −61 | −1·7 |
| 1881 | – | – | – | – | 8,978 | −1,998 | −18·2 | 6,225 | −1,391 | −16·9 | 2,753 | −607 | −18·0 |
| 1891 | 4,301 | – | – | 2·65 | 11,373 | +2,395 | +26·6 | 8,539 | +2,114 | +33·9 | 2,839 | +81 | +2·9 |
| 1901 | 2,649 | −1,652 | −38·4 | 2·59 | 6,869 | −4,504 | −39·6 | 4,916 | −3,623 | −42·3 | 1,953 | −886 | −31·2 |
| 1921 | 1,760 | −880 | −33·2 | 3·01 | 5,306 | −1,563 | −22·7 | 3,254 | −1,662 | −33·8 | 2,054 | +101 | +5·1 |
| 1931 | 1,561 | −199 | −11·4 | 2·87 | 4,484 | −822 | −15·5 | 2,852 | −402 | −12·3 | 1,632 | −422 | −20·5 |

Note

The statistics of people sleeping on board boats are particularly difficult to find; this is made worse by the fact that for each census they seem to appear in a different place. The 1911 figure proved too elusive, if indeed it exists. For the sake of brevity the sources of these statistics are given with the *first* volume listed for each census year, 1851–1931, in the Bibliography under the heading *The Census*. However, the derivation of the figures for 1851 needs further explanation. The total number of people said to be sleeping on board boats on canals in *Great Britain* in 1851 was 12,919, i.e. 10,390 (male), 2,529 (female), in *Census of Great Britain, 1851*, vol. I, *Report and Summary Tables*, 1852 [1631], table XXI, p. xliv. The total sleeping in 'Barges on Canals' in 1851 in *England and Wales* was given as 12,562 in *Census 1861*, vol. III, *General Report*, 1863 [7865], table 18, p. 87. By taking the figure of 2,503 'Females in and connected with barges' in *England and Wales* from *Census of England and Wales, 1851*, vol. II, part I, *Population Tables: Ages, etc.*, 1854 [1691–I], table XXV, p. ccxxvi, we arrive at a final total of 12,562 people sleeping on board boats in England and Wales in 1851; made up of 10,059 males and 2,503 females.

# APPENDIX V

# *The Census (ii)*

The relevant sections of the Local Government Board Regulations[1] read as follows:

III 8*b*. A cabin occupied as a sleeping place by a husband and wife shall not at any time while in such occupation be occupied as a sleeping place by any other person of the female sex above the age of twelve years, or by any other person of the male sex above the age of fourteen years:

Provided that in the case of a boat built prior to the thirtieth day of June, one thousand eight hundred and seventy eight, a cabin occupied as a sleeping place by a husband and wife may be occupied by one other person of the male sex above the age of fourteen years subject to the following conditions:-

(i) That the cabin be not occupied as a sleeping place by any other person than those above mentioned

(ii) That the part of the cabin which may be used as a sleeping place by the husband and wife shall, at all times while in actual use, be effectively separated from the part used as a sleeping place by the other occupant of the cabin, by means of a sliding or otherwise moveable screen or partition of wood or other solid material, so constructed or placed as to provide for efficient ventilation.

III 8*c*. A cabin occupied as a sleeping place by a person of the male sex above the age of fourteen years shall not at any time be occupied as a sleeping place by a person of the female sex above the age of twelve years, unless she be the wife of the male occupant.

Whether a boat was physically overcrowded or not depended upon the amount of air space in the cabin which could vary from one boat to another. In the lists of boats and their occupants taken from the census books and drawn up below the following standard has been adopted for narrow-boat cabins:

More than three-and-a-half adults = physically overcrowded.
More than two adults and three children = physically overcrowded.
    (A child is less than twelve years old. Two children are equivalent to one adult.)

On the wide boats at Wigan:
More than three adults (two children counting as one adult) in a boat with an aft cabin only = physically overcrowded.
More than three adults fore and three aft (assuming there to be two cabins) = physically overcrowded.

There is no way of knowing whether a boat had two cabins or not; hence we have made allowances for both possibilities, by working out overcrowding looked at in the best light possible (i.e. two cabins), or the worst (one cabin). On the narrow boats this 'worst' and 'best' depends on the provision of a movable screen as outlined in III 8*b* (ii) of the Local Government Board Regulations.

The following abbreviations have been used:

| | | | |
|---|---|---|---|
| B | Brother | D | Daughter |
| F | Female | FA | Father |
| GD | Granddaughter | GS | Grandson |
| M | Male | Mo. | Mother |
| Ne. | Niece | Nep. | Nephew |
| S | Son | SD | Stepdaughter |
| Sis. | Sister | FB | Family boat |

All relationships are to the master of the boat except where indicated.

A family boat is defined as one with any female on board and one with any child of the master under 12 on board.

Braces denote a single family travelling on more than one boat.

#### NOTE TO APPENDIX FIVE

[1] *Regulations by the Local Government Board under the Canal Boats Act of 1877*, 1878 (103), LXIV.

v*b* OVERCROWDING AND INDECENT OCCUPATION ON CANAL NARROW BOATS FOUND IN THE 1871 CENSUS ENUMERATION BOOKS

| | Name of boat | Place | Master | Wife | 11 | 10 | 9 | 8 | 7 | 6 | 5 | 4 | 3 | 2 | 1 | under 1 (age in months) |
|---|---|---|---|---|---|---|---|---|---|---|---|---|---|---|---|---|
| 1 | – | Smethwick | 34 | 35 | | | | S | | | | | S | | | S, 8m. |
| 2 | – | ,, | 25 | | | | | | | | | | | | | |
| 3 | – | ,, | 47 | | | | | | | | | | | | | |
| 4 | – | ,, | 23 | 21 | | | | | | D | | | | | | |
| 5 | – | ,, | 25 | | | | | | | | | | | | | |
| 6 | Eliza | Crescent Wharf, Birmingham | 49 | | | | | | | | | | | | | |
| 7 | Joseph | ,, | 39 | 34 | D | | | | S | S | S | | D | | | |
| 8 | Herd | ,, | 25 | | | | | | | | | | | | | |
| 9 | Shadow | ,, | 42 | 44 | | | | | | | | | | | | |
| 10 | Gainsborough | ,, | 36 | 34 | D | | D | D | | | S | | | | | |
| 11 | Samuel | ,, | 26 | | | | | | | | | | | | | |
| 12 | – | ,, | 43 | 42 | | D | | D | S | | S | | | | | D, 1m. |
| 13 | Emily | ,, | 33 | 30 | | | | D | | | | | | | | |
| 14 | Henry & Ann | ,, | 36 | 30 | | | | | | S | D | S | S | | | |
| 15 | Sarah | ,, | 24 | | | | | | | | | | | | | |
| 16 | Juno | ,, | 35 | 35 | | | | | | D | S | S | S | S | | |
| 17 | – | Manchester | 43 | 32 | | D | | | | D | S | | D | | | D, 2m. |
| {18 | No. 7 | Salford | 53 | 49 | | | | | | | | | | | | |
| {19 | No. 8 | ,, | | | | | | | | | S | S | | | | |
| {20 | Milo | ,, | 37 | 36 | S | | | | | | | | | | | |
| {21 | Midas | ,, | | | | | | | | S | S | D | | | | |
| {22 | Una | ,, | 27 | 28 | | | | | | | | | | | | |
| {23 | Ina | ,, | | | | | | | | | | | | | | |
| 24 | Sarah | ,, | absent | | S | | | | | | | | | | | |
| {25 | Eleanor | ,, | 50 | 41 | D | | | | | | | | | | | |
| {26 | Anne | ,, | | | | | S | | | | | D | | | | |
| {27 | Elizabeth | ,, | 22 | | | | | | | | | | | | | |
| {28 | Martha | ,, | 49 | 34 | | | | | | | S | | | | | |
| {29 | Sarah Anne | ,, | absent | | | | | | | | | | | | | |
| {30 | Emma | ,, | | | | | | | 7 females absent | | | | | | | |
| 31 | William | ,, | 35 | 35 | | | | | | | | | S | S | | |
| 32 | Frank | ,, | absent | | | | | | | | | | | | | |
| 33 | The Larch | ,, | 69 | 67 | | | | | | | | | | | | |
| 34 | Nottingham | ,, | 55 | 52 | | | | | | | | | | | | |
| 35 | Polly | ,, | absent | 45 | | | | | | | | | | | | |
| 36 | Bonnie Lassie | Bugbrook Wharf | 36 | 34 | | | | | | | | | | | | |
| 37 | Bessie | ,, | 24 | 21 | | | | | | | | | | | | |
| 38 | – | West Bromwich | 52 | | | | | | | | | | | | | |
| 39 | – | ,, | 56 | | | | | | | | | | | | | |
| 40 | – | ,, | 25 | 20 | | | | | | | | | | | S | |
| 41 | – | ,, | 20 | 22 | | | | | | | | | | | | |
| 42 | – | ,, | 55 | 51 | | | | | | | | | | | | |
| 43 | – | ,, | 43 | 46 | | | | | | | | | | | | |

| Other children of 12 and over of master—age and sex | Others not sons or daughters of master—age and sex | Physically overcrowded | Indecently overcrowded | | Family boat |
|---|---|---|---|---|---|
| | | | Worst | Best | |
| D, 14 | | Yes | Yes | Yes | FB |
| | B, 21 | No | No | No | |
| | M, 14 M, 14 | No | No | No | |
| | | | | | FB |
| | | No | No | No | |
| S, 18 | | No | No | No | |
| S, 15 | M, 24 | Yes | Yes | Yes | FB |
| | B, 20 | No | No | No | |
| | | No | No | No | FB |
| | | Yes | No | No | FB |
| | M, 66 B, 20 | No | Yes | Yes | FB |
| S, 12 | | Yes | No | No | FB |
| S, 12 | | No | No | No | FB |
| | F, 14 | Yes | Yes | Yes | FB |
| | | No | No | No | |
| | | Yes | No | No | FB |
| | M, 35 M, 40 | Yes | Yes | Yes | FB |
| D, 21 D, 13 | | Yes | Yes | Yes | FB |
| S, 19 S, 16 | | No | No | No | FB |
| D, 13 | | No | Yes | Yes | FB |
| S, 16 | | No | No | No | FB |
| | | No | No | No | FB |
| | M, 33 | No | No | No | |
| | M, 17 | No | No | No | FB |
| | | No | No | No | FB |
| | M, 23 | No | No | No | FB |
| | (Sons of 49: M, 7 M, 11) M, 20 | No | No | No | FB |
| D, 14 | | No | Yes | Yes | FB |
| | M, 14 | No? | Yes | No | FB |
| | | No? | Yes | No | FB |
| S, 13 | | Yes | No | No | FB |
| | M, 40 | No | No | No | |
| | GD, 15 | No | Yes | Yes | FB |
| | Nep, 8 | No | Yes | No | FB |
| | M, 31 M, 11 | No | Yes | No | FB |
| D, 13 | | No | Yes | Yes | FB |
| | M, 18 | No | Yes | No | FB |
| | M, 17 | No | No | No | |
| S, 16 | | No | No | No | |
| | M, 19 | No | Yes | Yes | FB |
| | | No | No | No | FB |
| | M, 16 | No | Yes | No | FB |
| S, 12 | M, 66 | No | Yes | Yes | FB |

| Name of boat | Place | Master | Wife | 11 | 10 | 9 | 8 | 7 | 6 | 5 | 4 | 3 | 2 | 1 | under 1 (age in months) |
|---|---|---|---|---|---|---|---|---|---|---|---|---|---|---|---|
| 44 – | ,, | 44 | 45 | S | | | D | | | | | | | | |
| 45 – | ,, | 54 | 51 | S | | | | S | S | | | | | | |
| 46 – | ,, | 50 | 39 | S | | | | 2S | | | | | | | |
| 47 – | ,, | 70 | 75 | | | | | | | | | | | | |
| 48 – | ,, | 28 | 27 | | | | | | | | | | | | |
| 49 – | ,, | 55 | 55 | S | | D | | | | | | | | | |
| 50 – | ,, | 35 | 27 | S | | | | S | | | | | | | |
| 51 Dolphin | Oldbury | 22 | 25 | | | | | | | | | | | | |
| 52 Hatton | ,, | 36 | | | | | | | | | | | | | |
| 53 Thomas | ,, | 24 | 22 | | | | | | | | | D | | | S, 7m. |
| 54 John | ,, | 46 | 50 | | | | | | | | | | | | |
| 55 Henry | ,, | 19 | 20 | | | | | | | | | | | | S, 3m. |
| 56 Enterprise | ,, | 27 | 27 | | | | | | | | | S | D | | |
| 57 Lilley | ,, | 23 | | | | | | | | | | | | | |
| 58 Prince of Wales | ,, | 55 | 52 | S | | | | | | | | | | | |
| 59 Black Eagle | ,, | 42 | 36 | D | D | | D | | | | | | | | S, 1m. |
| 60 No. 3 | ,, | 44 | 40 | | | | | | | | | | | | |
| 61 Unity | ,, | 29 | 27 | | | | | | | | | | D | | S, 2m. |
| 62 Newport | ,, | 55 | 50 | S | | | | | | | | | | | |
| 63 Raywell | ,, | 30 | | | | | | | | | | | | | |
| 64 Swansey | ,, | 41 | 40 | | | | | | | D | | D | | | D, 1m. |
| 65 Providence | ,, | 21 | | | | | | | | | | | | | |
| 66 Elizabeth | Kings Norton | 49 | | | | | | | | | | | | | |
| 67 – | ,, | 44 | | | | | | | | | | | | | |
| 68 Neptune | ,, | 38 | | | | | | | | | | | | | |
| 69 William | ,, | Age not known | | | | | | | two sons | | | | | | |
| 70 Envy None | ,, | 40 | 32 | | | | | | | | | S | | | |
| 71 – | ,, | 25 | 26 | | | | | | | | | | | | |
| 72 Harriet | Selly Oak | 30 | | | | | | | | | | | | | |
| 73 – | ,, | 31 | 29 | S | | D | | S | | S | | | | | |
| 74 – | ,, | 30 | | | | | | | | | | | | | |
| 75 Severn | Chester | 53 | | | | | | | | | | | | | |
| 76 Wolverhampton | ,, | 29 | 29 | | | | | | S | D | S | | | | |
| 77 Reindeer | ,, | | 54(master) | | | | | | | | | | | | |
| 78 Clyde | ,, | | | | | | | | | | | | | | |
| 79 Ram | ,, | 48 | | | | | | | | | | | | | |
| 80 Rapid | ,, | 23 | 24 | | | | | | | | | | | | D, 1m. |
| 81 Ruth | ,, | 42 | 33 | | | | | | | | | | | | |
| 82 Bittern | ,, | 40 | 34 | S | | | S | | S | | | | | | |
| 83 Preston | ,, | 47 | | | | | | | | | | | | | |
| 84 Drayton | ,, | 23 | | | | | | | | | | | | | |
| 85 Stour | ,, | 22 | 23 | | | | | | | | S | S | | | |
| 86 Avon | ,, | 38 | 37 | | | S | | S | | S | D | | | | |
| 87 Jessie | ,, | 39 | | | | | | | fly boat | | | | | | |
| 88 Chatterley | ,, | 42 | 38 | S | | S | D | D | S | S | | | | | |
| 89 Dale | ,, | 40 | | S? | | | | | | | | | | | |
| 90 Bleyer | ,, | | | | | | | | | | | | | | |
| 91 Ravensdale | ,, | 46 | 40 | | | | | | S | S | S | | | | |

| Other children of 12 and over of master—age and sex | Others not sons or daughters of master—age and sex | Physically overcrowded | Indecently overcrowded | | Family boat |
|---|---|---|---|---|---|
| | | | Worst | Best | |
| D, 15 S, 15 | F, 27 F, 21 | Yes | Yes | Yes | FB |
| S, 14 D, 19 D, 16 | | Yes | Yes | Yes | FB |
| | | No | No | No | FB |
| | GS, 25 | No | Yes | No | FB |
| | F, 8 | No | No | No | FB |
| D, 16 | | Yes | Yes | Yes | FB |
| | | No | No | No | FB |
| | | No | No | No | FB |
| | | No | No | No | |
| | M, 8 | No | No | No | FB |
| | M, 18 | No | Yes | No | FB |
| | F, 8 | No | No | No | FB |
| | | No | No | No | FB |
| | F, 20, daughter of F, 65 | No | Yes | Yes | FB |
| | | No | No | No | FB |
| D, 12 | | Yes | Yes | Yes | FB |
| | F, 16 | No | Yes | Yes | FB |
| | | No | No | No | FB |
| S, 16 | | No | Yes | No | FB |
| | M, 22 M, 13 | No | No | No | |
| D, 20 S, 14 | | Yes | Yes | Yes | FB |
| | B? 14 | No | No | No | |
| | M, 21 | No | No | No | |
| | | No | No | No | |
| S, 12 | Nep., 22 | No | Yes | Yes | FB |
| | | No | No | No | FB |
| S, 14 | | No | No | No | FB |
| | M, 14 | No | No | No | FB |
| S, 16 | | No | No | No | FB |
| | | Yes | No | No | FB |
| | M, 17 | No | No | No | |
| | M, 19 M, 17 M, 21 | No | No | No | |
| SD, 15 | | Yes | Yes | Yes | FB |
| | F, 19 | No | No | No | FB |
| | M, 14 M, 12 | No | No | No | |
| | F, 17 | No | Yes | Yes | FB |
| | M, 9 | No | No | No | FB |
| | M, 17 | No | Yes | No | FB |
| D, 12 | | Yes | No | No | FB |
| S, 21 | M, 19 | No | No | No | |
| | M, 19 | No | No | No | |
| | M, 17 M, 19 | Yes | Yes | Yes | FB |
| D, 16 | | Yes | Yes | Yes | FB |
| | M, 23 M, 30 M, 20 | No | No | No | |
| D, 13 | | Yes | Yes | Yes | FB |
| S? 14 | M, 16 | No | No | No | FB |
| | M, 18 | No | No | No | |
| D, 14 | | Yes | Yes | Yes | FB |

*Abstract (1871) – 1*

Total number of boats: 91.

Number of family boats: 69, *i.e.* 75·8% of all boats.

Number of boats physically overcrowded: 20, *i.e.* 22·0% of all boats and 29·0% of family boats.

Number of boats indecently overcrowded (worst): 36, *i.e.* 39·5% of all boats and 52·1% of family boats.

Number of boats indecently overcrowded (best): 26, *i.e.* 28·5% of all boats and 37·6% of family boats.

*Source* Public Record Office, *census 1871*.

V *c* OVERCROWDING AND INDECENT OCCUPATION ON CANAL WIDE BOATS IN AND NEAR WIGAN, FOUND IN THE 1871 CENSUS ENUMERATION BOOKS

| Name of boat | Place | Age | | Children of master under 12 | | | | | | | | | | | |
|---|---|---|---|---|---|---|---|---|---|---|---|---|---|---|---|
| | | Master | Wife | 11 | 10 | 9 | 8 | 7 | 6 | 5 | 4 | 3 | 2 | 1 | under 1 (age in months) |
| 1 John | Wallgate, Wigan | 41 | | | | | | | | | | | | | |
| 2 Two Sisters | Wigan | 26 | 25 | | | | | | | | | | | | |
| 3 Margaret Ellen | ,, | 46 | 36 | S | | | | | D | | D | | D | | |
| 4 Lily | Ince | 20 | | | | | | | | | | | | | |
| 5 – | ,, | 34 | | | | | | | | | | | | | |
| 6 – | ,, | 24 | | | | | | | | | | | | | |
| 7 April | ,, | 77 | 72 | | | | | | | | | | | | |
| 8 Tom | ,, | 19 | | | | | | | | | | | | | |
| 9 Danube | ,, | 36 | | | | | | | | | | | | | |
| 10 Feller | ,, | 30 | | | | | | | | | | | | | |
| 11 Polly | ,, | 50 | 50 | | | | | | | | 2D | | | | |
| 12 Ellen | ,, | 23 | 27 | | | | | D | | 2S | | | | | |
| 13 Mark & Louise | ,, | | | | | | | | | | | | | | |
| 14 Margaret | ,, | | | | | | | | | | | | | | |
| 15 Defiance | ,, | 40 | 40 | | | | | | | | | | | | |
| 16 Hope | ,, | | | | | | | | | | | | | | |
| 17 Margaret | ,, | 40 | 36 | | | | S | | | D | | | | | |
| 18 – | ,, | 27 | 29 | | | | | | | | S | | | | |
| 19 – | ,, | 33 | 30 | S | | S (no age given) | | | | | | | | | |
| 20 – | ,, | 21 | 21 | | | | | | | | | | | | |
| 21 – | Appley Bridge, Wigan | 39 | 46 | | D | | | | | D S | | | | S, 3m. |
| 22 – | ,, | 56 | | | | | | | | | | | | | |
| 23 – | ,, | 26 | 24 | S | | | | | | D | | | | | |

*Source*    Public Record Office, *census 1871.*

| | |
|---|---|
| 1–5 | RG 10 3088 (16), p. 53. |
| 6–16 | ,,  ,,  3089 (1),  pp. 26–7. |
| 17 | ,,  ,,  4060 (19), p. 70. |
| 18–31 | ,,  ,,  4022 (10), pp. 74–7. |
| 32–5 | ,,  ,,  4023 (16), p. 21. |
| 36–7 | ,,  ,,  2982 (27), p. 144. |
| 38–50 | ,,  ,,  2986 (25), pp. 163–4. |
| 51–65 | ,,  ,,  2977 (22), p. 94. |
| 66–71 | ,,  ,,  3077 (7),  p. 105. |
| 72–4 | ,,  ,,  3084 (6),  p. 150. |
| 75 | ,,  ,,  3722 (7),  p. 93. |
| 76–86 | ,,  ,,  3722 (5),  p. 37. |
| 87–91 | ,,  ,,  3721 (1),  p. 42. |

| Other children of 12 and over of master—age and sex | Others not sons or daughters of master—age and sex | Physically overcrowded | Indecently overcrowded | | Family boat |
|---|---|---|---|---|---|
| | | | Worst | Best | |
| | | No | No | No | |
| | | No | No | No | FB |
| | | Yes    No | No | No | FB |
| | M, 18 | No | No | No | |
| | M, 20 F, 30 F, 20 | Yes    No | Yes | No | FB |
| | M, 22 F, 21 (wife of M, 22) M, 1 (son of M, 22) | Yes    No | Yes | No | FB |
| | M, 30 M, 20 | Yes    No | Yes | No | FB |
| | M, 17 | No | No | No | |
| | M, 46 | No | No | No | |
| | M, 16 M, 12 | No | No | No | |
| D, 20 D, 13 | | Yes    No | Yes | No | FB |
| | M, 16 | Yes    No | Yes | No | FB |
| | M, 35 | No | No | No | |
| | M, 20 | No | No | No | |
| | | No | No | No | FB |
| | M, 18 | No | No | No | |
| | FA? 70 | Yes    No | Yes | No | FB |
| | M, 19, F, 20 (sister? of wife) | Yes    No | Yes | No | FB |
| | | No | No | No | FB |
| | | No | No | No | FB |
| S, 12 | | Yes    No | No | No | FB |
| | M, 40 | | | | |
| | | No | No | No | FB |

| Name of boat | Place | Age | | Children of master under 12 | | | | | | | | | | | |
|---|---|---|---|---|---|---|---|---|---|---|---|---|---|---|---|
| | | Master | Wife | 11 | 10 | 9 | 8 | 7 | 6 | 5 | 4 | 3 | 2 | 1 | under 1 (age in months) |
| 24 Ada | Aspull or Blackrod | 42 | 40 | | | | | | S | | | | S | | |
| 25 — | ,, | 50 | 47 | | | | | | | D | | | | | |
| 26 Alice | ,, | 39 | 38 | | | | S | | | D | | | | | S, 8m. |
| 27 Fire King | ,, | | 39(master) | | | | | | | | | | | | |
| 28 Edward Tootal | ,, | 28 | 24 | | | | | D | | S | | | | | |
| 29 Margaret | ,, | 38 | 36 | | | | | | | | D | | D | | |
| 30 Anna | ,, | | | | | | | | | | | | | | |
| 31 Harold | ,, | | | | | | | | | | | | | | |
| 32 Dol | ,, | 37 | 39 | | | | S | D | | | D | | | | |
| { 33 Catus | ,, | 38 | 34 | | | | | | | | D | S | | S | |
| { 34 James | ,, | | | | | | S | D | | | | | | | |
| 35 Petronius | ,, | 25 | 24 | | | | | | | | | | | | |
| 36 James | Ashton in Makerfield | 40 | 35 | | | | | | | | | | | | |
| 37 Oak | ,, | — | | | | | | | | | | | | | |
| 38 — | Brynn Colliery | 33 | 30 | D | | | D | S | | | D | | | | S, 10m. |
| 39 — | ,, | 36 | 37 | S | | | | | | | | | | | |
| 40 — | ,, | 45 | 42 | | | | | | | | | | | | |
| 41 — | ,, | 45 | | | | S | | | | | | | | | |

*Abstract (1871) – II*

Total number of boats: 41.

Number of family boats: 28, *i.e.* 68·3% of all boats.

Number of boats physically overcrowded (worst): 15, *i.e.* 36·6% of all boats and 53·5% of family boats.

Number of boats physically overcrowded (best): 0, *i.e.* 0% of all boats and 0% of family boats.

Number of boats indecently overcrowded (worst): 11, *i.e.* 27·0% of all boats and 39·2% of family boats.

Number of boats indecently overcrowded (best): 0, *i.e.* 0% of all boats and 0% of family boats.

v d OVERCROWDING AND INDECENT OCCUPATION ON CANAL NARROW BOATS, FOUND IN THE 1861 CENSUS ENUMERATION BOOKS

| Name of boat | Place | Age | | Children of master under 12 | | | | | | | | | | | |
|---|---|---|---|---|---|---|---|---|---|---|---|---|---|---|---|
| | | Master | Wife | 11 | 10 | 9 | 8 | 7 | 6 | 5 | 4 | 3 | 2 | 1 | under 1 (age in months) |
| 1 Indus | Stafford, Radford Wharf | 25 | 25 | | | | | | | | | S | D | | |
| 2 Gipsy | ,, | 30 | 30 | | | | | | | | | | D | S | |
| 3 Emilea | Tunstall | 55 | | | | | | D | | S | | | | | |
| 4 Live and let live | ,, | 44 | 39 | | | | | | | | | | | | |

| Other children of 12 and over of master—age and sex | Others not sons or daughters of master—age and sex | Physically overcrowded | Indecently overcrowded | | Family boat |
|---|---|---|---|---|---|
| | | | Worst | Best | |
| D, 14 | | Yes   No | Yes | No | FB |
| S, 26 D, 12 | | Yes   No | Yes | No | FB |
| S, 16 | | Yes   No | Yes | No | FB |
| | M, 14 F, 12 M, 5 | Yes   No | No | No | FB |
| | | No | No | No | FB |
| D, 14 | | Yes   No | Yes | No | FB |
| | M, 30 | No | No | No | |
| | M, 14 | No | No | No | |
| | | No | No | No | FB |
| | | No | No | No | FB |
| D, 13 | | No | No | No | FB |
| | | No | No | No | FB |
| | M, 14 | No | No | No? | FB |
| S, 20 | M ? | No | No | No | |
| | | Yes   No | No | No | FB |
| | | No | No | No | FB |
| | M, 10 | No | No | No | FB |
| S, 17 | | No | No | No | |

*Source*   Public Record Office, *Census 1871*.

| 1 | RG 10 3887 (23), p. 46. |
| 2–3 | „ „ 3888 (31), p. 63. |
| 4–12 | „ „ 3892 (20), p. 131. |
| 13–17 | „ „ 3893 (22), p. 58. |
| 18–20 | „ „ 3893 (23), p. 87. |
| 21–3 | „ „ 3881 (7), p. 160. |
| 24–30 | „ „ 3883 (6), p. 4. |
| 31–5 | „ „ 3883 (6), p. 4. |
| 36–7 | „ „ 3898 (1), p. 13 |
| 38–41 | „ „ 3898 (4), p. 84. |

| Other children of 12 and over of master—age and sex | Others not sons or daughters of master—age and sex | Physically overcrowded | Indecently overcrowded | | Family boat |
|---|---|---|---|---|---|
| | | | Worst | Best | |
| | F, 17 | Yes | Yes | Yes | FB |
| | M, 16 | Yes | Yes | Yes | FB |
| S, 14 | | No | No | No | FB |
| S, 19 | | No | Yes | No | FB |

| Name of boat | Place | Age | | Children of master under 12 | | | | | | | | | | | |
|---|---|---|---|---|---|---|---|---|---|---|---|---|---|---|---|
| | | Master | Wife | 11 | 10 | 9 | 8 | 7 | 6 | 5 | 4 | 3 | 2 | 1 | under 1 (age in months) |
| 5 Wrekin | ,, | | 60 (master) | | | | | | | | | | | | |
| 6 Harriet | ,, | 35 | | | | | | | | | | | | | |
| 7 Eliza | ,, | 23 | 22 | | | | | | | | | | | | |
| 8 Brentford | ,, | 64 | | | | | | | | | | | | | |
| 9 Speedwell | ,, | | | | | | | | | | | | | | |
| 10 Emma | ,, | 52 | 46 | | | | | | D | | | | | | |
| 11 Liverpool | ,, | 29 | | | | | | | | | | | | | |
| 12 C.C. | ,, | 54 | | | | | | | | | | | | | |
| 13 Triumph | ,, | 25 | 21 | | | | | | | | | D | | | D, 3m. |
| 14 Britannia | ,, | 29 | | | | | | | | | | | | | |
| 15 Cefn | ,, | 22 | | | | | | | | | | | | | |
| 16 H. | ,, | 20 | 21 | | | | | | | | | | | | S, 3m. |
| 17 Rose in June | ,, | 42 | | | | | | | | | | | | | |
| 18 Thistle | ,, | 33 | | | | | | | | | | | | | |
| 19 Aston | ,, | 50 | 48 | | D | | | | | | S | | | | |
| 20 James Hayes | ,, | 45 | 40 | | | | | | | | | | | | |
| 21 Eliza Jane | ,, | 42 | | | | | | | | | | | | | |
| 22 Echo | ,, | 42 | | | | S | | | | | | | | | |
| 23 Albim | ,, | 45 | | | | | | | | | | | | | |
| 24 Who' ha' thought it | ,, | 36 | | | | | | | | | | | | | |
| 25 Lillah | ,, | 28 | 25 | | | | | | | | | | | | D, 8m. |
| 26 – | ,, | 36 | 34 | S | | S | D | | | | | | | | |
| 27 William | ,, | 38 | | | S | | | | | | | | | | |
| 28 – | Coventry | 50 | | | | | | | | | | | | | |
| 29 – | ,, | 40 | 37 | | | | | | | | | | | | |
| 30 Neva | ,, | 19 | | | | | | | | | | | | | |
| 31 Major | ,, | 20 | | | | | | | | | | | | | |
| 32 Nimrod | Sladeheath | 46 | 46 | S | | D | D | | S | | | | | | |
| 33 Hebe | ,, | 43 | 38 | | | | | | S | | S | | | | |
| 34 – | Alderley Junction | 57 | | | | | | | | | | | | | |
| 35 – | ,, | 24 | 22 | | | | | | | | | | | | |
| 36 Newport | ,, | 38 | 44 | | | | | | | | | | | | |
| 37 – | ,, | 37 | 27 | | | | | | | | | | | | |
| 38 – | ,, | 52 | 53 | | | | | | | | | | | | |
| 39 Thistle | ,, | 27 | 28 | | | | | | D | | | D | | | S, 9m. |
| 40 – | ,, | 37 | | | | | | | | | | | | | |
| 41 – | ,, | 15 | | | | | | | | | | | | | |
| 42 – | ,, | 47 | 39 | | | | | | | | | | | | |
| 43 – | ,, | 40 | 35 | | | | | | D | | | | | | |
| 44 – | ,, | 21 | 20 | | | | | | | | | | | | |
| 45 – | ,, | 62 | | | | | | | | | | | | | |
| 46 – | ,, | 37 | 37 | | | | | | | | | D | S | | |
| 47 – | ,, | 38 | 36 | | | | | | | | | | | | |
| 48 – | ,, | 24 | 22 | | | | | | | | | | | | |
| 49 – | ,, | 47 | 26 | | | | | | | | | | | | |
| 50 – | ,, | 36 | 32 | | | | | | D | | DD | | DS | | |

| Other children of 12 and over of master—age and sex | Others not sons or daughters of master—age and sex | Physically overcrowded | Indecently overcrowded | | Family boat |
|---|---|---|---|---|---|
| | | | Worst | Best | |
| D, 20 S, 17 | G,D. 12 | Yes | Yes | Yes | FB |
| | M, 50 | No | No | No | |
| | Sis., 12 | No | No | No | FB |
| | M, 12 | No | No | No | |
| | M, 15 | No | No | No | |
| S, 16 | | No | Yes | Yes | FB |
| | M, 18 M, 13 | No | No | No | |
| | M, 15 | No | No | No | |
| | | No | No | No | FB |
| | M, 17 | No | No | No | |
| | M, 20 | No | No | No | |
| | | No | No | No | FB |
| | M, 20 | No | No | No | |
| | M, 20 | No | No | No | |
| D, 12 | | Yes | No | No | FB |
| | M, 26 | No | Yes | No | FB |
| | M, 16 F, 9 (sister of M, 16) | No | No | No | FB |
| S, 15 | | No | No | No | FB |
| S? 23 | M, 16 | No | No | No | |
| | M, 42 | No | No | No | |
| | | No | No | No | FB |
| S, 13 | | Yes | Yes | Yes | FB |
| S? 14 | | No | No | No | FB |
| | M, 18 | No | No | No | |
| | | No | No | No | FB |
| | M, 27 | No | No | No | |
| | M, 19 | No | No | No | |
| | | Yes | No | No | FB |
| D, 12 | | Yes | No | No | FB |
| | M, 52 | No | No | No | |
| | M, 19 | No | Yes | No | FB |
| SD, 16 | | No | Yes | Yes | FB |
| | | No | No | No | FB |
| S, 22 D, 18 S, 15 | | Yes | Yes | Yes | FB |
| | | No | No | No | FB |
| | M, 16 M, 11 | No | No | No | |
| | Mo, 49 B, 10 M, 23 | Yes | Yes | Yes | FB |
| S, 14 | | No | No | No | FB |
| D, 12 | M, 15 | Yes | Yes | Yes | FB |
| | M, 13 | No | No | No | FB |
| S, 15 D, 26 | | No | Yes | Yes | FB |
| S, 18 D, 16 | | Yes | Yes | Yes | FB |
| | M, 27 | No | Yes | No | FB |
| | M, 21 | No | Yes | No | FB |
| | F, 6 | No | No | No | FB |
| D, 12 | | Yes | No | No | FB |

| Name of boat | Place | Age | | Children of master under 12 | | | | | | | | | | | |
| --- | --- | --- | --- | --- | --- | --- | --- | --- | --- | --- | --- | --- | --- | --- | --- |
| | | Master | Wife | 11 | 10 | 9 | 8 | 7 | 6 | 5 | 4 | 3 | 2 | 1 | under 1 (age in months) |
| 51 — | ,, | 19 | 18 | | | | | | | | | | | | |
| 52 — | ,, | 60 | 55 | | | | | | | | | | | | |
| 53 — | ,, | 30 | 26 | | | | | | | | | S | | | |
| 54 William | Wheaton Aston | 47 | 37 | | | S | | | | | | | | | |
| 55 Neptune | ,, | 34 | 28 | | | | S | | | | | | D | | |
| 56 William | Brereton | 40 | | | | | | | | | | | | | |
| 57 No. 3 | ,, | 31 | 27 | | | S | | | | | | D | D | | |
| 58 No. 1 | ,, | 50 | | | | | | | | | | | | | |
| 59 Lady of the Lake | ,, | 38 | | | | | | | | | | | | | |
| 60 Vanguard | ,, | 55 | | | | | | | | | | | | | |
| 61 No. 4 | ,, | 42 | 40 | | D | | D | | | D | | S | | | |
| 62 No. 1 | ,, | 39 | | | | | | | | | | | | | |
| 63 Harriet | ,, | 28 | | | | | | | | | | | | | |
| 64 Amelia | ,, | | | | | | | | | | | | | | |
| 65 Trent | Horninglow | 43 | | | | | | | fly boat? | | | | | | |
| 66 James | ,, | 49 | | | | | | | | | | | | | |
| 67 Havelock | ,, | 35 | | | | | | | | | | | | | |
| 68 Pilkington | ,, | 35 | | | | | | | fly boat? | | | | | | |
| 69 — | ,, | 32 | 32 | | | | | | | S | | | D | | |
| 70 — | Froghall | 20 | | | | | | | | | | | | | |
| 71 — | ,, | 31 | | | | | | | | | | | | | |
| 72 — | ,, | 35 | 27 | | | | | | | S | S | | | | |
| 73 — | ,, | 52 | | | | | | S | | | | | | | |
| 74 — | ,, | 25 | | | | | | | | | | | | | |
| 75 — | ,, | 45 | 45 | | | | | | | | | | | | |
| 76 — | Ipstones | 50 | | | | | | | | | | | | | |
| 77 Mary | ,, | 62 | 42 | | | | | | | | | | | | |
| 78 Gould Intended | ,, | 43 | 29 | | | | | | | | | | | | |
| 79 Justice | ,, | 27 | | | | | | | | | | | | | |
| 80 Alona | ,, | 19 | | | | | | | | | | | | | |
| 81 — | ,, | 28 | 25 | | | | | | | | | S | D | | |
| 82 Jane Hannah | ,, | 46 | 50 | | | | | S | | | | | | | |
| 83 Fairey Queen | ,, | 52 | 57 | | | | | | | | | | | | |
| 84 — | ,, | 35 | 46 | D | | | | | | | | | | | |
| 85 Kate | ,, | 17 | | | | | | | | | | | | | |
| 86 — | ,, | 12 | | | | | | | | | | | | | |
| 87 Sapper | ,, | 25 | | | | | | | | | | | | | |
| 88 Elizabeth | ,, | 43 | 43 | | | | | | | | | | | | |
| 89 Industry | ,, | 28 | 27 | | | | | | | D | S | | | | D, 4m. |
| 90 — | ,, | 24 | 21 | | | | | | | | | S | | | |
| 91 Rifle Man | ,, | 43 | | | | | | | D | S | | | | | |
| 92 Elizabeth | Barton-under-Needwood | 48 | 47 | | | | | | | | | | | | |
| 93 Colchester | Burton Extra | 40 | | | | | | | | | | | | | |
| 94 Ann | ,, | 63 | 60 | | | | | | | | | | | | |
| 95 Winchester | ,, | 21 | | | | | | | | | | | | | |
| 96 Atherstone | ,, | 36 | 38 | | | | S | S | | D | | S | | | |

| Other children of 12 and over of master—age and sex | Others not sons or daughters of master —age and sex | Physically overcrowded | Indecently overcrowded | | Family boat |
|---|---|---|---|---|---|
| | | | Worst | Best | |
| | M, 25 | No | Yes | No | FB |
| S, 23 S, 19 S, 14 | GD, 13 | Yes | Yes | Yes | FB |
| | | No | No | No | FB |
| S, 14 | | No | No | No | FB |
| | | No | No | No | FB |
| S, 15 | | No | No | No | |
| | | No | No | No | FB |
| | M, 21 | No | No | No | |
| S, 13 | | No | No | No | |
| | M, 20 | No | No | No | |
| D, 17 S, 13 D, 12 | | Yes | Yes | Yes | FB |
| | M, 17 | No | No | No | |
| | M, 38 M, 17 | No | No | No | |
| | M, 20 | No | No | No | |
| | M, 50 M, 20 M, 22 | No | No | No | |
| S, 16 | M, 29 | No | No | No | |
| S, 13 | M, 20 | No | No | No | |
| S, 13 | M, 27 M, 23 | No | No | No | |
| | M, 16 | Yes | Yes | Yes | FB |
| | M, 27 | No | No | No | |
| | M, 22 | No | No | No | |
| | | No | No | No | FB |
| S, 20 S, 18 S, 16 | | Yes | No | No | FB |
| | F, 15 | No | Yes | Yes | FB |
| | M, 18 | No | Yes | No | FB |
| S, 21 S, 17 | | No | No | No | |
| | M, 14 | No | No | No | FB |
| D, 17 D, 15 | M, 16 | Yes | Yes | Yes | FB |
| | M, 20 | No | No | No | FB |
| | M, 16 | No | No | No | FB |
| | | No | No | No | FB |
| | M, 15 | No | Yes | Yes | FB |
| D, 17 D, 15 D, 14 | | | | | |
| D, 12 | | Yes | Yes | Yes | FB |
| | M, 12 | No | No | No | FB |
| | B? 14 | No | No | No | |
| | M, 17 | No | No | No | |
| | M, 15 | No | No | No | |
| | M, 15 | No | Yes | No | FB |
| | M, 21 | Yes | Yes | Yes | FB |
| | | No | No | No | FB |
| D, 17 D, 13 | | Yes | Yes | Yes | FB |
| | M, 18 | No | Yes | No | FB |
| | M, 40 M, 20 M, 40 | No | No | No | |
| | M, 28 | No | Yes | No | FB |
| | M, 30 M, 21 M, 19 | No | No | No | |
| | M, 16 | Yes | Yes | Yes | FB |

| Name of boat | Place | Age | | Children of master under 12 | | | | | | | | | | | |
| | | Master | Wife | 11 | 10 | 9 | 8 | 7 | 6 | 5 | 4 | 3 | 2 | 1 | under 1 (age in months) |
|---|---|---|---|---|---|---|---|---|---|---|---|---|---|---|---|
| 97 Alice | ,, | 54 | | | | | | | | | | | | | |
| 98 Mersey | Newport S.U.C. | 36 | | | | | | | | | | | | | |
| 99 Robert | ,, | 44 | 36 | | | | | | | | | | | | |
| 100 Hannah | ,, | | | | | | | | | | | | | | |
| 101 Invincible | ,, | 36 | | | | | | | | | | | | | |
| 102 Hero | ,, | 47 | 47 | S | | S | | | | S | | | | | |
| 103 No. 15 | Radford Wharf, Stafford | 46 | | | | | | | D | | | | | | |
| 104 Hazard | ,, | 41 | 35 | D | | | | | | | | | | D | S |
| 105 Dundas | ,, | 48 | 50 | | | | | | | S | D | | | | |
| 106 Lincoln | Woodside, Staffordshire | 40 | 33 | S | | | | | | | S | | | | D |
| 107 Success | Alrewas | 19 | | | | | | | | | | | | | |
| 108 — | ,, | 36 | 30 | | | | | | | | | | | | |
| 109 — | Fradley Junction | 42 | | | | | | | | | | | | | |

*Abstract (1861)*

Total number of boats: 109

Number of family boats: 68, *i.e.* 62·4% of all the boats.

Number of boats physically overcrowded: 23, *i.e.* 21·1% of all boats and 33·7% of family boats.

Number of boats indecently overcrowded (worst): 34, *i.e.* 31·2% of all boats and 50·0% of family boats.

Number of boats indecently overcrowded (best): 24, *i.e.* 22·0% of all boats and 35·3% of family boats.

| Other children of 12 and over of master—age and sex | Others not sons or daughters of master —age and sex | Physically overcrowded | Indecently overcrowded | | Family boat |
|---|---|---|---|---|---|
| | | | Worst | Best | |
| | | No | No | No | |
| | M, 34 M, 14 | No | No | No | |
| | | No | No | No | FB |
| | M, 23 M, 26 M, 35 | No | No | No | |
| | M, 17 | No | No | No | |
| D, 16 S, 14 S, 12 | | Yes | Yes | Yes | FB |
| D, 16 | | No | Yes | Yes | FB |
| | | No | No | No | FB |
| D, 16 S, 14 | | Yes | Yes | Yes | FB |
| | | No | No | No | FB |
| | M, 16 | No | No | No | |
| | | No | No | No | FB |
| | M, 20 | No | No | No | |

_Source_ Public Record Office, _Census 1861._

| | |
|---|---|
| 1–2 | RG 9 1911, pp. 144–5. |
| 3–27 | ,, ,, 1926, pp. 139–63. |
| 28–33 | ,, ,, 1981, pp. 15–20. |
| 34–55 | ,, ,, 1981, pp. 60–81. |
| 56–64 | ,, ,, 1978, pp. 102–10. |
| 65–9 | ,, ,, 1967, p. 32–6. |
| 70–5 | ,, ,, 1951, p. 112. |
| 76–91 | ,, ,, 1951, pp. 163–78. |
| 92 | ,, ,, 1964, p. 42. |
| 93–7 | ,, ,, 1966, pp. 92–6. |
| 98–102 | ,, ,, 1903, pp. 86–90. |
| 103–5 | ,, ,, 1907, pp. 2–4. |
| 107–9 | ,, ,, 1976, pp. 140–2. |
| 106 | Source lost. |

# APPENDIX VI

*Details of infringements
of the Canal Boats Acts
1877 and 1884
on canal boats, 1887–1914*

| Infringement | 1887 | 1889 | 1890 | 1891 | 1892 | 1893 | 1894 | 1895 | 1896 | 1897 | 1898 |
|---|---|---|---|---|---|---|---|---|---|---|---|
| 1 Boats not registered | 220 | 312 | 252 | 217 | 185 | 190 | 210 | 151 | 198 | 142 | 163 |
| 2 Non-notification of change of master[a] | – | 29 | 108 | 60 | 47 | 95 | 86 | 73 | 20 | 17 | 14 |
| 3 Boats without certificate | 521 | 673 | 637 | 559 | 599 | 503 | 511 | 501 | 534 | 479 | 557 |
| 4 Certificate not identifying owner and boat | 4 | 135 | 122 | 125 | 118 | 114 | 121 | 132 | 111 | 135 | 85 |
| 5 Boats not properly marked | 498 | 493 | 400 | 361 | 394 | 338 | 307 | 306 | 353 | 331 | 306 |
| *Registration* | 1,243 | 1,642 | 1,519 | 1,322 | 1,343 | 1,240 | 1,235 | 1,163 | 1,216 | 1,104 | 1,125 |
| 6 Cabins overcrowded | 143 | 110 | 121 | 112 | 109 | 108 | 97 | 67 | 103 | 90 | 87 |
| 7 No proper partition and separation of sexes | 166 | 66 | 41 | 46 | 60 | 48 | 52 | 42 | 48 | 47 | 36 |
| 8 Females over 12 improperly occupying | – | 27 | 48 | 27 | 26 | 19 | 36 | 24 | 23 | 14 | 18 |
| *Decency* | 309 | 203 | 210 | 185 | 195 | 175 | 185 | 133 | 174 | 151 | 141 |
| As a % of all boats inspected[b] | – | – | 0·7 | 0·6 | 0·6 | 0·5 | 0·5 | 0·4 | 0·5 | 0·4 | 0·4 |
| 9 Cabins not in cleanly condition | 564 | 257 | 404 | 319 | 337 | 224 | 212 | 155 | 176 | 183 | 169 |
| 10 Cabins not sufficiently ventilated | – | 84 | 172 | 24 | 41 | 41 | 86 | 41 | 79 | 68 | 79 |
| 11 Cabins required to be painted | – | 340 | 546 | 358 | 355 | 530 | 502 | 497 | 520 | 519 | 479 |
| 12 Woodwork of cabins delapidated | 60 | 164 | 270 | 417 | 448 | 417 | 478 | 467 | 488 | 437 | 385 |
| 13 Removal of bilge water not attended to | – | 38 | 26 | 31 | 56 | 34 | 31 | 28 | 10 | 20 | 21 |
| 14 Boats being without pump | 30 | 39 | 24 | 20 | 20 | 12 | 65 | 66 | 42 | 13 | 21 |
| 15 Refused to admit local inspector | 5 | 4 | 3 | 2 | 5 | 1 | 2 | 2 | 1 | 5 | 3 |
| 16 Boats without proper water vessel | 71 | 120 | 87 | 90 | 79 | 105 | 125 | 109 | 154 | 146 | 165 |
| 17 Without requisite double bulkhead | 52 | 53 | 56 | 33 | 44 | 49 | 36 | 48 | 30 | 30 | 36 |
| *Cleanliness, health etc., excluding 15 and 18* | 777 | 1,095 | 1,585 | 1,292 | 1,380 | 1,412 | 1,535 | 1,411 | 1,499 | 1,416 | 1,355 |
| 18 Non-notification of infectious disease[c] | – | 14 | 19 | 11 | 14 | 36 | 23 | 25 | 32 | 17 | 21 |
| *Total* | 2,334 | 2,958 | 3,336 | 2,812 | 2,937 | 2,864 | 2,850 | 2,734 | 2,922 | 2,693 | 2,645 |

| 1899 | 1900 | 1901 | 1902 | 1903 | 1904 | 1905 | 1906 | 1907 | 1908 | 1909 | 1910 | 1911 | 1912 | 1913 |
|---|---|---|---|---|---|---|---|---|---|---|---|---|---|---|
| 222 | 112 | 160 | 142 | 191 | 34 | 134 | 162 | 119 | 89 | 120 | 106 | 144 | 129 | 109 |
| 37 | 10 | – | – | – | – | – | – | – | – | – | – | – | – | – |
| 494 | 473 | 501 | 599 | 552 | 581 | 533 | 499 | 544 | 444 | 445 | 503 | 509 | 483 | 571 |
| 132 | 48 | 107 | 112 | 99 | 99 | 94 | 118 | 87 | 110 | 86 | 98 | 101 | 76 | 103 |
| 248 | 283 | 261 | 349 | 366 | 352 | 382 | 385 | 344 | 331 | 377 | 440 | 389 | 408 | 438 |
| 1,133 | 926 | 1,029 | 1,202 | 1,208 | 1,066 | 1,143 | 1,264 | 1,094 | 974 | 1,028 | 1,147 | 1,143 | 1,096 | 1,221 |
| 94 | 73 | 83 | 127 | 123 | 120 | 118 | 113 | 138 | 113 | 129 | 116 | 129 | 124 | 90 |
| 19 | 42 | 31 | 32 | 23 | 29 | 41 | 59 | 54 | 58 | 53 | 22 | 32 | 40 | 28 |
| 29 | 7 | 16 | 22 | 49 | 22 | 22 | 19 | 13 | 8 | 8 | 16 | 9 | 9 | 20 |
| 142 | 122 | 130 | 181 | 195 | 171 | 181 | 191 | 205 | 179 | 190 | 154 | 170 | 173 | 138 |
| 0·4 | 0·3 | 0·4 | 0·5 | 0·6 | 0·5 | 0·5 | 0·5 | 0·5 | 0·5 | 0·5 | 0·4 | 0·4 | 0·5 | 0·4 |
| 143 | 165 | 231 | 286 | 306 | 362 | 286 | 315 | 498 | 310 | 364 | 283 | 277 | 305 | 284 |
| 57 | 41 | 43 | 76 | 147 | 151 | 132 | 107 | 82 | 82 | 75 | 83 | 84 | 79 | 84 |
| 417 | 424 | 417 | 556 | 552 | 560 | 522 | 465 | 541 | 498 | 520 | 717 | 807 | 764 | 784 |
| 362 | 376 | 410 | 558 | 621 | 560 | 619 | 412 | 636 | 520 | 641 | 742 | 753 | 800 | 833 |
| 16 | 24 | 24 | 29 | 31 | 33 | 63 | 36 | 44 | 33 | 38 | 41 | 34 | 29 | 38 |
| 28 | 12 | 19 | 21 | 47 | 50 | 45 | 37 | 28 | 37 | 23 | 31 | 38 | 32 | 25 |
| 1 | – | 6 | 3 | 3 | 5 | 1 | 3 | 3 | 2 | 2 | 4 | 5 | 2 | 2 |
| 156 | 167 | 173 | 240 | 278 | 311 | 267 | 220 | 258 | 269 | 229 | 226 | 292 | 238 | 214 |
| 31 | 22 | 35 | 36 | 24 | 7 | 17 | 18 | 18 | 24 | 14 | 6 | 13 | 21 | 2 |
| 1,210 | 1,231 | 1,352 | 1,802 | 2,006 | 2,034 | 1,951 | 1,610 | 2,105 | 1,775 | 1,904 | 2,129 | 2,298 | 2,268 | 2,264 |
| – | – | – | 1 | – | – | – | – | 1 | – | – | – | – | – | 1 |
| 2,486 | 2,279 | 2,517 | 3,189 | 3,412 | 3,276 | 3,276 | 2,968 | 3,408 | 2,928 | 3,124 | 3,434 | 3,616 | 3,539 | 3,626 |

*Notes*

[a]  Soon became a dead letter.

[b]  Boats infringing the 'decency' regulations must have been even fewer in number than indicated here since there must often have been two and even three 'decency' infringements upon one boat. The numbers of boats inspected are listed in Table 10, p. 140.

[c]  The earlier figures were in fact notifications of infectious diseases rather than infringements.

*Source*  Compiled from the 'Annual Report of the Inspector of Canal Boats', found in the *Annual Reports of the Local Government Board* (1890–1913). Figures are for England and Wales.

# BIBLIOGRAPHY

I  MANUSCRIPT SOURCES

(a)   At the British Transport Historical Records Office, Porchester Road, London W.2
(now the Public Record Office)

*Documents relating to the Birmingham Canal Company (coded under BCN)*
Birmingham Canal Committee Minute Books: BCN 1/1, 1767–71; BCN 1/2, 1770–2; BCN 1/3, 1773–4; BCN 1/4, 1775–84; BCN 1/7A, 1793–9.
Journals and Cash Books: BCN 4/29, 1770–1; BCN 4/30, 1771–2; BCN 4/32, 1773–4; BCN 4/33, 1777–8; BCN 4/131, 1771.
Letter Books: BCN 4/371B, 1793–1804; BCN 4/372, 1813–17; BCN 4/373, 1817–22.
General Assembly Minutes: BCN 1/42.

*Birmingham and Liverpool Junction Canal Company (BLC)*
Committee Minutes: BLC 1/1, 1830–40; BLC 1/2, 1840–4 (also includes Select Committee Minutes, 1843).
Sub-Committee Minutes: BLC 1/3, 1835–9.
Minutes of Proprietors' Meetings: BLC 1/4, 1826–45.

*Grand Junction Canal Company (GJC)*
Minutes of the Proceedings of the Select Committee: GJC 1/1 to GJC 1/24, 1816–95 (i.e. twenty-four documents).

*Oxford Canal Company (OXC)*
Committee Book: OXC 1/4, 1787–97.
Letter Books and letters: OXC 4/51 to OXC 4/53, 1831–46 (i.e. three books); OXC 4/59, 1822; OXC 4/60, 1829–30; OXC 4/80/1–6, loose inward letters in a separate folder for each year, 1793–8; OXC 4/81/1–2, 1799–1800 (as with 4/80/1–6).
Oxford Canal Guard Book: OXC 4/110, 1787–1900.

*Pickfords (PIC)*
PIC 3/1, Letter of License.
PIC 4/1, Pickfords, Old Newspaper Cuttings and other Historical Documents.
PIC 4/26, Short Histories, etc. (for the diary of Josiah Baxendale).
PIC 4/27, Collection of Original Letters.

*Shropshire Union Railways and Canal Company (SURC)*
Traffic Committee Book: SURC 1/2, 1849.
Finance Minutes: SURC 1/9, 1847–8.
Executive Committee Minute Books: SURC 1/10 to SURC 1/27, 1849–1919 (i.e. eighteen books).
Canal Committee Minute Book: SURC 1/37, 1847–8.
Staff Register: SURC 15/2, 1879–97.

*Staffordshire and Worcester Canal Company (STW)*
Committee Book: STW 1/4, 1806–23.

*Worcester and Birmingham Canal Company (WOBC)*
Proceedings of the General Assembly: WOBC 1/2, 1834–74.
Proceedings of the Worcester and Birmingham Canal Company: WOBC 1/9, 1831–9; WOBC 1/10, 1839–45; WOBC 1/11, 1845–52.

See also GEN 4/857/1–4 listed under Newspapers.


*(b) At the House of Lords Record Office, Victoria Tower, House of Lords, London*

*Minutes of Evidence for railway and canal bills in date order.*

*House of Commons evidence*
Manchester and Sheffield Railway Bill, 1831.
Birmingham and Gloucester Railway Bill, vol. 1, 1836.
Birmingham and Derby and Stonebridge Railway Bill, vol. 1, 1836.
Manchester and Cheshire Railway Bill, vol. 20, 1836.
Manchester and Cheshire Junction Railway Bill, vol. 21, 1836.
Manchester and Leeds Railway Bill, vol. 23, 1836.
Manchester and Salford Canal Bill, vol. 24, 1836.
North Midland Railway Bill, vol. 32, 1836.
Manchester, Cheshire and Staffordshire Railway Bill, vol. 20, 1837.
Birmingham Canal Bill, vol. 3, 1839.
Weaver Churches Bill, 1840.
Manchester Bury and Rossendale and the Leeds and Manchester (Bury Branch) Railway Bill, vol. 27, 1844.

*House of Lords evidence*
Birmingham Canal Bill, 1791.
Cromford Canal Bill, 1789.
Paddington Canal Bill, 1812.
Liverpool and Manchester Railroad Bill, 1826.
London and Birmingham Railway Bill, 1832.
Weaver Churches Bill, 1840.


*(c) At the Public Record Office*

*Portugal Street*
Enumeration Books for: 1851 Census, HO 107; 1861 Census, RG 9; 1871 Census, RG 10.

*Chancery Lane*
MH 12/11645.

MH 25/106.
MH 32/94, John Brydone's Correspondence, 1883–99.
ED 11/1, Replies to Circular 283 for 1887 and 1893.
ED 11/40, Education of children in canal boats, including summaries of annual returns, 1902–5.
ED 11/41, Summary of Returns for 1905.
ED 11/87, Summary of Returns, 1912–15.


*(d) At various County and City Record Offices, Libraries and Museums, in alphabetical order*

*Birmingham Reference Library*
Diary of G. R. Bird, wharfinger and carrier of Birmingham, including weather reports and their effects upon canal traffic, 1820–30, 662750.

*Cheshire County Record Office, Chester*
Poor Law Settlement Papers.
Register of Boats and Barges, 1795–1812 (Referred to as Boat Register 1795.)
Wills at Chester.

*Chester City Record Office*
Registers of Boats, 1879–1914.

*Coventry City Record Office*
Canal Boats Box.
Registers of Canal Boats, 1879–1914.

*Derbyshire County Record Office, Matlock*
Cromford Canal Permit Books, 501 B/B1, B2, B4, B45.
Register of Boats and Barges, 1795 (i.e. Boat Register 1795).

*Gloucestershire County Record Office, Gloucester*
Register of Barges and Trows . . . , 1795 (i.e. Boat Register 1795), Q/RR 1.

*Ilkeston Public Library*
Registers of Canal Boats, 1879–1914.

*Lancashire County Record Office, Preston*
Register of Boats, Barges and Vessells, Pursuant to the Statute of 35 Geo. III, Cap. 58, 1795 (i.e. Boat Register 1795), QDV/16/1.

*Leicestershire County Record Office, Leicester*
Register of Boats and Barges, 1795 (i.e. Boat Register 1795).

*Nottinghamshire County Record Office, Nottingham*
Poor Law Settlement Papers, P.R. 85.

*Oxford Local History Library*
Register of Canal Boats, 1879–1914.

*Oxfordshire County Record Office, Oxford*
Petitions and Evidence relative to the Oxford Canal Bill, 1829, OX vi/ii/i.

*Reading Public Library ( Tilehurst)*
Register of Canal Boats, 1877–1914.

*Staffordshire Record Office, Stafford*
Register of Boats and Barges, 1795–7 (i.e. Boat Register 1795), QR UB1.
Poor Law Settlement Papers.

*Stoke Bruerne (British Waterways Museum)*
Diary of W. H. King—Canal Contractor, 1895.
Letter Book of Oxford Canal Company, 1790–1, WD 63/44.
Wages Book of the Coventry Canal Company, 1840–4.

*Warwickshire County Record Office, Warwick*
Register of Boats and Barges, 1795 (i.e. Boat Register 1795), QS. 95/1–9.

*Public Health Offices at Burnley, Daventry, Hinckley, Leigh, Manchester, Nantwich, Nottingham,*
*Paddington, Tring, West Drayton and Wigan*
Documents relative to the enforcement of the Canal Boats Acts of 1877 and 1884, i.e.
registers of canal boats, 1879–1914, journals of inspection, and correspondence, not all of
which are necessarily to be found at all of the above offices.

## II PRINTED SOURCES

### (a) Parliamentary Papers (in date order)

*Report and Evidence of the S. C. on the Observance of the Sabbath Day* 1831–2 (697), VIII (re-
ferred to in the text as *S. C. on the Observance of the Sabbath,* 1832).
*Select Committee on Inquiry into Drunkenness,* 1834 (559), VIII.
*First Report of the Commissioners appointed to inquire as to the best Means of establishing an Ef-*
*ficient Constabulary Force in the Counties of England and Wales,* 1839 (169), XIX (referred to
as *Constabulary Force Report,* 1839).
'Evidence of the S. C. on Sunday trading on canals and navigable rivers and railways',
*House of Lords Journal,* 4th and 5th Victoria, vol. 73, appendix 2 (referred to as *S. C. on*
*Sunday trading,* 1841).
*Reports and Evidence of the S. C. on Railway and Canal Bills,* 1852–3 (79, 170, 246, 736) (re-
ferred to as *S. C. on Railway and Canal Bills,* 1852–3).
*Report of the Commissioners appointed to enquire into the working of the Factory and Workshops*
*Act . . . ,* vol. 1, *Report Appendix and Index,* 1876 [C.1443], XXIX; vol. II, *Minutes of Evi-*
*dence,* 1876 [C. 1443–1], XXX (referred to as the *Factory and Workshops Commission,* 1876)..
*Regulations by the Local Government Board under the Canal Boats Act of 1877,* 1878 (103), LXIV.
*Reports and Evidence of the S. C. on Canals,* 1883 (252), XIII.
*Reports and Evidence of the S. C. on the Canal Boats Act (1877) Amendment Bill,* 1884 (263), VIII
(referred to as *S. C. on Canal Boats,* 1884).
*First Report of the Royal Commission for enquiry into the Housing of the Working Classes with*
*Evidence,* 1884–5 [C. 4402–1], XXXI.
*Returns of Wages published between 1830 and 1886,* 1887 [C. 5172].
*Royal Commission on Labour (group B), Transport and Agriculture,* vol. III, 1893–4 [C.
6894–VIII], XXXIII (referred to as *R. C. on Labour (group B),* 1893–4).
*Supplement to the 55th Annual Report of the Registrar General of Births, Deaths and Marriages in*
*England, Part II,* 1897 [C. 8503], XXI (abbreviated to *55th Report of Registrar General (Sup-*
*plement),* 1897).

*Supplement to the 65th Annual Report of the Registrar General, Part II*, 1908 [Cd. 2619], XVII
    (abbreviated to *65th Report of Registrar General (Supplement)*, 1908).
*First Report of the Royal Commission on Canals and Inland Navigations in the United Kingdom*
    (1906–9): vol. I, 1906, [Cd. 3183–4], XXXII; vol. V, part II, 1909 [Cd. 4840], XIII; vol.
    VIII, 1910 [Cd. 5204], XII (title abbreviated to *R. C. on Canals*, 1906–9).


### (b) Annual Reports of the Local Government Board, 1883–1914

*14th Annual Report of the L. G. B. for 1884* (1884–5) [C. 4515], XXXII.
*15th for 1885* (1886) [C. 4844], XXXI.
*16th for 1886* (1887) [C. 5131], XXXVI.
*17th for 1887* (1888) [C. 5526], XLIX.
*18th for 1888* (1889) [C. 5813], XXXV.
*19th for 1889–90* (1890) [C. 6141], XXXIII.
*20th for 1890* (1890–1) [C. 6460], XXXIII.
*21st for 1891* (1892) [C. 6745], XXXVIII.
*22nd for 1892* (1893–4) [C. 7180], XLIII.
*23rd for 1893* (1894) [C. 7500], XXXVIII.
*24th for 1894* (1895) [C. 7867], L.
*25th for 1895* (1896) [C. 8212], XXXVI.
*26th for 1896* (1897) [C. 8583], XXXVI.
*27th for 1897* (1898) [C. 8978], XXXIX.
*28th for 1898* (1899) [C. 9444], XXXVII.
*29th for 1899–1900* (1900) [Cd. 292], XXXIII.
*30th for 1900* (1901) [Cd. 746], XXV.
*31st for 1901* (1902) [Cd. 1231], XXXV.
*32nd for 1902* (1903) [Cd. 1700], XXIV.
*33rd for 1903* (1904) [Cd. 2214], XXV.
*34th for 1904* (1905) [Cd. 2661], XXXI.
*35th for 1905* (1906) [Cd. 3105], XXXV.
*36th for 1906* (1907) [Cd. 3665], XXVI.
*37th for 1907* (1908) [Cd. 4347], XXX.
*38th for 1908* (1908–9), part I [Cd. 4786].
*39th for 1909* (1910), part II [Cd. 5275], XXXVIII.
*40th for 1910* (1911), part II [Cd. 5978], XXXI.
*41st for 1911* (1912–13), part II [Cd. 6331], XXXV.
*42nd for 1912* (1913), part III [Cd. 6982], XXXI.
*43rd for 1913* (1914) [Cd. 7611], XXXVIII.

### (c) The Census

The exact sources of the numbers sleeping on board boats are given with the *first* volume
in each census year from 1851, but see Appendix IV*d*, note 1 for a detailed derivation of the
1851 figures.

The exact sources of the numbers of bargemen, watermen and lightermen, and the
numbers of women listed in the 'Occupational Returns', are given with the *second* volume
in each census year from 1851.

*Population Census of England and Wales, 1841: Occupation Abstract,* 1844.

*Census of Great Britain,* 1851, vol. I, *Report and Summary Tables,* 1852 [1631], table XXI, p. xliv.

*Census of Great Britain, 1851,* vol. II, part I, *Population tables: Ages, Civil Condition, Occupations and Birthplaces,* 1854 [1691–1], table XXV, pp. ccxxiii and ccxxvi.

*Census of England and Wales* (henceforward *Census*), *1861,* vol. III, *General Report,* 1863 [7865], tables 18 and 19, pp. 87–8.

*Census 1861,* vol. II, *Population Tables: Ages (etc.),* 1863 [5597], table XIX, p. xlv.

*Census 1871,* vol. I, *Population Tables: Area, Houses and Inhabitants,* 1872, table XII, p. xl.

*Census 1871,* vol. IV, *General Report,* 1873 [C. 872–1], p. 94.

*Census 1881,* vol. II, *Population Tables: Area (etc.),* 1883 [C. 3563], table IV, p. xix.

*Census 1881,* vol. III, *Population Tables: Ages (etc.),* 1883 [C. 3722], p. xi.

*Census 1891,* vol. IV, *General Report,* 1893 [C. 7222], p. 24 (males), and *ibid.,* vol. II, *Population Tables: Area (etc.),* 1893 [C. 6948–1], table VII, p. xxxiv (females).

*Census 1891,* vol. III, *Population Tables: Ages (etc.),* 1893 [C. 7058], p. xii.

*Census 1901: General Report,* 1904 [Cd. 2174], section IX, p. 164.

*Census 1901: Summary Tables,* 1903 [Cd. 1523], table XXXV, p. 118.

*Census 1911,* vol. X, part I, *Occupations and Industries,* 1914 [Cd. 7018], table 3, p. 14. (No figures for sleeping on board available in 1911.)

*Census 1921: General Tables,* 1925, table 31–(17), p. 126.

*Census 1921: Occupation Tables,* 1924, table 1, p. 16.

*Census 1931: General Tables,* 1935, table 16–(16), p. 124.

*Census 1931: Occupation Tables,* 1934, table 1, p. 10.

### (d) Contemporary printed sources

**Books**

Anon, *History of Inland Navigation* (1766) (catalogued under James Brindley in the Manchester University Library).

Aubertin, C. J., *A Caravan Afloat* (London, *c.* 1918), Simkin, Marshall, Hamilton, Kent & Co.

*Fourth International Congress on Inland Navigation* (Manchester, 1890).

Hassell, John, *A Tour of the Grand Junction Canal in 1819* (London, 1968 reprint, with notes and introduction by John Cranfield), Cranfield and Bonfield Books.

'Hercules', *British Railways and Canals* (London, *c.* 1885), Field & Tuer.

Hoare, E. A., *Notable Workers in Humble Life* (London, 1887), Nelson & Sons (for the article on George Smith).

Hodder, Edwin, *George Smith [of Coalville]: The Story of an Enthusiast* (London, 1896), Nisbet & Co.

Leland, Charles G., *The Gypsies* (London, 1882), Trubner & Co.

Meteyard, Eliza, *Life of Josia Wedgewood,* two volumes (London, 1865), Hurst & Blackett.

Phillips, John, *A General History of Inland Navigation* (Newton Abbot, 1970 reprint of the 1805 ed.; 1st ed. 1792), David & Charles.

Pommeuse, Huerne de, *Les Canaux navigable,* vol. 2 (Paris, 1822), Bachelier and Huzard.

Rees, Abraham, *Cyclopaedia,* vol. VI (London, 1819), Longmans (for the article on 'Canals', written around 1806).

Stevenson, R. L., *An Inland Voyage* (London, 1919 ed.; 1st ed. 1888), Chatto & Windus.

Smith, George, *Our Canal Population: The Sad Condition of the Women and Children—With Remedy* (London, 1875), Houghton & Co.

—*Our Canal Population: a Cry from the Boat Cabins—With Remedy* (London, 1879), Houghton & Co.

—*Canal Adventures by Moonlight* (London, 1881), Hodder & Stoughton.

Sutcliffe, John, *A Treatise on Canals and Reservoirs* (Rochdale, 1816).

Temple Thurston, E., *The Flower of Gloster* (Newton Abbot, 1968 reprint of 1911 ed.), David & Charles.

Thacker, F. S., *The Thames Highway*, vol. I, *General History* (Newton Abbot, 1968 reprint of 1914 ed.), David & Charles.

—*The Thames Highway*, vol. II, *Locks and Weirs* (Newton Abbot, 1968 reprint of 1920 ed.), David & Charles.

*Articles*

Ellis-Martin, Benjamin, 'Through London by canal', *Harpers Monthly Magazine*, vol. 70 (1885), pp. 857–76.

'On the canal', *Household Words* (conducted by Charles Dickens), 11, 18 and 25 September 1858, pp. 289–93, 318–23, 354–60.

Rideing, William H., 'The waterways of New York', *Harpers New Monthly Magazine*, vol. 48 (December 1873), pp. 1–17.

Whitman, James S., 'Down the Thames in a birch-bark canoe', *Harpers Monthly Magazine*, vol. 62 (1880–1), pp. 211–18.

Wood, G. H., 'Real wages and the standard of comfort since 1850', *Journal of the Royal Statistical Society* (1909).

*Annual Reports, newspapers, periodicals, pamphlets, etc.*

*Annual Reports of the Medical Officer of Health of the City of Birmingham* (1886–1914), and especially the *Report* for 1905 containing the *Supplement* entitled 'Report on the conditions of life under which canal boat children are reared'.

*Annual Reports of the Medical Officers of Health* to 1914 for the towns and cities of Burnley, Leicester, Nantwich, Nottingham, Reading and Wigan.

*Annual Reports of the Incorporated Seamen and Boatmen's Friend Society (Birmingham District)*, 1899–1924, Birm. R. L., 239999.

*Annual Reports of the Incorporated Seamen and Boatmen's Friend Society (North-eastern District)*, 1901–17, Leeds Central Reference Library, 266 IN 2L.

*Aris's Birmingham Gazette*, as in C. P. Weaver's 'Extracts from *Aris's Birmingham Gazette*, 1760–1809, relating to canals', British Transport Historical Records Office, GEN 4/857/1–4.

*Articles of Agreement made between the Members of a Society who have agreed to meet at the House of Mr John Jones – The Waggon and Horses in Summer Row, Birmingham* (Birmingham, 1808), Birm. R. L., 72294.

*Birmingham and London Junction Canal Petitions* (1830), Birm. R. L., 26200.

*Canal Boatmen's Magazine* (London, 1829–32), the monthly magazine of The Paddington Society for Promoting Christian knowledge among Canal Boatmen and Others, British Museum, PP. 1090 c.

*Fellows Morton and Clayton Ltd: Memorandum of Association* (1889), Birm. R. L., 663022.

*Fellows Morton and Clayton Ltd: 1st, 9th and 17th Directors' Reports*, 1890, 1898, 1906, Birm. R. L., 663023.

Hansard, *Parliamentary Debates*, 1840–2.

*History and Reminiscences of the Mersey Mission to Seamen* (Runcorn, 1921), Runcorn Public Reference Library.

*Hope Iron Boat Club Rules and Regulations* (Birmingham, 1856), Birm. R. L., 72220.

Osborne, G. H., 'Newspaper Cuttings relating to Canals', Birm. R. L., 243972 (especially for the article 'Maritime Birmingham' in the *Mail*, 8 February 1886, p. 3).

*Seamen's Institute, Runcorn* (Runcorn, 1906).

*Staffordshire Advertiser*.

*The Waterman*, 1909–15, the monthly magazine of the Incorporated Seamen and Boatmen's Friend Society, Birm. R. L., 219389.

*Miscellaneous*

Ministry of Health, *Report and Minutes of Evidence* (two volumes) *of the Departmental Committee Appointed to inquire into the practice of Living-in on Canal Boats in England and Wales and to report whether any alteration in the practice is desirable*, 1921 (referred to as *Committee on Living-in*, 1921). I am grateful to the Librarian of the Department of the Environment who made these two documents available. They are numbered:- H.V. 3164 M.66, pamphlet box (the *Report*), and H.V. 3164 M.661, pamphlet box (*Minutes of evidence*).


*(e) Modern printed sources*

*Books*

Anglade, Jean, *Vie quotidienne dans le Massif Central au 19e siècle* (Paris, 1971), Hachette.

Bowley, A. L., *Wages and Income in the United Kingdom since 1860* (Cambridge, 1937), Cambridge University Press.

Clébert, Jean Paul, *The Gypsies* (London, 1963), Vista Books (translated by Charles Duff).

Clew, Kenneth R., *The Kennet and Avon Canal* (Newton Abbot, 1968), David & Charles.

—*The Somersetshire Coal Canal* (Newton Abbot, 1970), David & Charles.

Coleman, Terry, *The Railway Navvies* (London, 1965), Hutchinson.

De Maré, Eric, *The Canals of England* (London, 1950; 1968 ed.), Architectural Press.

Dubois, Armand Budington, *The English Business Company after the Bubble Act, 1720–1800* (New York, 1938), The Commonwealth Fund.

Gladwin, D. D. and White, J. M., *English Canals*, part III, *Boats and Boatmen* (Lingfield, 1969), Oakwood Press.

Hadfield, Charles, *British Canals* (Newton Abbot, 1966; 1st ed. 1950), David & Charles.

—*The Canal Age* (Newton Abbot, 1968), David & Charles.

—and Biddle, Gordon, *The Canals of North West England*, vols. I and II (Newton Abbot, 1970), David & Charles.

Household, Humphrey, *The Thames and Severn Canal: Birth and Death of a Canal* (Newton Abbot, 1969), David & Charles.

Hunt, Bishop Carleton, *The Development of the Business Corporation in England, 1800–67* (Cambridge, Mass., 1936), Harvard University Press.

Mather, F. C., *After the Canal Duke: a Study of the Industrial Estates administered by the Trustees of the Third Duke of Bridgewater in the Age of Railway Building, 1825–72* (Oxford, 1970), Clarendon Press.

Ministry of Housing and Local Government and the Welsh Office, *Gypsies and other Travellers* (London, 1967), H.M.S.O.

Mitchell, B. R. and Deane, P., *Abstract of British Historical Statistics* (Cambridge, 1962; 1971 ed.), Cambridge University Press.

Redford, A., *Labour Migration in England, 1800–50* (Manchester; 1926; 1964 ed.), Manchester University Press (edited and revised by W. H. Chaloner).

Rolt, L. T. C., *Narrow Boat* (London, 1944; 1965 ed.), Eyre & Spottiswood.

—*The Inland Waterways of England* (London, 1950, 1962 ed.), George Allen & Unwin.

—*Navigable Waterways* (London, 1969), Longmans.

Stevenson, Peter, *The Nutbrook Canal: Derbyshire* (Newton Abbot, 1970), David & Charles.

Thompson, E. P. and Yeo, Eileen, *The Unknown Mayhew – Selections from the Morning Chronicle*, 1849–50 (London, 1971), Merlin Press.

*Transport Saga, 1646–1947: the History of Pickfords* (London, 1947), loaned by Pickfords Ltd.

Vine, P. A. L., *London's Lost Route to the Sea* (Newton Abbot, 1965), David & Charles.

—*London's Lost Route to Basingstoke* (Newton Abbot, 1968), David & Charles.

Willan, T. S., *River Navigation in England, 1600–1750* (London, 1936; 1964 ed.), Frank Cass.

—*The Navigation of the River Weaver in the 18th Century* (Manchester, 1951), Chetham Society.

*Articles*

Albert, William, 'The justices rates for land carriage, 1748–1827, reconsidered', *Transport History*, I (1968), pp. 105–29.

Blaug, Mark, 'The myth of the old Poor Law and the making of the new', *Journal of Economic History*, XXIII, 2 (June 1963), pp. 151–84.

Broadbridge, S. R., 'Living conditions on midland canal boats', *Transport History*, III (1970), pp. 36–51.

Chaloner, W. H., 'Salt in Cheshire, 1600–1870', *Transactions of the Lancashire and Cheshire Antiquarian Society*, LXXI (1961), pp. 58–74.

Harrison, Brian, 'The Sunday trading riots of 1855', *Historical Journal*, VIII, 2 (1965), pp. 219–45.

—'Two roads to social reform: Francis Place and the "Drunken Committee" of 1834', *Historical Journal*, XI, 2 (1968), pp. 272–300.

—and Trinder, B., 'Drink and sobriety in an early Victorian county town: Banbury 1830–60', *English Historical Review*, supplement 4 (1969), pp. 7–14.

Hauldren, A. B., 'The hygienic and welfare aspects of waterway transport, (a) Living conditions on the canal', *The Royal Sanitary Institute Journal*, 75, No. 5 (May 1955).

Jones, Barbara, 'The rose and the castle', *Architectural Review* (December 1946).

Lewis, R. A., 'Transport for 18th-century ironworks', *Economica*, new series, 18 (August 1951), pp. 278–84.

McKeon, T. and Record, R. G., 'Reasons for the decline of mortality in England and Wales during the nineteenth century', *Population Studies*, 16 (1962–3), pp. 94–121.

Macleod, Roy M., 'Social policy and the "Floating Population". The administration of the Canal Boats Acts 1877–99', *Past and Present* (1966), pp. 101–32.

Turnbull, Gerard L., 'Pickfords and the canal carrying trade 1780–1850', *Transport History*, VI (1973) (kindly loaned by the author before publication).

Wilson, Charles, 'Economy and society in late Victorian Britain', *Economic History Review*, 2nd series, vol. 18, No. 1 (August 1965), pp. 183–98.

*Newspapers*

Birmingham Newspaper Cuttings – Canals and Waterways (1946), Birm. R. L., 662820.

*Theses*

Iredale, D. A., 'Canal settlement: a study of the origin and growth of the canal settlement at Barnton in Cheshire between 1775 and 1845', unpublished Ph.D. thesis, of Leicester University, 1966 (abbreviated in text to 'Canal Settlement: Barnton, 1775–1845').

Malley, Edith, 'The financial administration of the Bridgewater estates, 1780–1800', unpublished M.A. thesis, Manchester University, 1929.

Martin, Florence M., 'Elementary education in the Poor Law Union of Runcorn, 1870–1903', unpublished M.Ed. Thesis, Durham University, 1970.

# INDEX